CAPTAIN AMERICA
MAN OUT OF TIME

AIN AMERICA: MAN OUT OF TIME. Contains material originally published in magazine form as CAPTAIN AMERICA: MAN OUT OF TIME #1-5 and AVENGERS #4. First printing 2011. ISBN# 978-0-7851-5129-6. hed by MARVEL WORLDWIDE, INC., a subsidiary of MARVEL ENTERTAINMENT, LLC. OFFICE OF PUBLICATION: 135 West 50th Street, New York, NY 10020. Copyright © 1963, 2010 and 2011 Marvel Characters, Inc. nts reserved. $16.99 per copy in the U.S. and $18.99 in Canada (GST #R127032852); Canadian Agreement #40668537. All characters featured in this issue and the distinctive names and likenesses thereof, and all d indicia are trademarks of Marvel Characters, Inc. No similarity between any of the names, characters, persons, and/or institutions in this magazine with those of any living or dead person or institution is intended, ny such similarity which may exist is purely coincidental. **Printed in the U.S.A.** ALAN FINE, EVP - Office of the President, Marvel Worldwide, Inc. and EVP & CMO Marvel Characters B.V.; DAN BUCKLEY, Publisher & ent - Print, Animation & Digital Divisions; JOE QUESADA, Chief Creative Officer; DAVID BOGART, SVP of Business Affairs & Talent Management; TOM BREVOORT, SVP of Publishing; C.B. CEBULSKI, SVP of Creator & nt Development; DAVID GABRIEL, SVP of Publishing Sales & Circulation; MICHAEL PASCIULLO, SVP of Brand Planning & Communications; JIM O'KEEFE, VP of Operations & Logistics; DAN CARR, Executive Director blishing Technology; SUSAN CRESPI, Editorial Operations Manager; ALEX MORALES, Publishing Operations Manager; STAN LEE, Chairman Emeritus. For information regarding advertising in Marvel Comics or on l.com, please contact John Dokes, SVP.Integrated Sales and Marketing, at jdokes@marvel.com. For Marvel subscription inquiries, please call 800-217-9158. **Manufactured between 10/26/2011 and 11/14/2011** R. DONNELLEY, INC., SALEM, VA, USA.

CAPTAIN AMERICA
MAN OUT OF TIME

Writer: **MARK WAID**

Pencils & Breakdowns: **JORGE MOLINA**

Inks & Finishes: **KARL KESEL** with **SCOTT HANNA** (Issue #3)

Colorist: **FRANK D'ARMATA**

Letterer: **VC'S JOE SABINO**

Cover Art: **BRYAN HITCH, PAUL NEARY & PAUL MOUNTS**

Associate Editor: **LAUREN SANKOVITCH**

Editor: **TOM BREVOORT**

CAPTAIN AMERICA CREATED BY
JOE SIMON & JACK KIRBY

Collection Editor: **JEFF YOUNGQUIST**

Editorial Assistants: **JAMES EMMETT & JOE HOCHSTEIN**

Assistant Editors: **ALEX STARBUCK & NELSON RIBEIRO**

Editors, Special Projects: **JENNIFER GRÜNWALD & MARK D. BEAZLEY**

Senior Vice President of Sales: **DAVID GABRIEL**

SVP of Brand Planning & Communications: **MICHAEL PASCIULLO**

Design: **SPRING HOTELING**

Editor in Chief: **AXEL ALONSO**

Chief Creative Officer: **JOE QUESADA**

Publisher: **DAN BUCKLEY**

Executive Producer: **ALAN FINE**

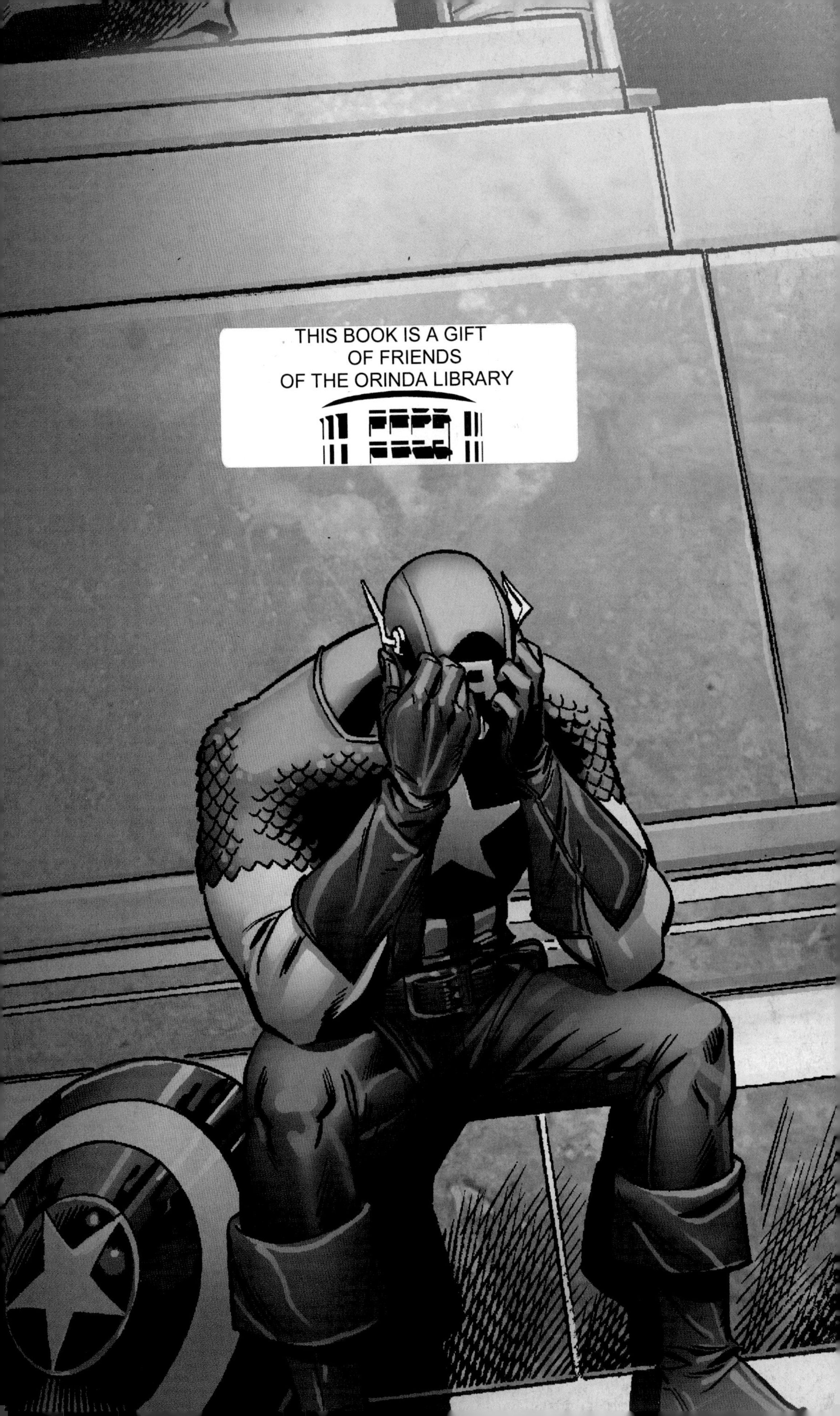

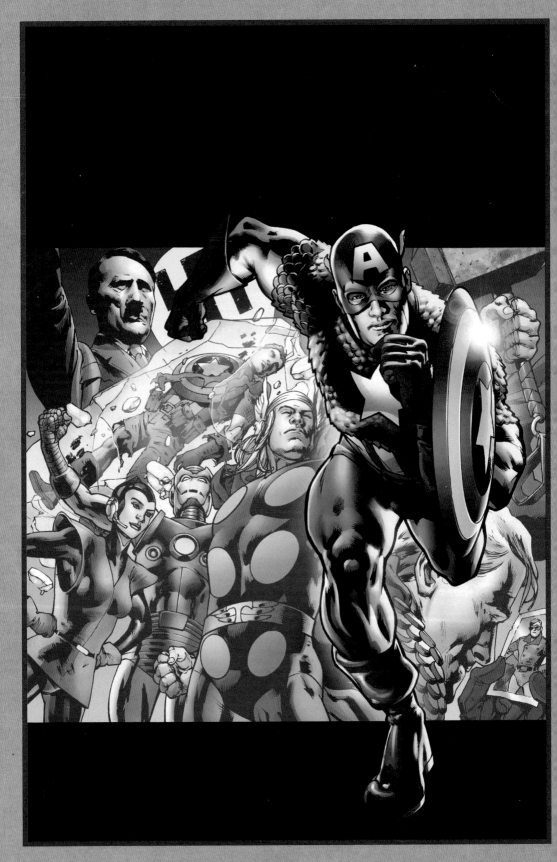

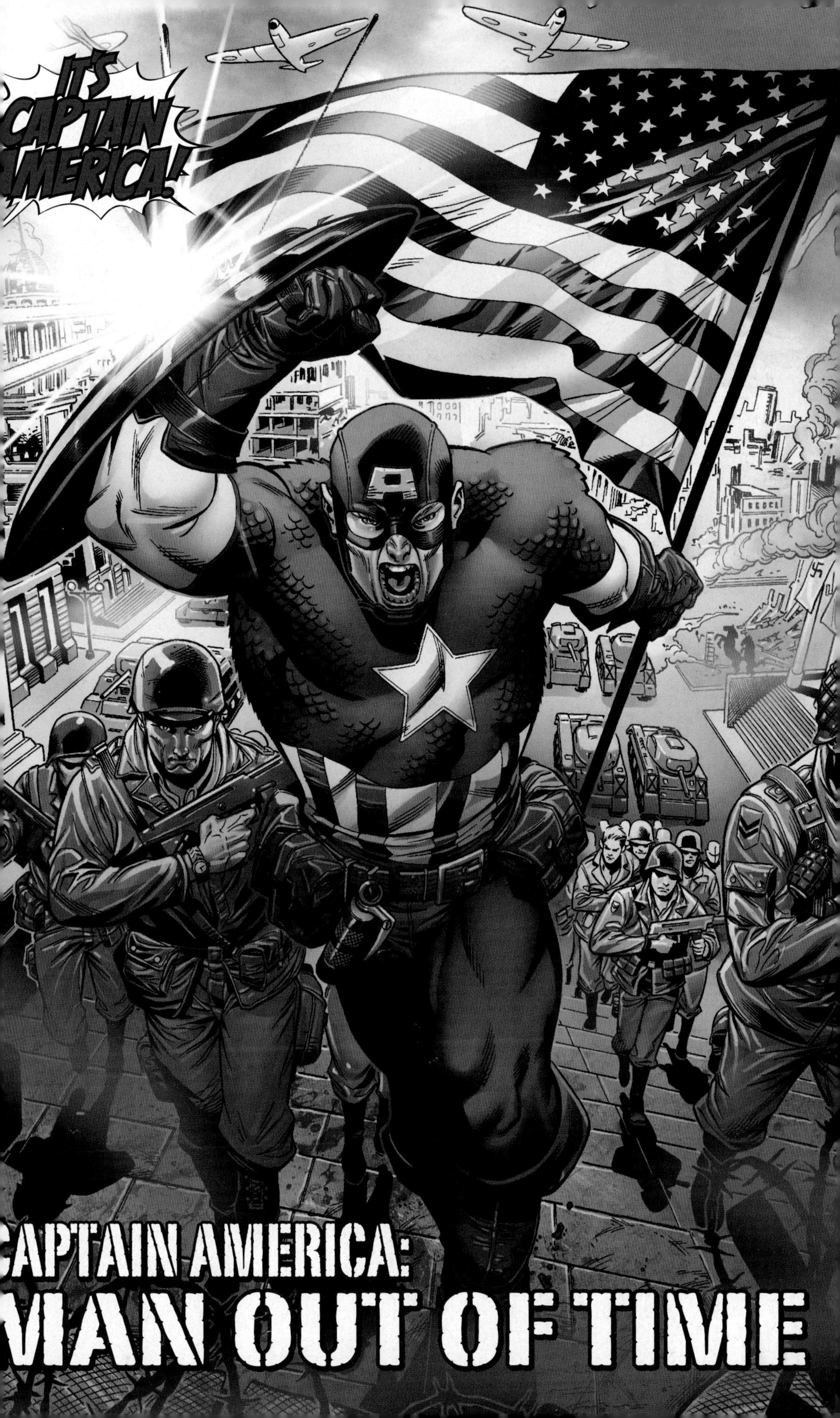
IT'S CAPTAIN AMERICA!
CAPTAIN AMERICA:
MAN OUT OF TIME

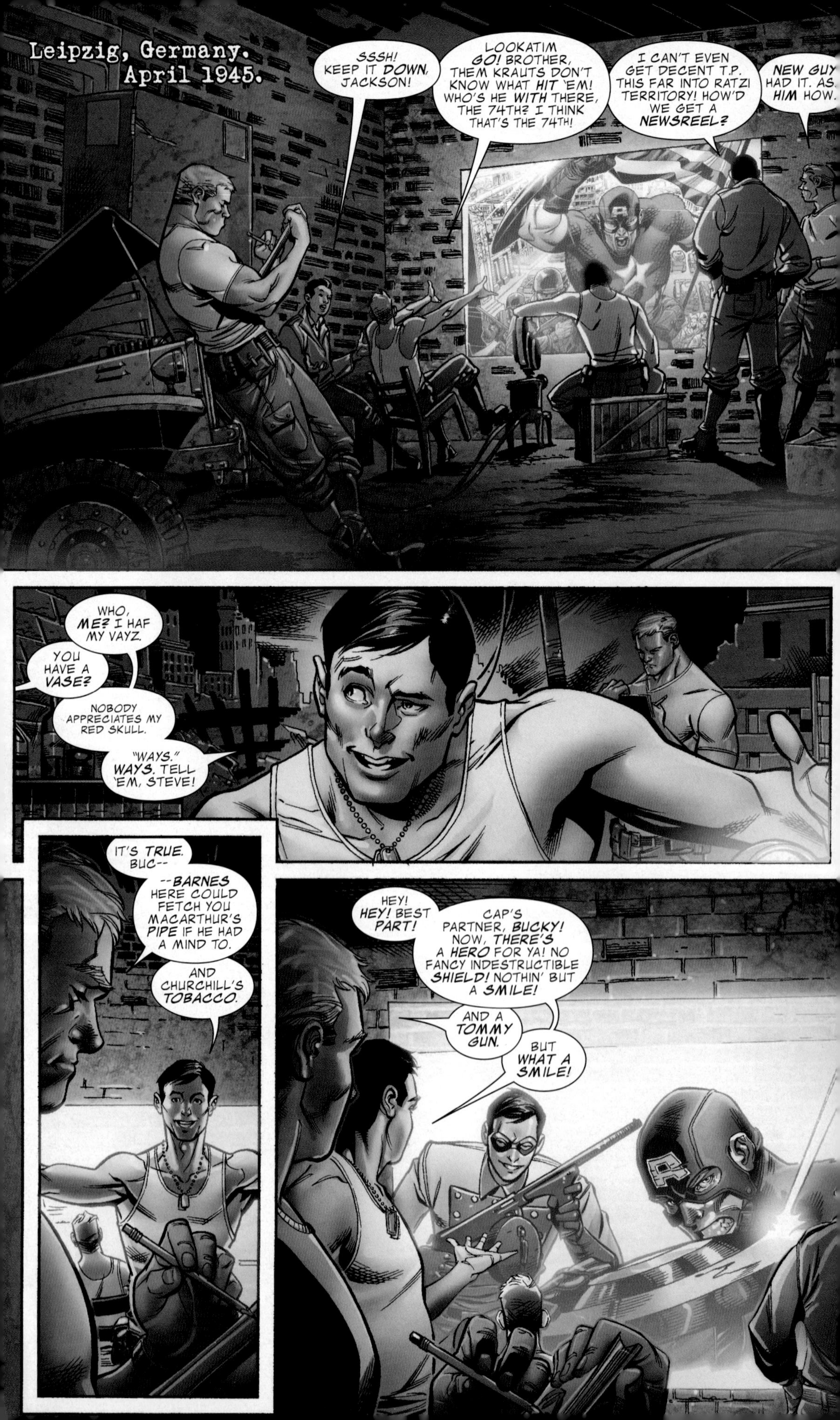

Leipzig, Germany. April 1945.
SSSH! KEEP IT DOWN, JACKSON!
LOOKATIM GO! BROTHER, THEM KRAUTS DON'T KNOW WHAT HIT 'EM! WHO'S HE WITH THERE, THE 74TH? I THINK THAT'S THE 74TH!
I CAN'T EVEN GET DECENT T.P. THIS FAR INTO RATZI TERRITORY! HOW'D WE GET A NEWSREEL?
NEW GUY HAD IT. AS HIM HOW.
WHO, ME? I HAF MY VAYZ.
YOU HAVE A VASE?
NOBODY APPRECIATES MY RED SKULL.
"WAYS." WAYS. TELL 'EM, STEVE!
IT'S TRUE. BUC--
--BARNES HERE COULD FETCH YOU MACARTHUR'S PIPE IF HE HAD A MIND TO.
AND CHURCHILL'S TOBACCO.
HEY! HEY! BEST PART!
CAP'S PARTNER, BUCKY! NOW, THERE'S A HERO FOR YA! NO FANCY INDESTRUCTIBLE SHIELD! NOTHIN' BUT A SMILE!
AND A TOMMY GUN.
BUT WHAT A SMILE!

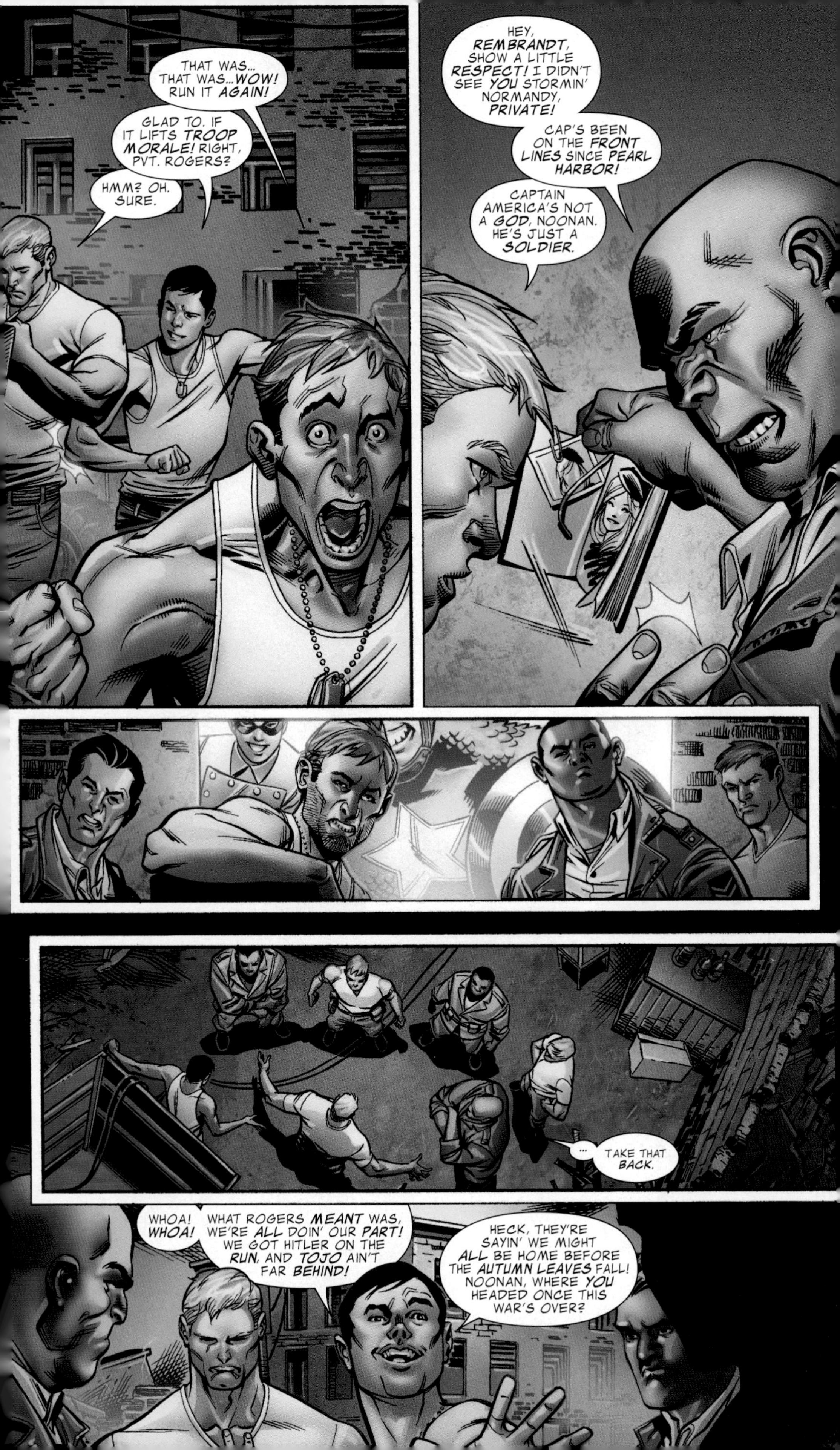

THAT WAS... THAT WAS...WOW! RUN IT AGAIN!
GLAD TO. IF IT LIFTS TROOP MORALE! RIGHT, PVT. ROGERS?
HMM? OH. SURE.
HEY, REMBRANDT, SHOW A LITTLE RESPECT! I DIDN'T SEE YOU STORMIN' NORMANDY, PRIVATE!
CAP'S BEEN ON THE FRONT LINES SINCE PEARL HARBOR!
CAPTAIN AMERICA'S NOT A GOD, NOONAN. HE'S JUST A SOLDIER.
...
TAKE THAT BACK.
WHOA! WHOA!
WHAT ROGERS MEANT WAS, WE'RE ALL DOIN' OUR PART! WE GOT HITLER ON THE RUN, AND TOJO AIN'T FAR BEHIND!
HECK, THEY'RE SAYIN' WE MIGHT ALL BE HOME BEFORE THE AUTUMN LEAVES FALL! NOONAN, WHERE YOU HEADED ONCE THIS WAR'S OVER?

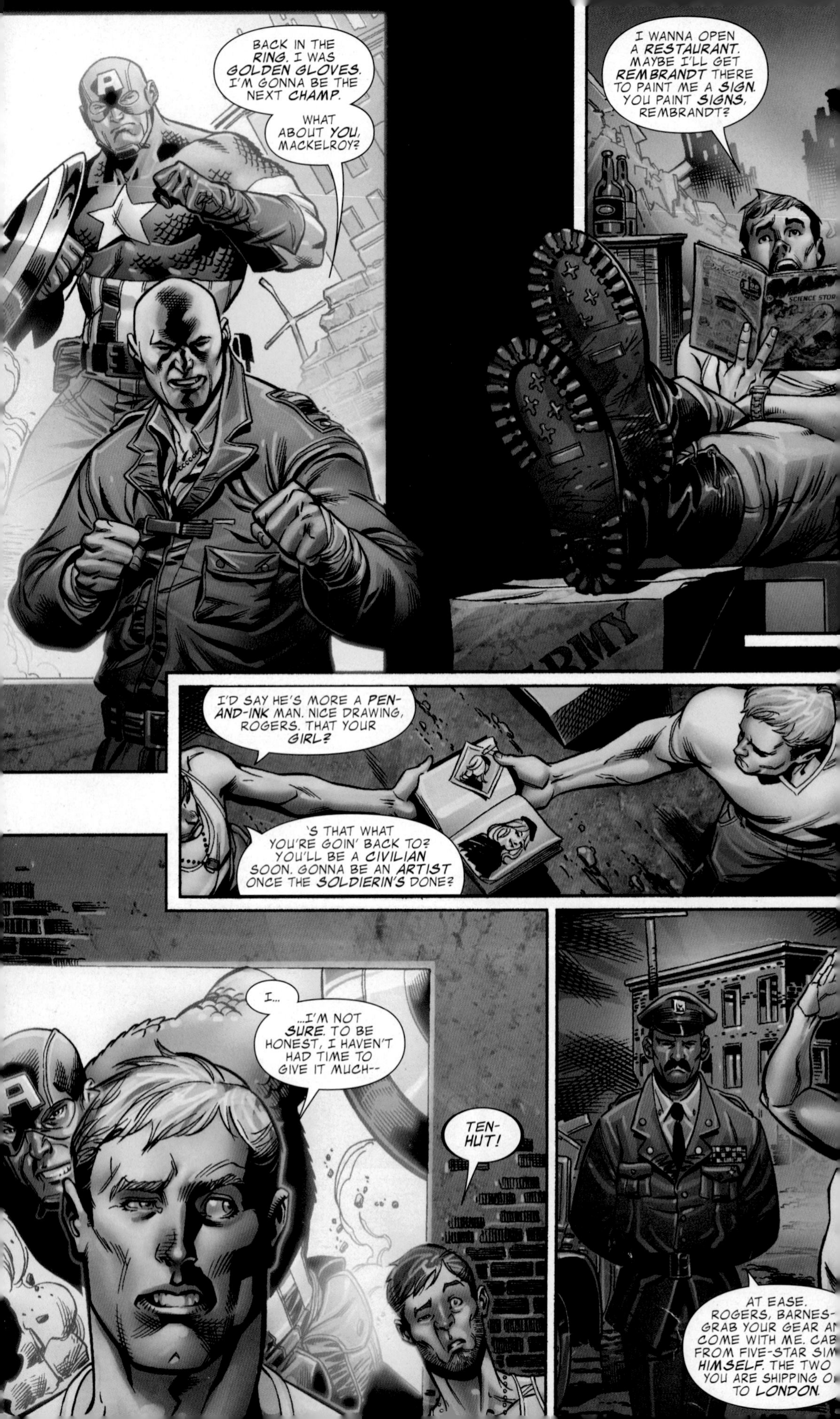
BACK IN THE RING. I WAS GOLDEN GLOVES. I'M GONNA BE THE NEXT CHAMP.
WHAT ABOUT YOU, MACKELROY?
I WANNA OPEN A RESTAURANT. MAYBE I'LL GET REMBRANDT THERE TO PAINT ME A SIGN. YOU PAINT SIGNS, REMBRANDT?
ARMY
I'D SAY HE'S MORE A PEN-AND-INK MAN. NICE DRAWING, ROGERS. THAT YOUR GIRL?
'S THAT WHAT YOU'RE GOIN' BACK TO? YOU'LL BE A CIVILIAN SOON. GONNA BE AN ARTIST ONCE THE SOLDIERIN'S DONE?
I...
...I'M NOT SURE. TO BE HONEST, I HAVEN'T HAD TIME TO GIVE IT MUCH--
TEN-HUT!
AT EASE. ROGERS, BARNES-- GRAB YOUR GEAR AN COME WITH ME. CAB FROM FIVE-STAR SIM HIMSELF. THE TWO YOU ARE SHIPPING O TO LONDON.

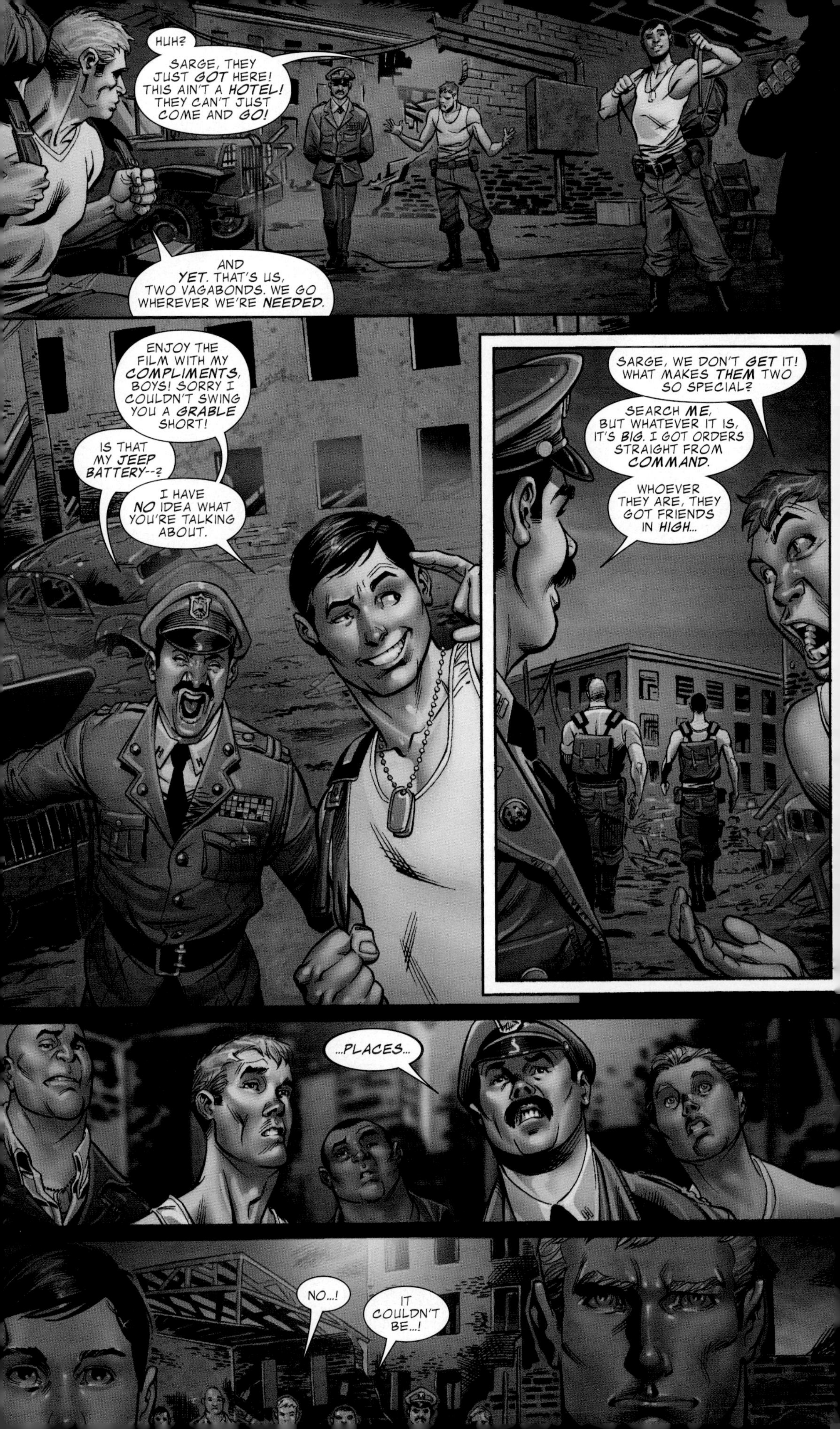
HUH?
SARGE, THEY JUST GOT HERE! THIS AIN'T A HOTEL! THEY CAN'T JUST COME AND GO!
AND YET. THAT'S US, TWO VAGABONDS. WE GO WHEREVER WE'RE NEEDED.
ENJOY THE FILM WITH MY COMPLIMENTS, BOYS! SORRY I COULDN'T SWING YOU A GRABLE SHORT!
IS THAT MY JEEP BATTERY--?
I HAVE NO IDEA WHAT YOU'RE TALKING ABOUT.
SARGE, WE DON'T GET IT! WHAT MAKES THEM TWO SO SPECIAL?
SEARCH ME, BUT WHATEVER IT IS, IT'S BIG. I GOT ORDERS STRAIGHT FROM COMMAND.
WHOEVER THEY ARE, THEY GOT FRIENDS IN HIGH...
...PLACES...
NO...!
IT COULDN'T BE...!

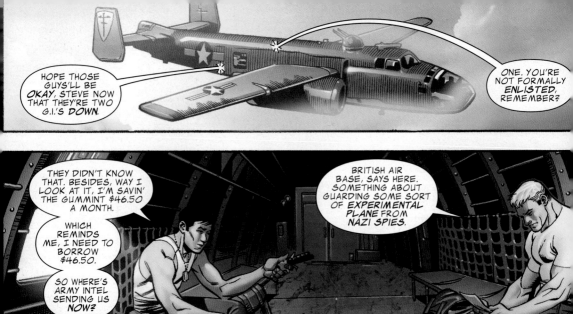

HOPE THOSE GUYS'LL BE *OKAY*, STEVE NOW THAT THEY'RE TWO G.I.'S *DOWN*.

ONE. YOU'RE NOT FORMALLY *ENLISTED*, REMEMBER?

THEY DIDN'T KNOW THAT. BESIDES, WAY I LOOK AT IT, I'M SAVIN' THE GUMMINT $46.50 A MONTH.

WHICH REMINDS ME, I NEED TO BORROW $46.50.

SO WHERE'S ARMY INTEL SENDING US *NOW*?

BRITISH AIR BASE, SAYS HERE. SOMETHING ABOUT GUARDING SOME SORT OF *EXPERIMENTAL* PLANE FROM *NAZI SPIES*.

PROBABLY MORE *UNDERCOVER* WORK, THEN. CRIMINY PETE. THIS WAR REALLY *IS* SLOWIN' DOWN, INNIT?

REALLY NICE SKETCH OF PEGGY, BY THE BY. YOU GOTTA TEACH ME HOW TO SLING A PENCIL ONE OF THESE DAYS.

THAT WHAT YOU WANT AFTER SERVICE? TO BE AN ART STUDENT?

NAH. I WAS THINKING MORE ALONG THE LINES OF PITCHING FOR THE *DODGERS*. MAYBE BEIN' A *MOVIE STAR*.

WELL, THAT'S SENSIBLE.

OKAY, SERIOUSLY? I WAS THINKING MAYBE *FOREST RANGER*.

SINCE *WHEN*?

AAAAAAAHH, IT'S JUST...

REDWOOD FORESTS, *GULF STREAM WATERS*, ALL THE *REST* OF THAT SONG...SUPPOSED TO BE *GORGEOUS*, RIGHT?

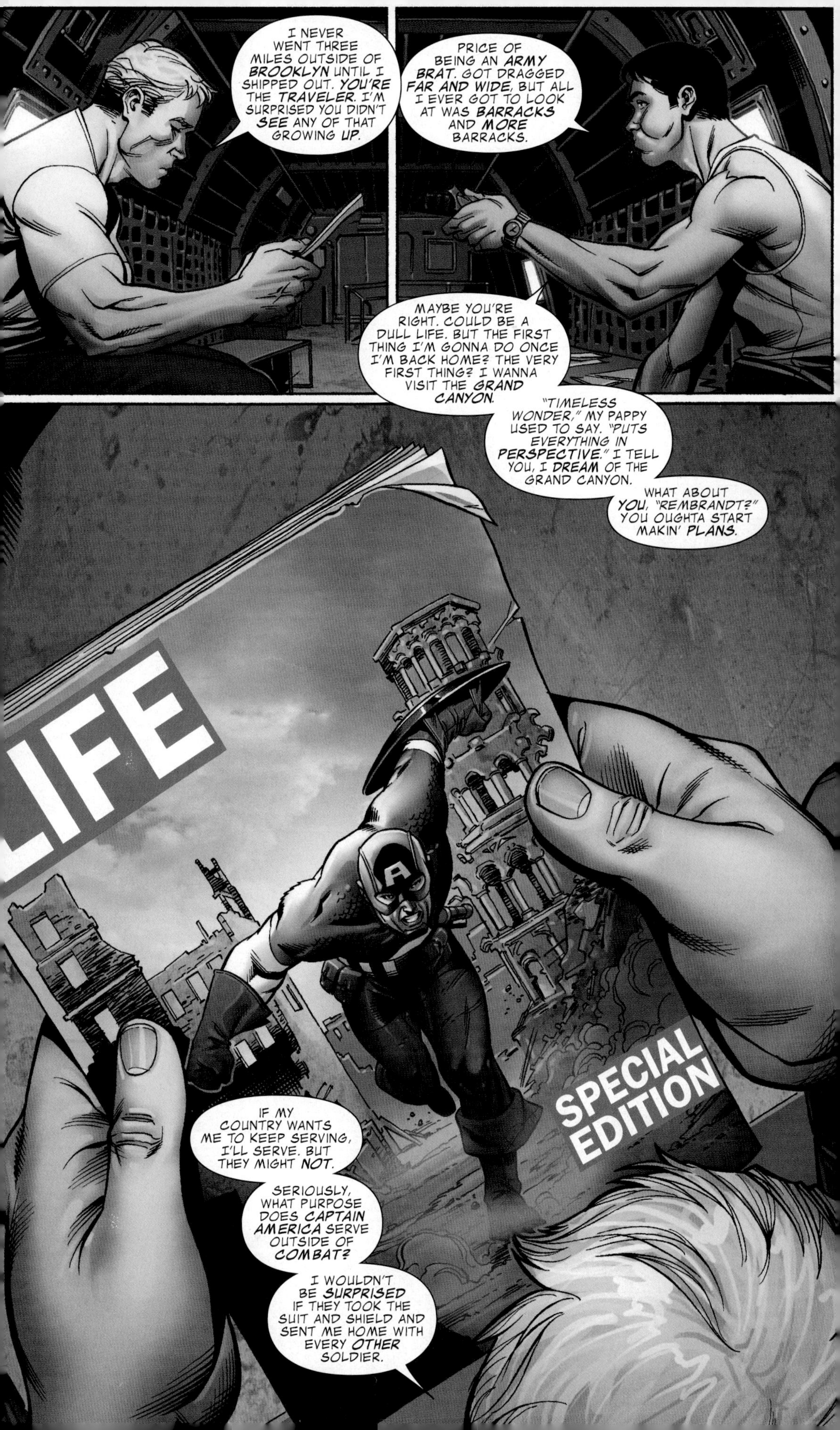
I NEVER WENT THREE MILES OUTSIDE OF BROOKLYN UNTIL I SHIPPED OUT. YOU'RE THE TRAVELER. I'M SURPRISED YOU DIDN'T SEE ANY OF THAT GROWING UP.
PRICE OF BEING AN ARMY BRAT. GOT DRAGGED FAR AND WIDE, BUT ALL I EVER GOT TO LOOK AT WAS BARRACKS AND MORE BARRACKS.
MAYBE YOU'RE RIGHT. COULD BE A DULL LIFE. BUT THE FIRST THING I'M GONNA DO ONCE I'M BACK HOME? THE VERY FIRST THING? I WANNA VISIT THE GRAND CANYON.
"TIMELESS WONDER," MY PAPPY USED TO SAY. "PUTS EVERYTHING IN PERSPECTIVE." I TELL YOU, I DREAM OF THE GRAND CANYON.
WHAT ABOUT YOU, "REMBRANDT?" YOU OUGHTA START MAKIN' PLANS.
LIFE
SPECIAL EDITION
IF MY COUNTRY WANTS ME TO KEEP SERVING, I'LL SERVE. BUT THEY MIGHT NOT.
SERIOUSLY, WHAT PURPOSE DOES CAPTAIN AMERICA SERVE OUTSIDE OF COMBAT?
I WOULDN'T BE SURPRISED IF THEY TOOK THE SUIT AND SHIELD AND SENT ME HOME WITH EVERY OTHER SOLDIER.

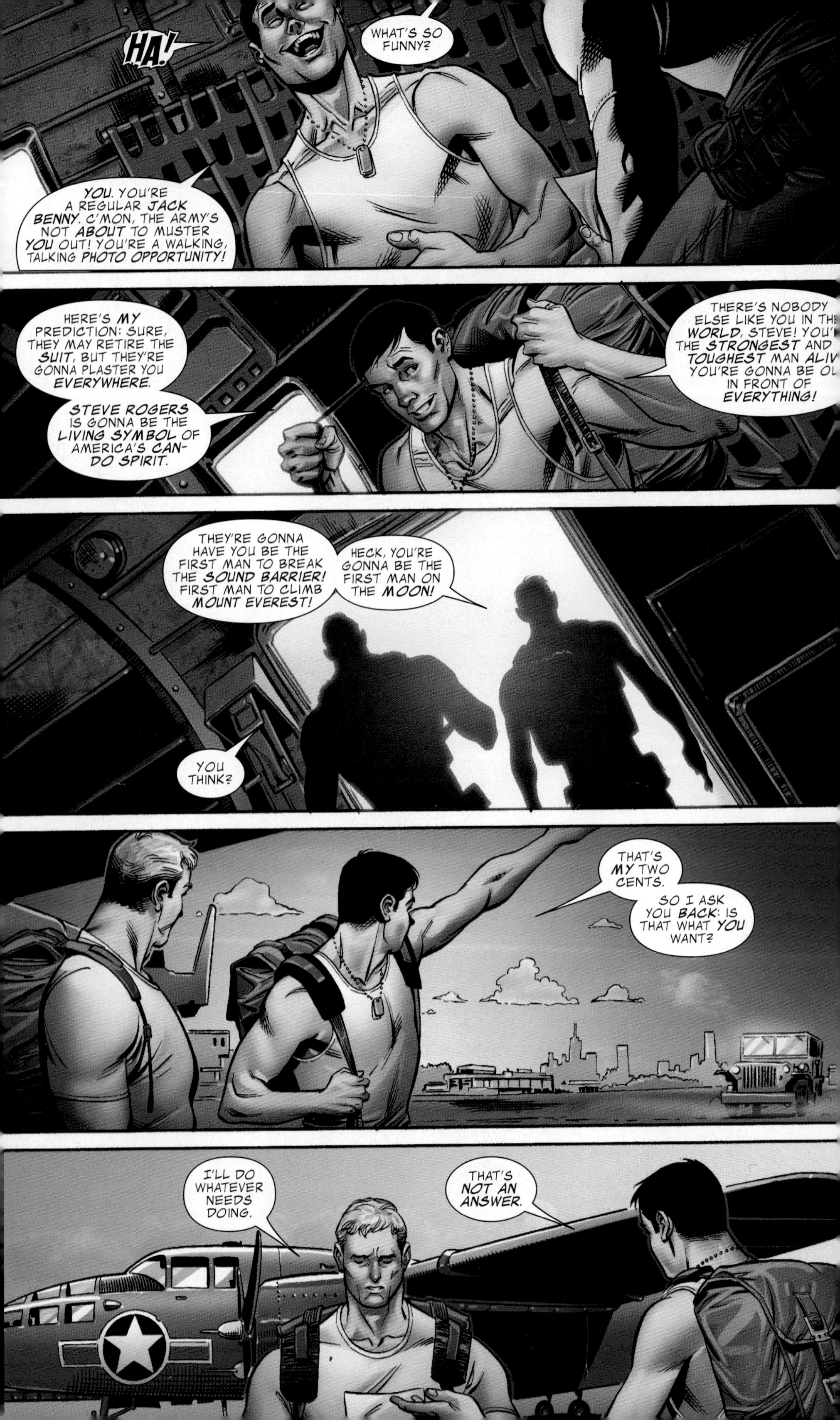
HA!
WHAT'S SO FUNNY?
YOU. YOU'RE A REGULAR JACK BENNY. C'MON, THE ARMY'S NOT ABOUT TO MUSTER YOU OUT! YOU'RE A WALKING, TALKING PHOTO OPPORTUNITY!
HERE'S MY PREDICTION: SURE, THEY MAY RETIRE THE SUIT, BUT THEY'RE GONNA PLASTER YOU EVERYWHERE.
STEVE ROGERS IS GONNA BE THE LIVING SYMBOL OF AMERICA'S CAN-DO SPIRIT.
THERE'S NOBODY ELSE LIKE YOU IN TH WORLD, STEVE! YOU' THE STRONGEST AND TOUGHEST MAN ALIV YOU'RE GONNA BE O IN FRONT OF EVERYTHING!
THEY'RE GONNA HAVE YOU BE THE FIRST MAN TO BREAK THE SOUND BARRIER! FIRST MAN TO CLIMB MOUNT EVEREST!
HECK, YOU'RE GONNA BE THE FIRST MAN ON THE MOON!
YOU THINK?
THAT'S MY TWO CENTS.
SO I ASK YOU BACK: IS THAT WHAT YOU WANT?
I'LL DO WHATEVER NEEDS DOING.
THAT'S NOT AN ANSWER.

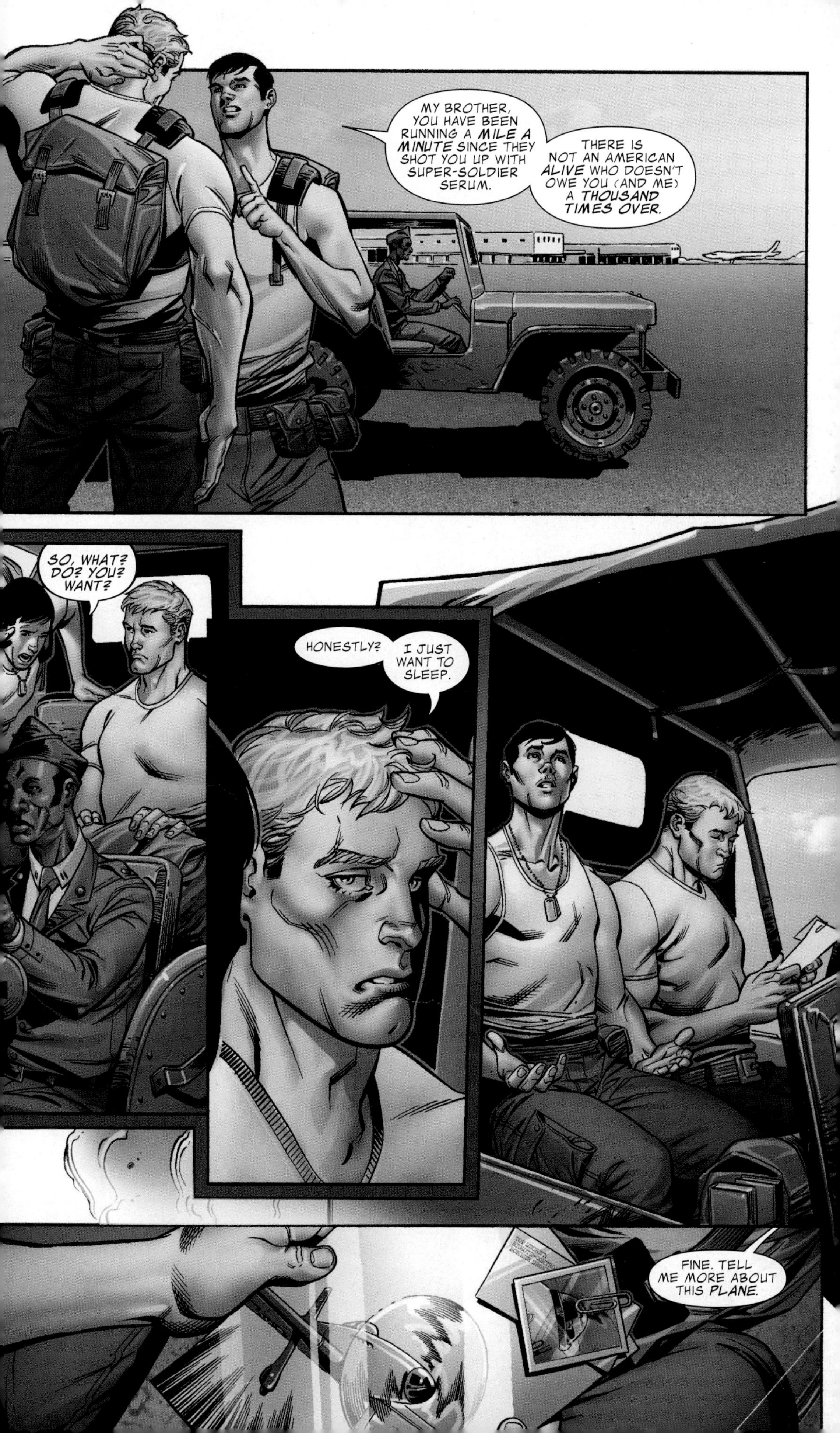
MY BROTHER, YOU HAVE BEEN RUNNING A MILE A MINUTE SINCE THEY SHOT YOU UP WITH SUPER-SOLDIER SERUM.
THERE IS NOT AN AMERICAN ALIVE WHO DOESN'T OWE YOU (AND ME) A THOUSAND TIMES OVER.
SO, WHAT? DO? YOU? WANT?
HONESTLY?
I JUST WANT TO SLEEP.
FINE. TELL ME MORE ABOUT THIS PLANE.

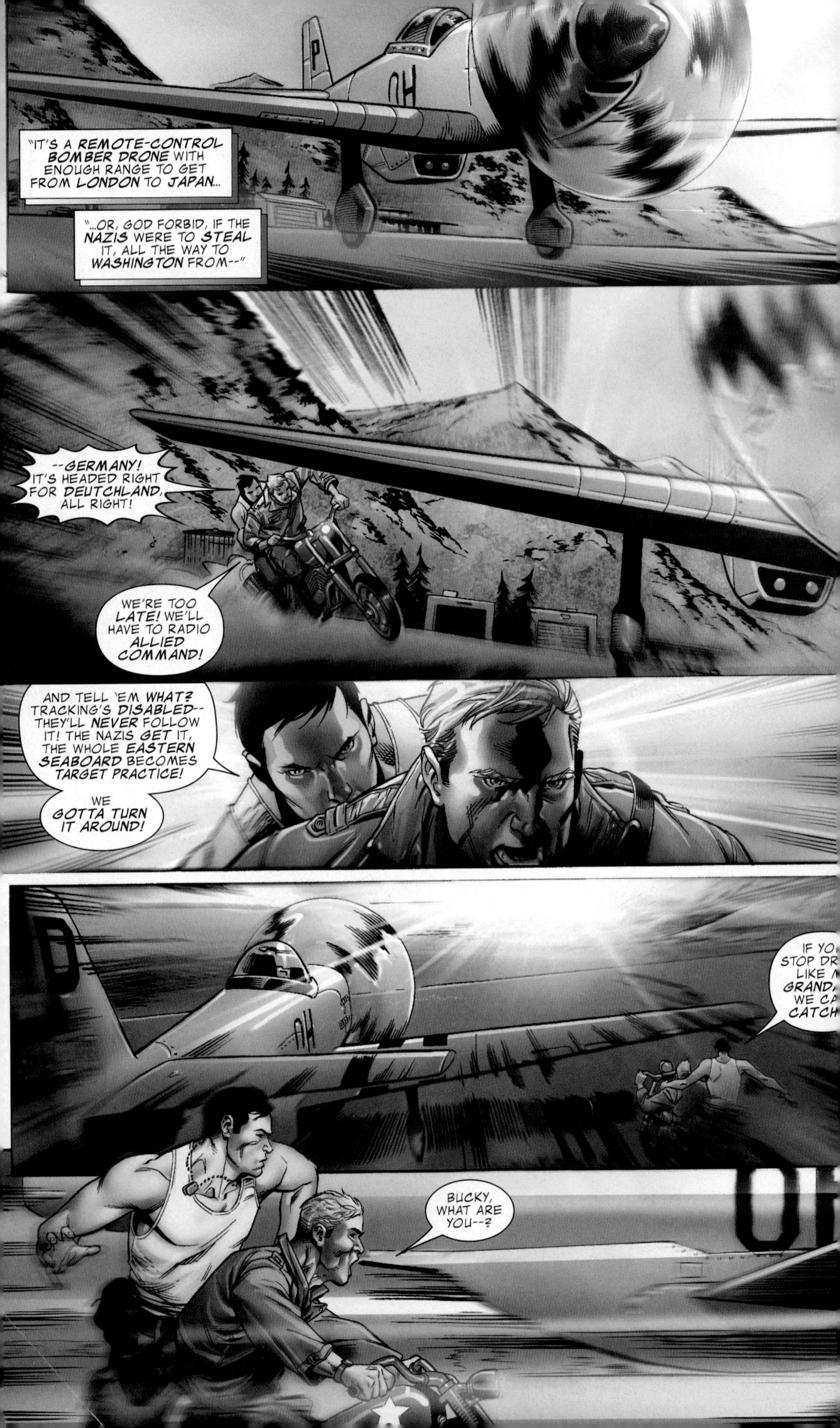
"IT'S A REMOTE-CONTROL BOMBER DRONE WITH ENOUGH RANGE TO GET FROM LONDON TO JAPAN...
"...OR, GOD FORBID, IF THE NAZIS WERE TO STEAL IT, ALL THE WAY TO WASHINGTON FROM--"
--GERMANY! IT'S HEADED RIGHT FOR DEUTCHLAND, ALL RIGHT!
WE'RE TOO LATE! WE'LL HAVE TO RADIO ALLIED COMMAND!
AND TELL 'EM WHAT? TRACKING'S DISABLED-- THEY'LL NEVER FOLLOW IT! THE NAZIS GET IT, THE WHOLE EASTERN SEABOARD BECOMES TARGET PRACTICE!
WE GOTTA TURN IT AROUND!
BUCKY, WHAT ARE YOU--?

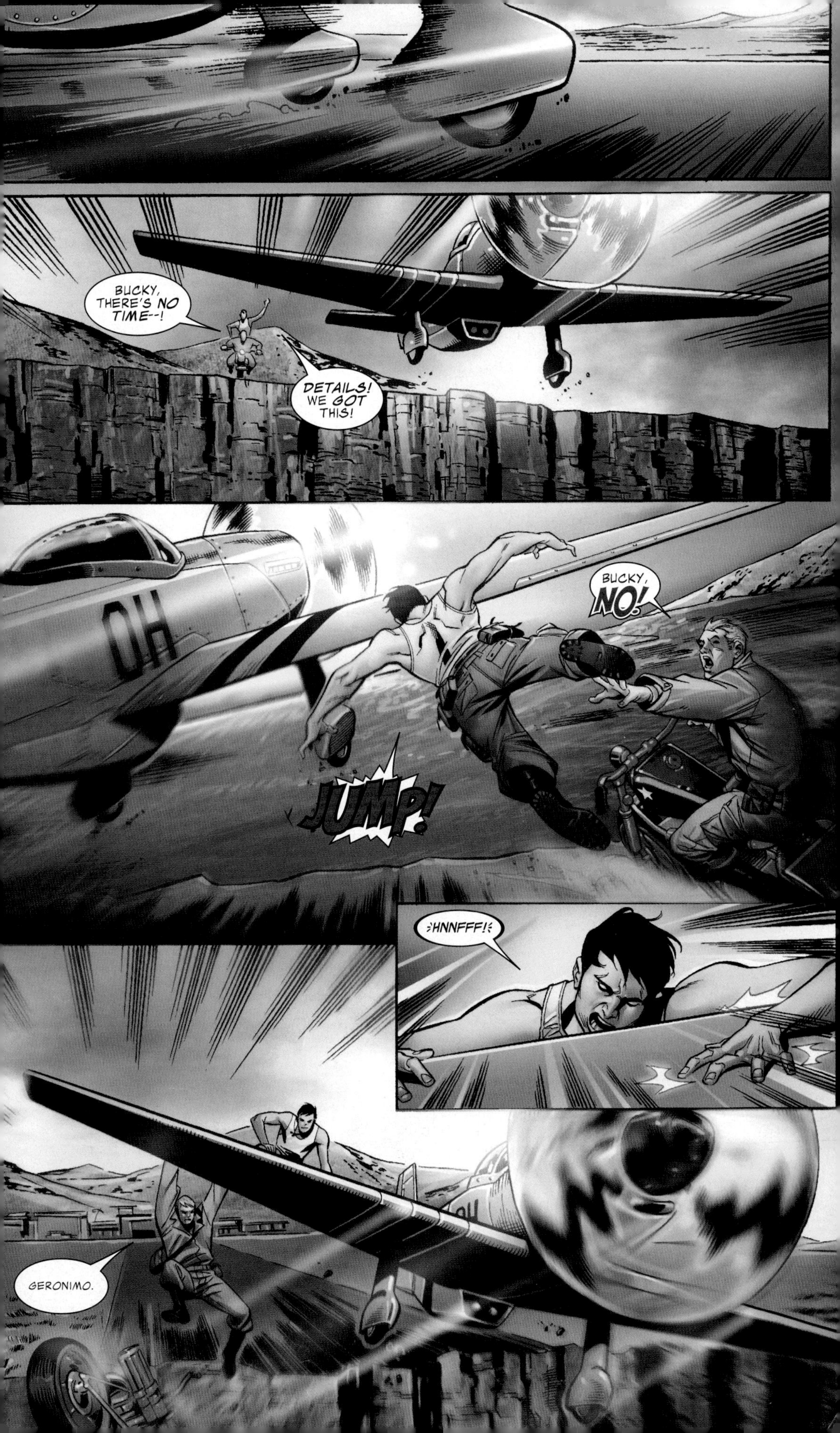
BUCKY, THERE'S NO TIME--!
DETAILS! WE GOT THIS!
BUCKY, NO!
JUMP!
HNNFFF!
GERONIMO.

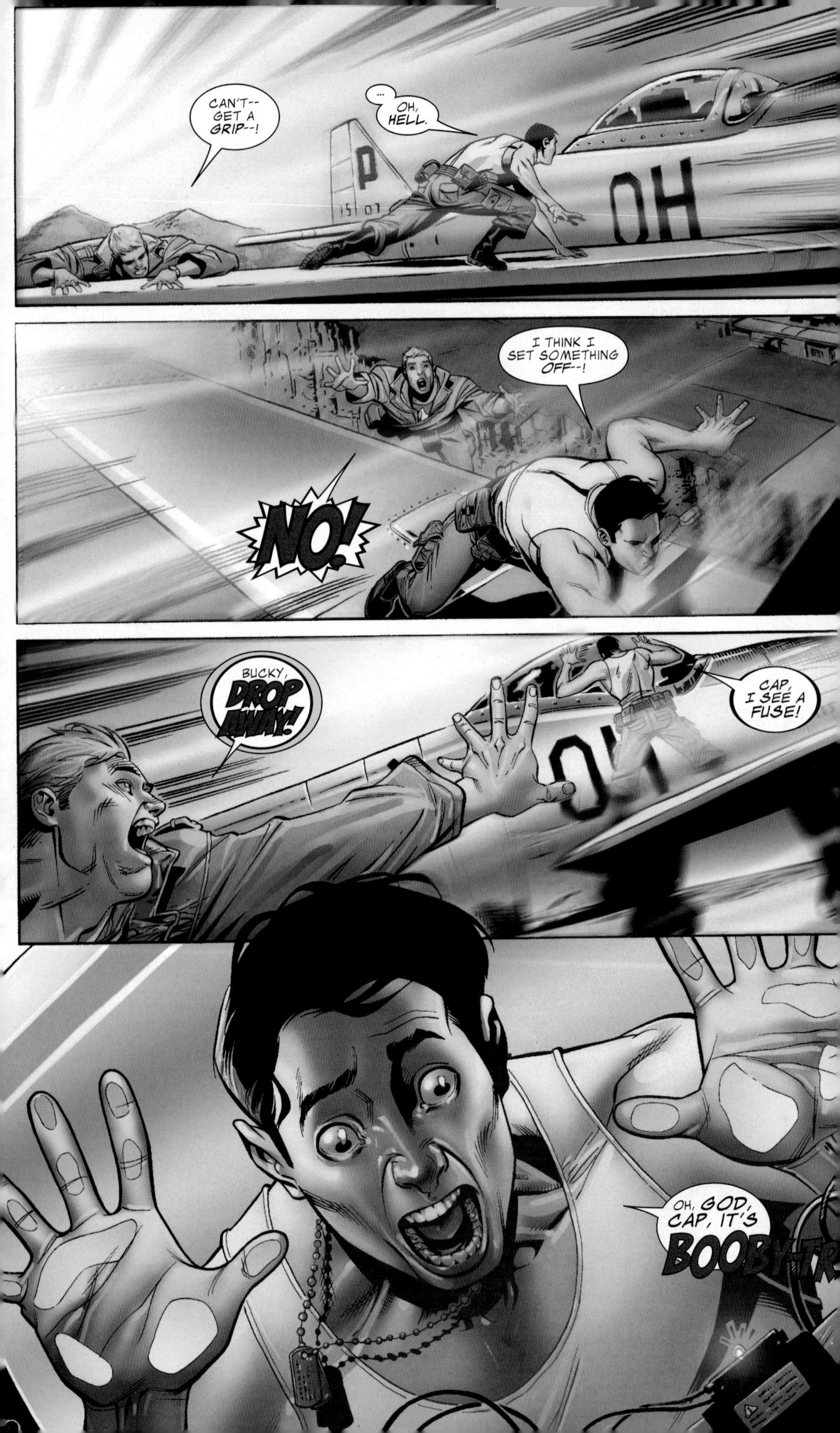
CAN'T-- GET A GRIP--!
... OH, HELL.
OH
I THINK I SET SOMETHING OFF--!
NO!
BUCKY, DROP AWAY!
CAP, I SEE A FUSE!
OH, GOD, CAP, IT'S BOOBY-TR

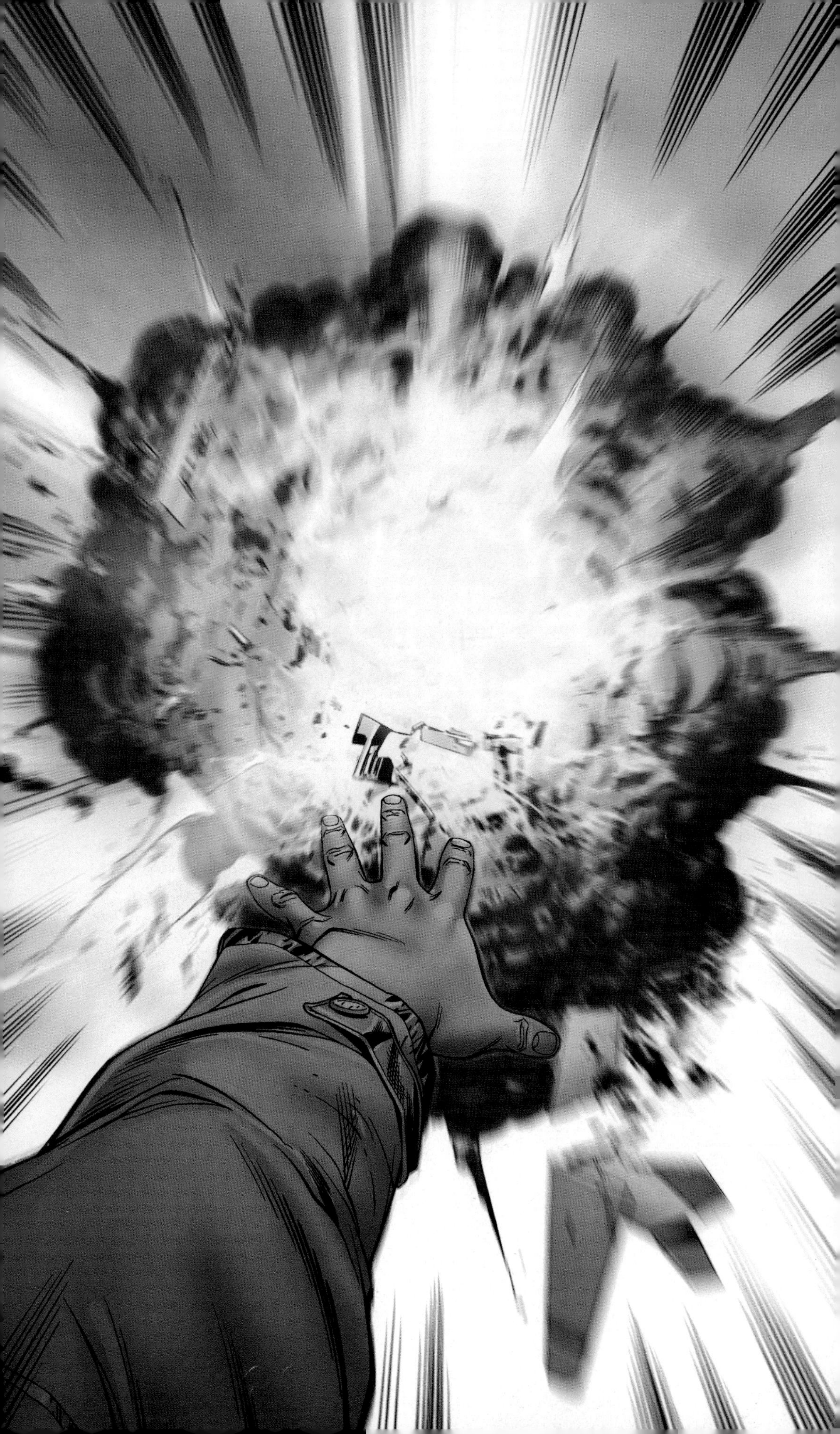

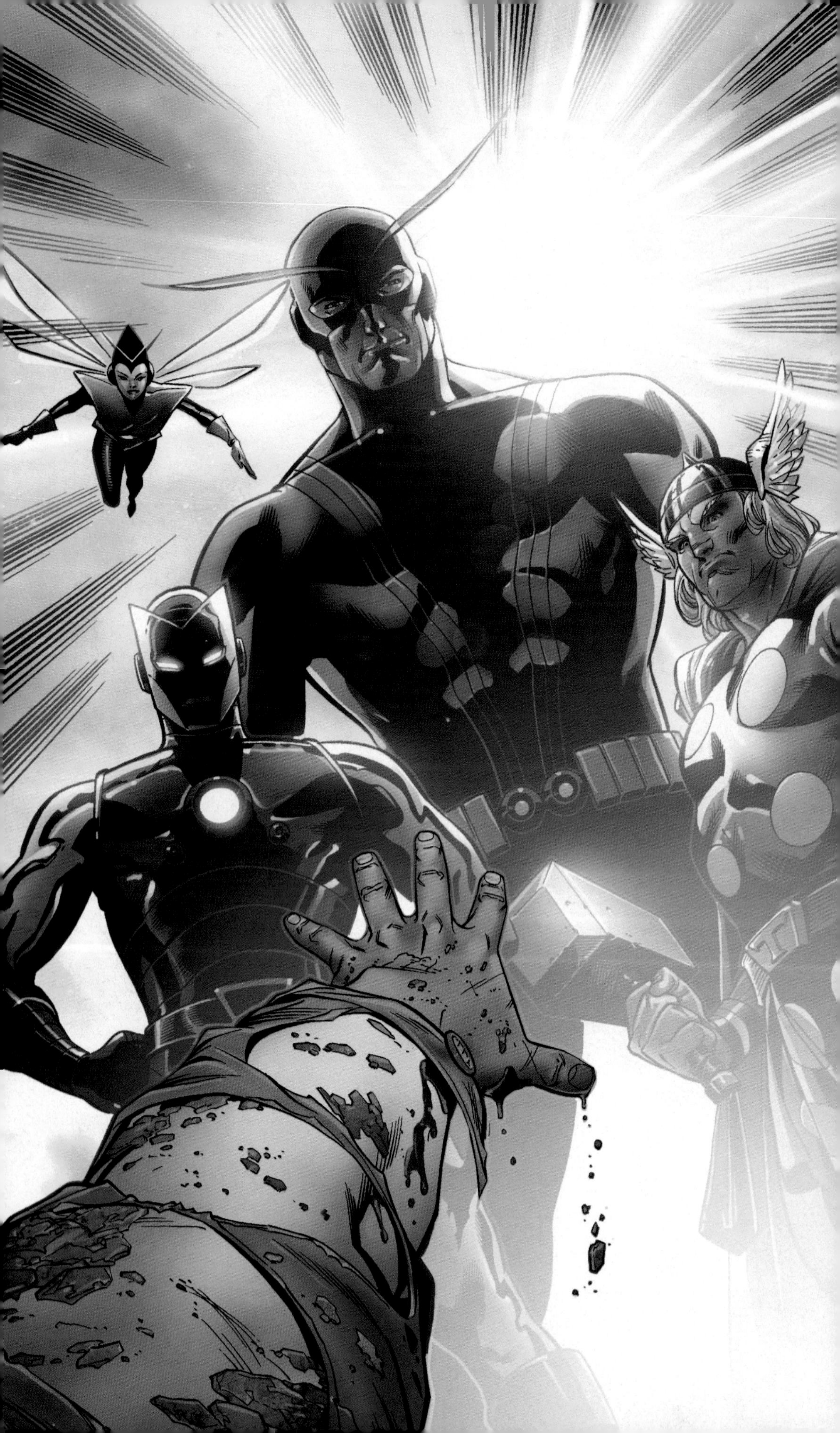

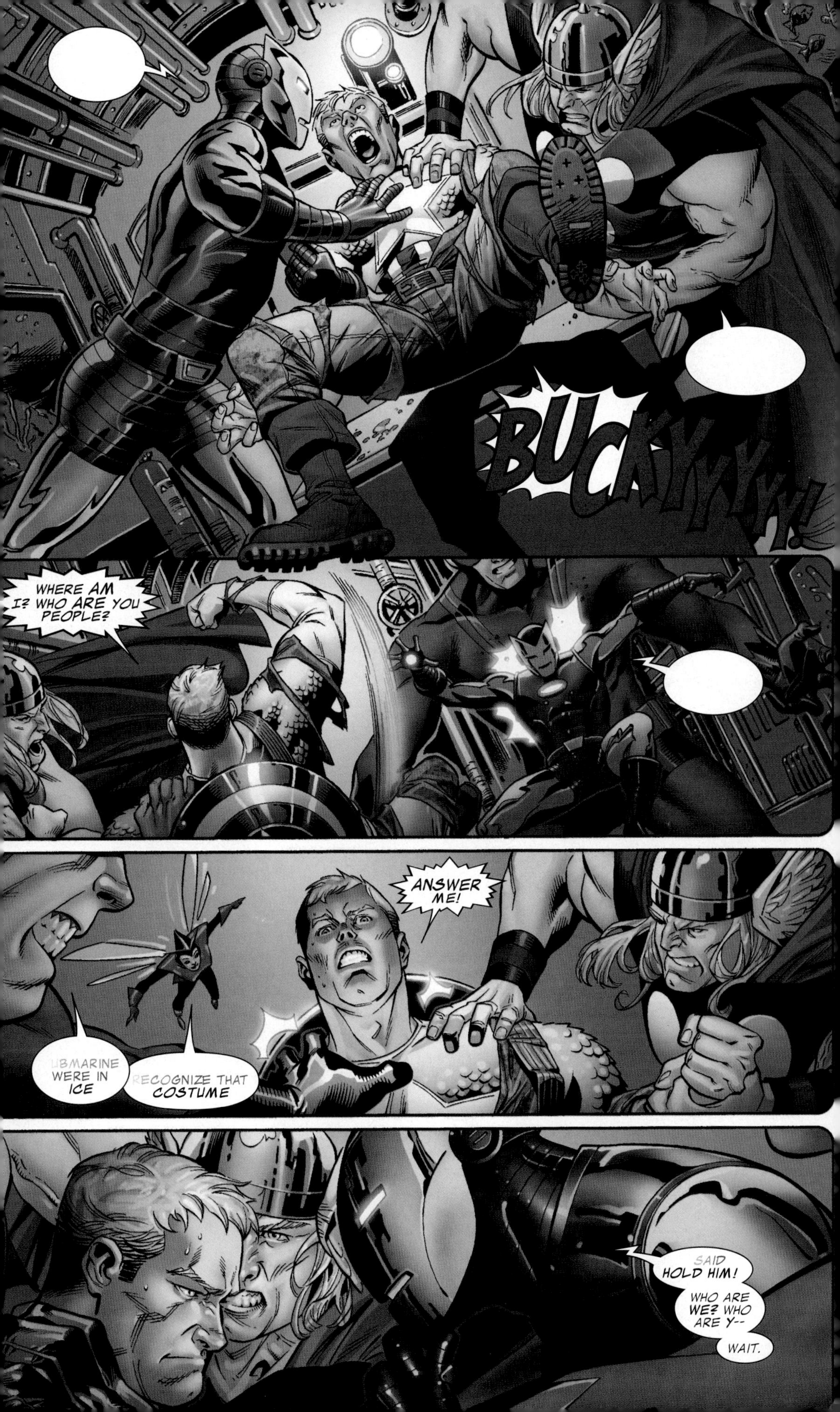
BUCKYYYY!
WHERE AM I? WHO ARE YOU PEOPLE?
ANSWER ME!
UBMARINE WERE IN ICE
ECOGNIZE THAT COSTUME
SAID HOLD HIM!
WHO ARE WE? WHO ARE Y--
WAIT.

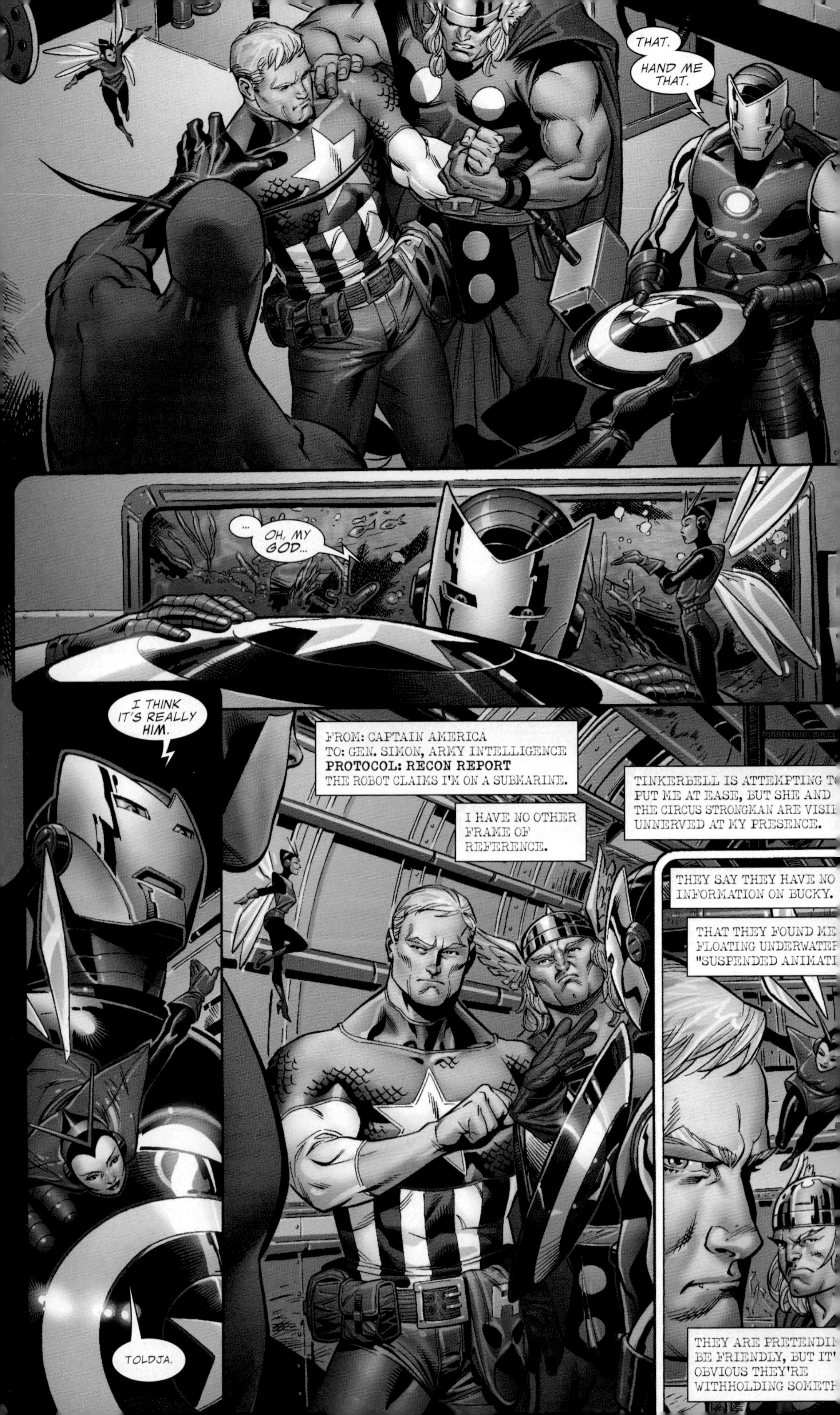

THAT.
HAND ME THAT.
... OH, MY GOD...
I THINK IT'S REALLY HIM.
TOLDJA.
FROM: CAPTAIN AMERICA
TO: GEN. SIMON, ARMY INTELLIGENCE
PROTOCOL: RECON REPORT
THE ROBOT CLAIMS I'M ON A SUBMARINE.
I HAVE NO OTHER FRAME OF REFERENCE.
TINKERBELL IS ATTEMPTING T PUT ME AT EASE, BUT SHE AND THE CIRCUS STRONGMAN ARE VISI UNNERVED AT MY PRESENCE.
THEY SAY THEY HAVE NO INFORMATION ON BUCKY.
THAT THEY FOUND ME FLOATING UNDERWATE "SUSPENDED ANIMATI
THEY ARE PRETENDI BE FRIENDLY, BUT IT' OBVIOUS THEY'RE WITHHOLDING SOMET

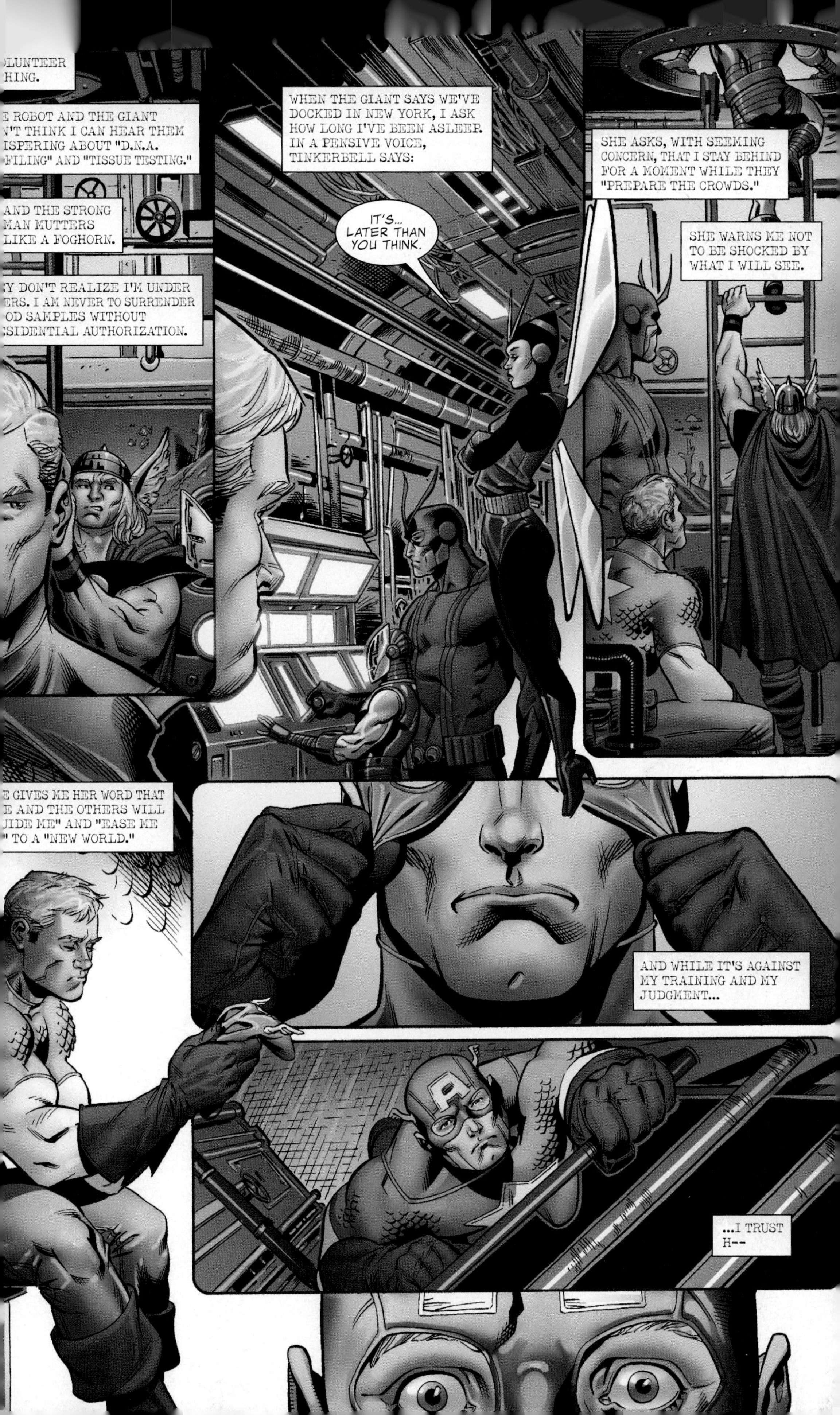
OLUNTEER
HING.
E ROBOT AND THE GIANT
N'T THINK I CAN HEAR THEM
ISPERING ABOUT "D.N.A.
FILING" AND "TISSUE TESTING."
AND THE STRONG MAN MUTTERS LIKE A FOGHORN.
Y DON'T REALIZE I'M UNDER
ERS. I AM NEVER TO SURRENDER
OD SAMPLES WITHOUT
SIDENTIAL AUTHORIZATION.
WHEN THE GIANT SAYS WE'VE DOCKED IN NEW YORK, I ASK HOW LONG I'VE BEEN ASLEEP. IN A PENSIVE VOICE, TINKERBELL SAYS:
IT'S... LATER THAN YOU THINK.
SHE ASKS, WITH SEEMING CONCERN, THAT I STAY BEHIND FOR A MOMENT WHILE THEY "PREPARE THE CROWDS."
SHE WARNS ME NOT TO BE SHOCKED BY WHAT I WILL SEE.
E GIVES ME HER WORD THAT
E AND THE OTHERS WILL
UIDE ME" AND "EASE ME
" TO A "NEW WORLD."
AND WHILE IT'S AGAINST MY TRAINING AND MY JUDGMENT...
...I TRUST H--

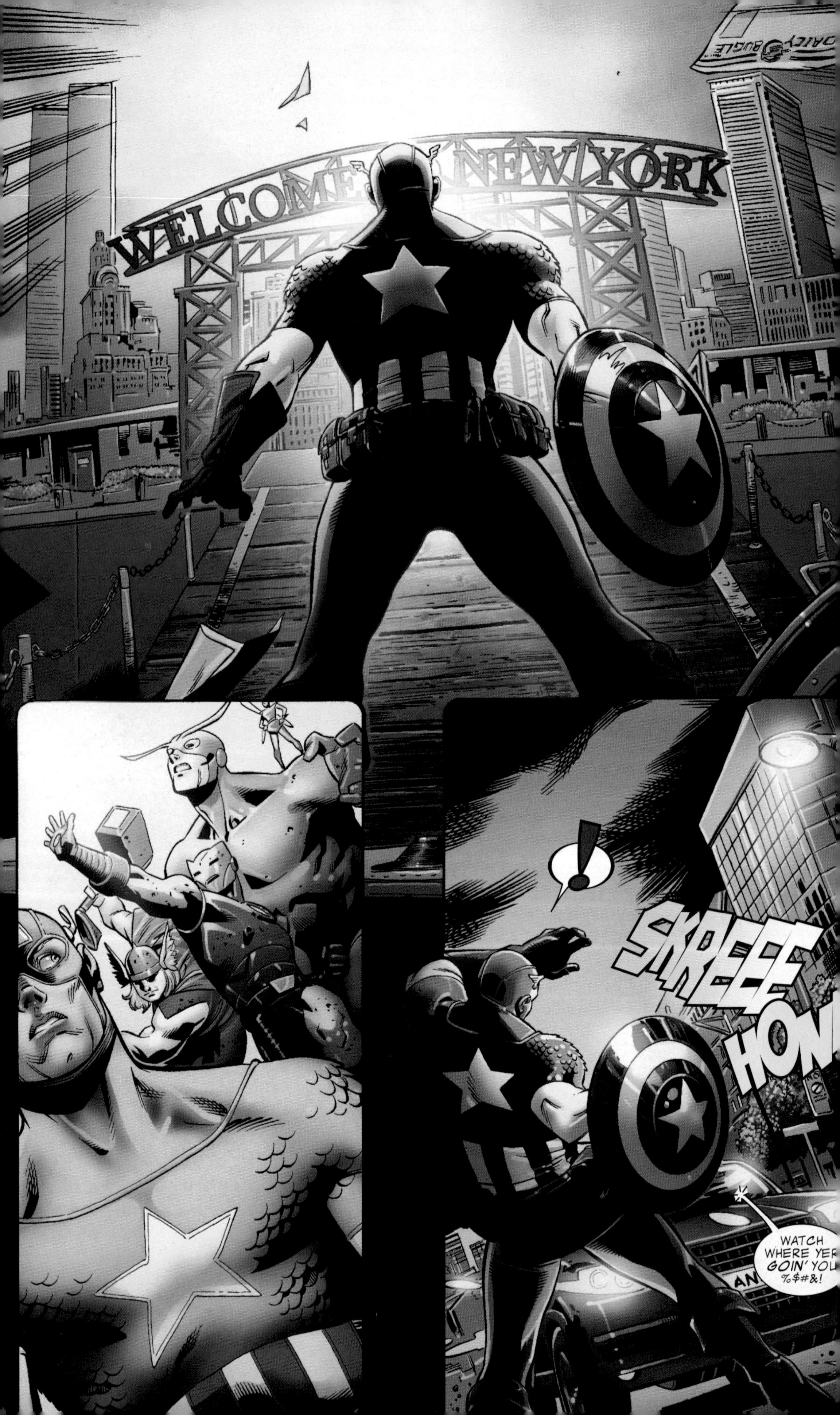
WELCOME
NEW YORK
!
SKREEE
HON
WATCH WHERE YER GOIN' YOU %$#&!

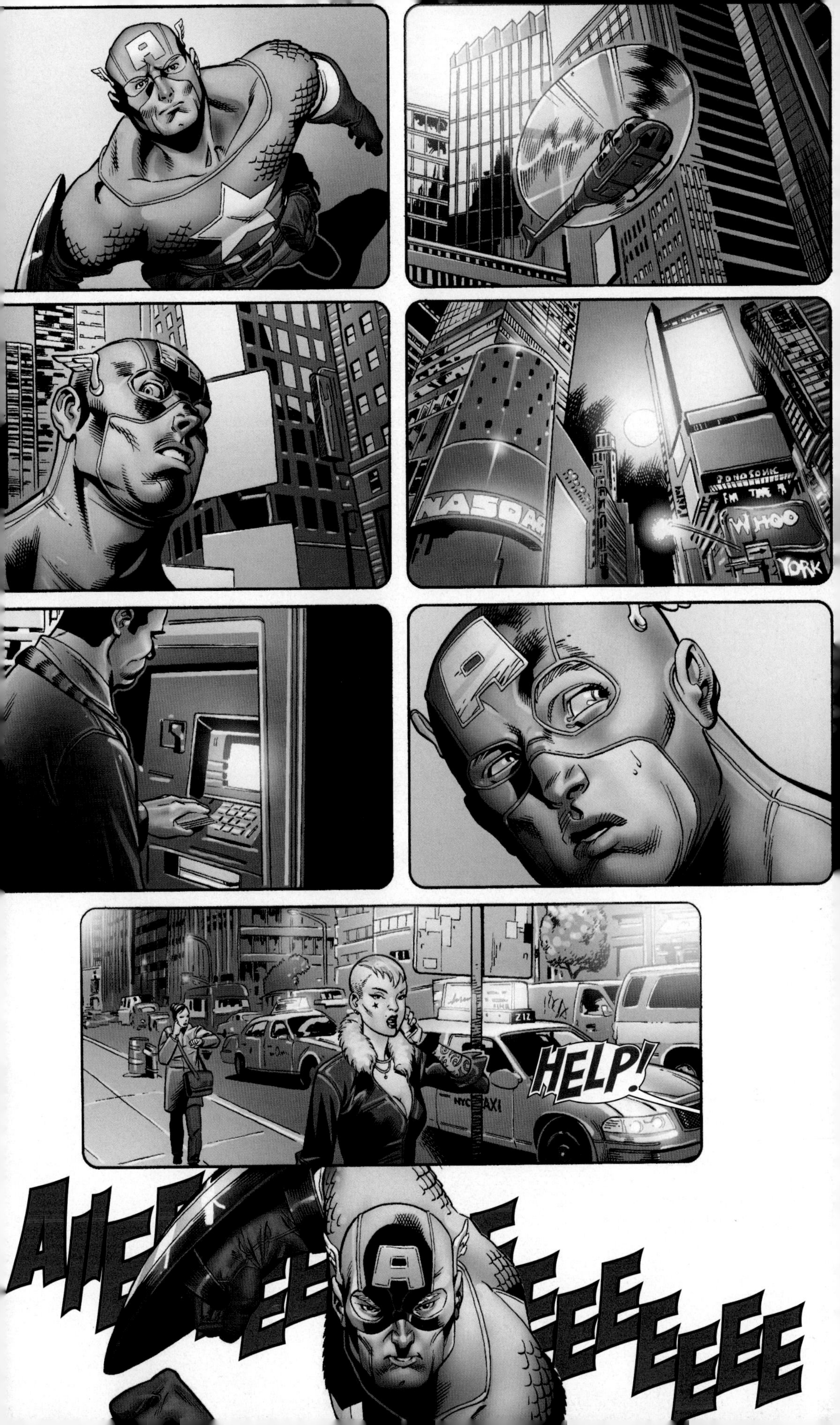
HELP!
AIEEEEEEEEEEEEEEEEE

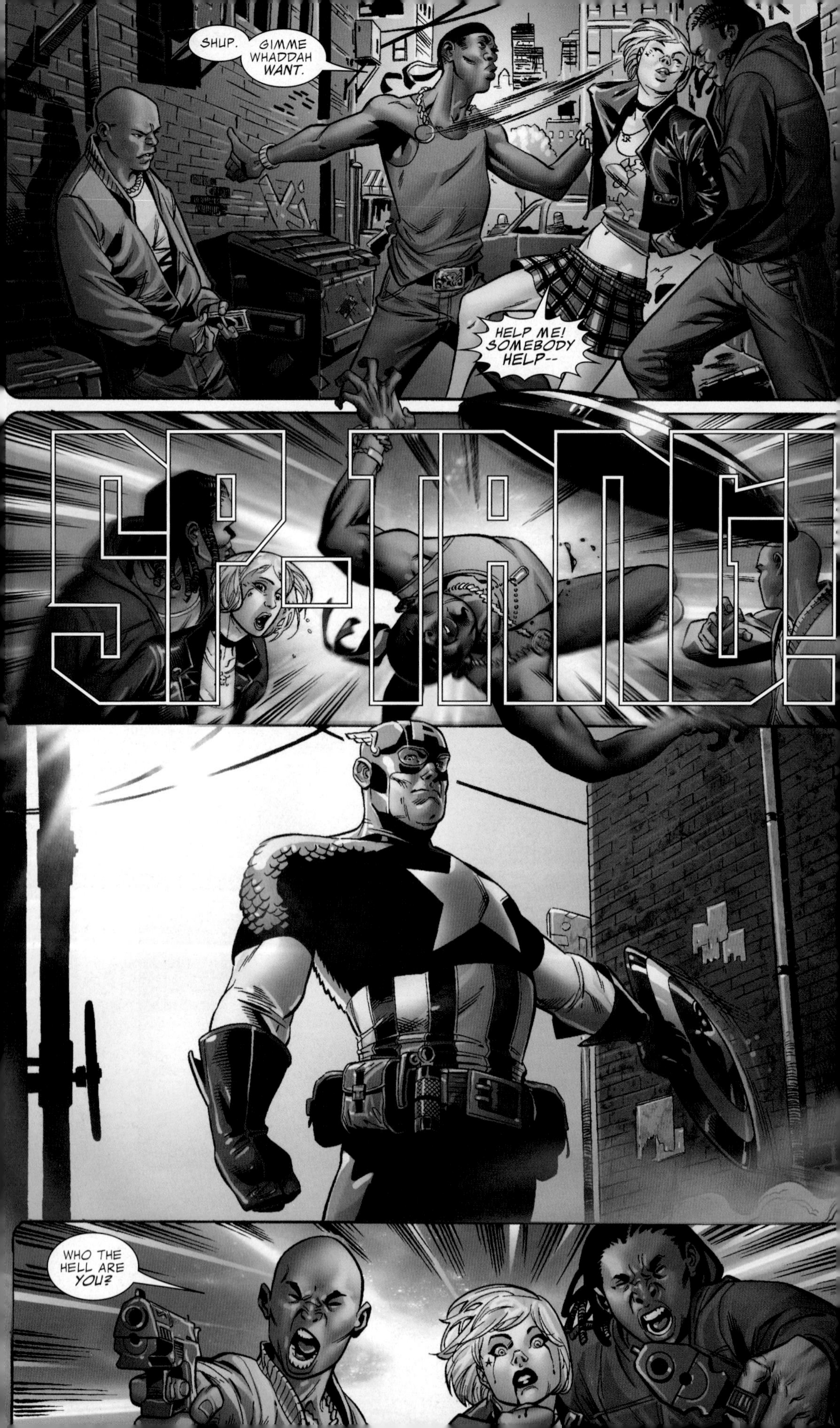

SHUP.
GIMME WHADDAH WANT.
HELP ME! SOMEBODY HELP--
SPTANG!
WHO THE HELL ARE YOU?

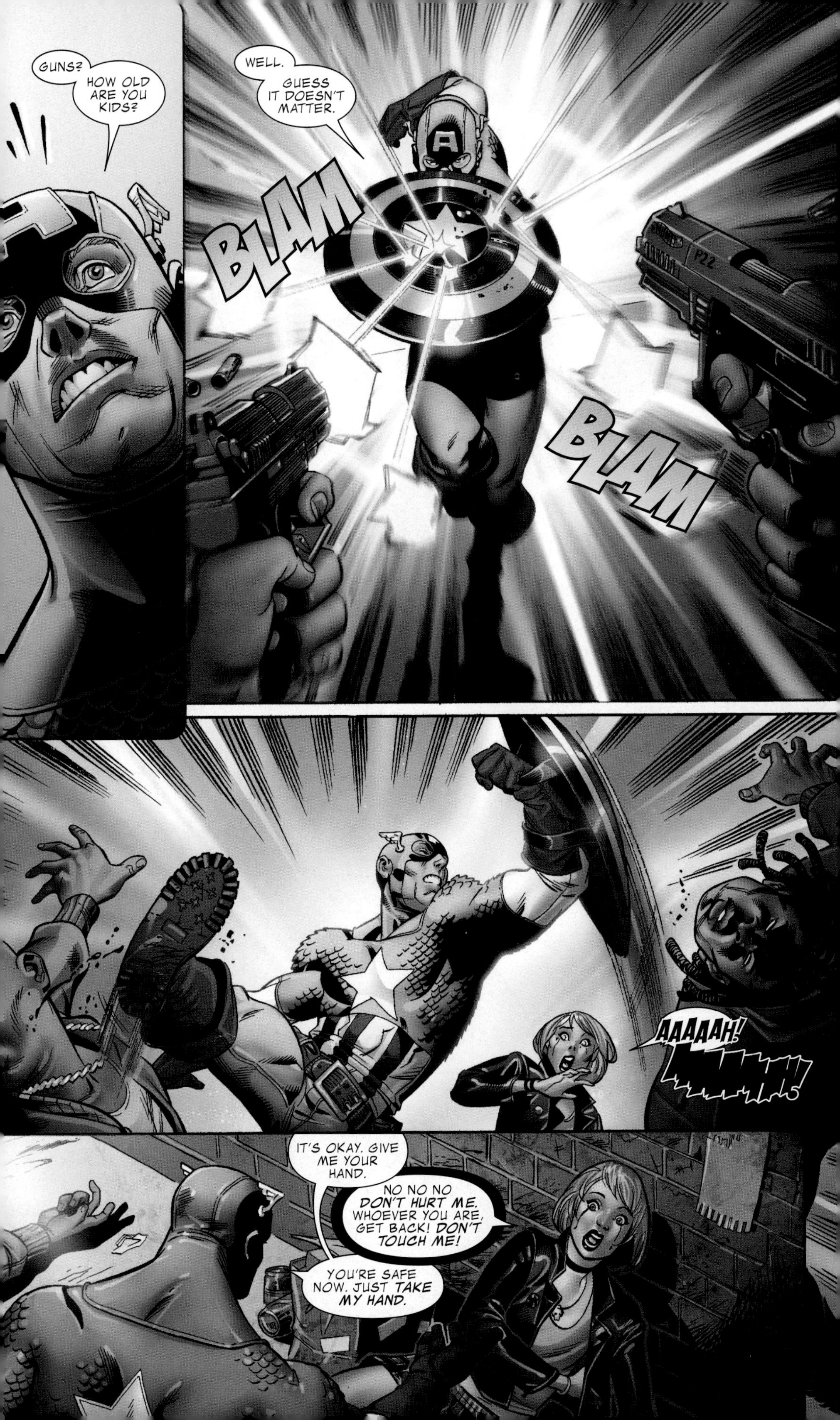
GUNS? HOW OLD ARE YOU KIDS?
WELL. GUESS IT DOESN'T MATTER.
BLAM
BLAM
AAAAAH!
IT'S OKAY. GIVE ME YOUR HAND.
NO NO NO DON'T HURT ME. WHOEVER YOU ARE, GET BACK! DON'T TOUCH ME!
YOU'RE SAFE NOW. JUST TAKE MY HAND.

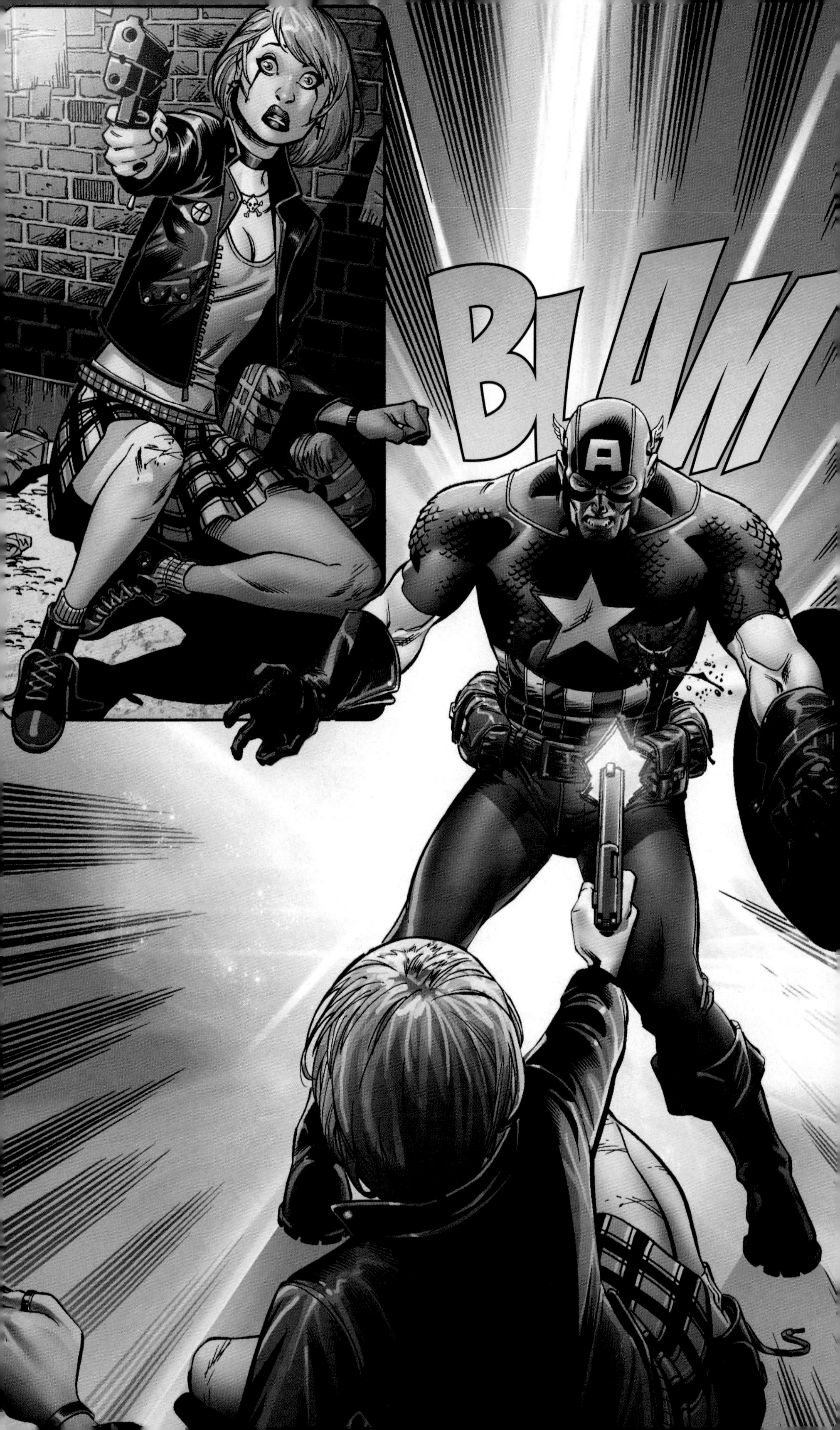
BLAM

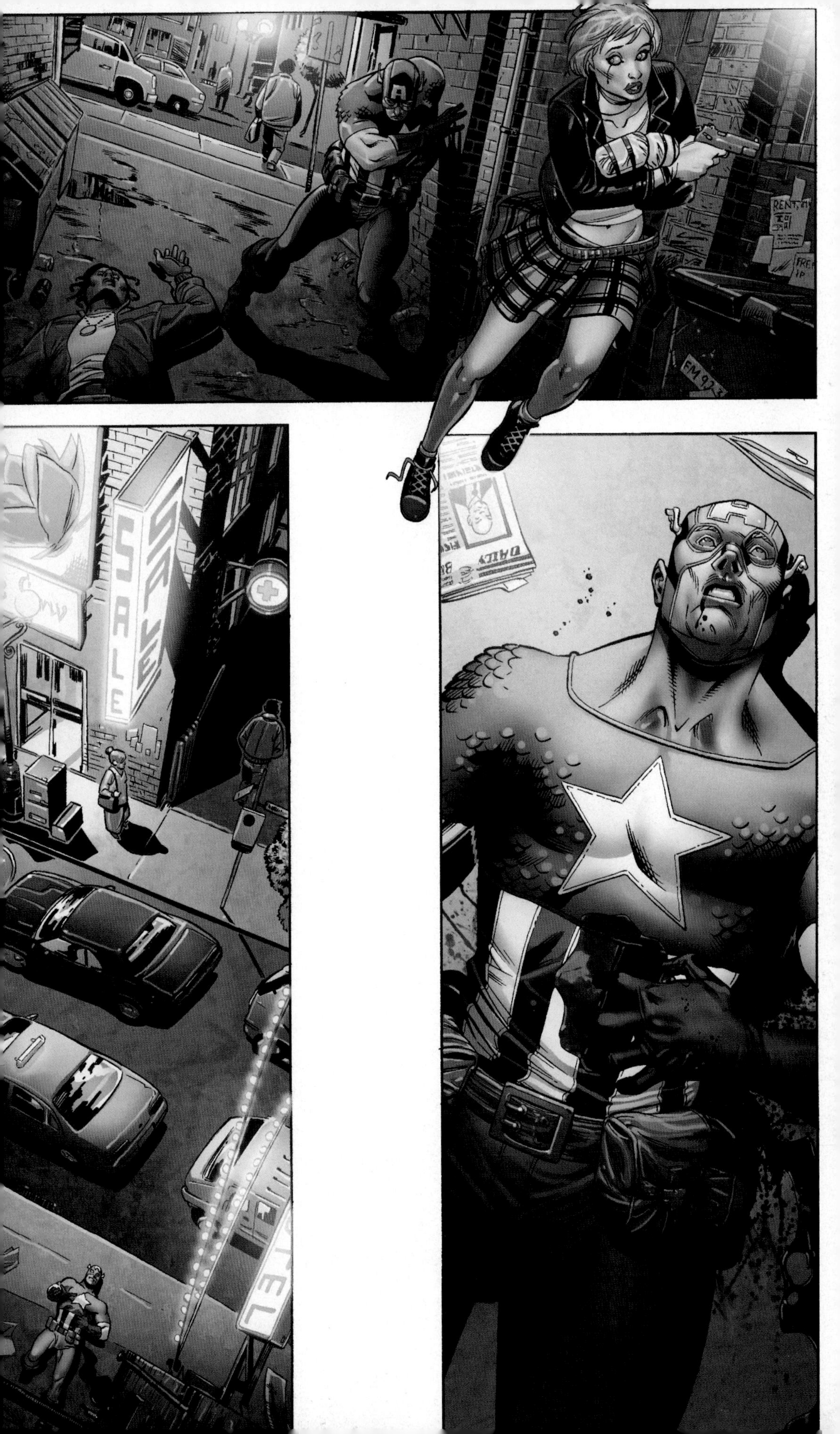
RENT
SALE

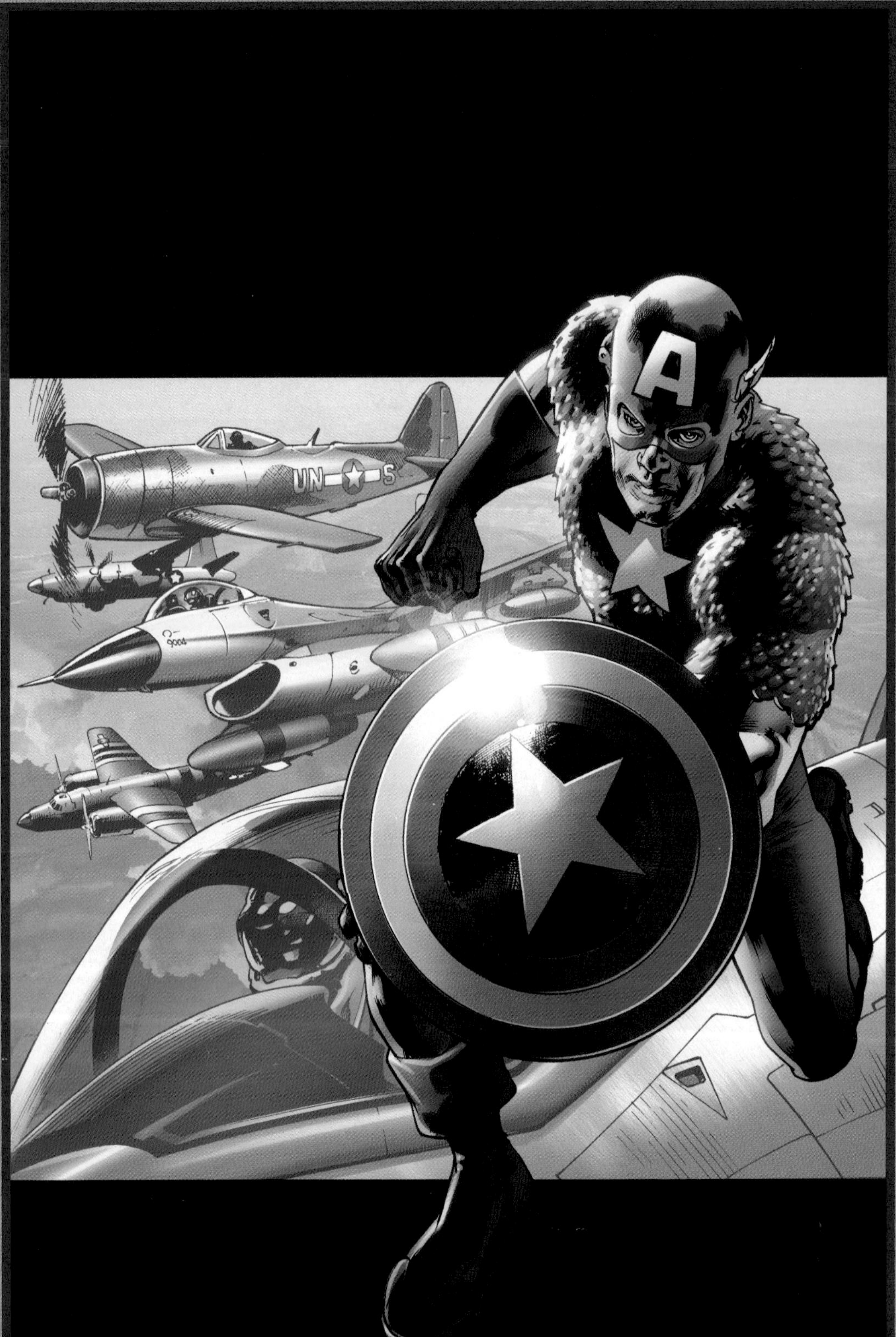
UN S
9004

[2]

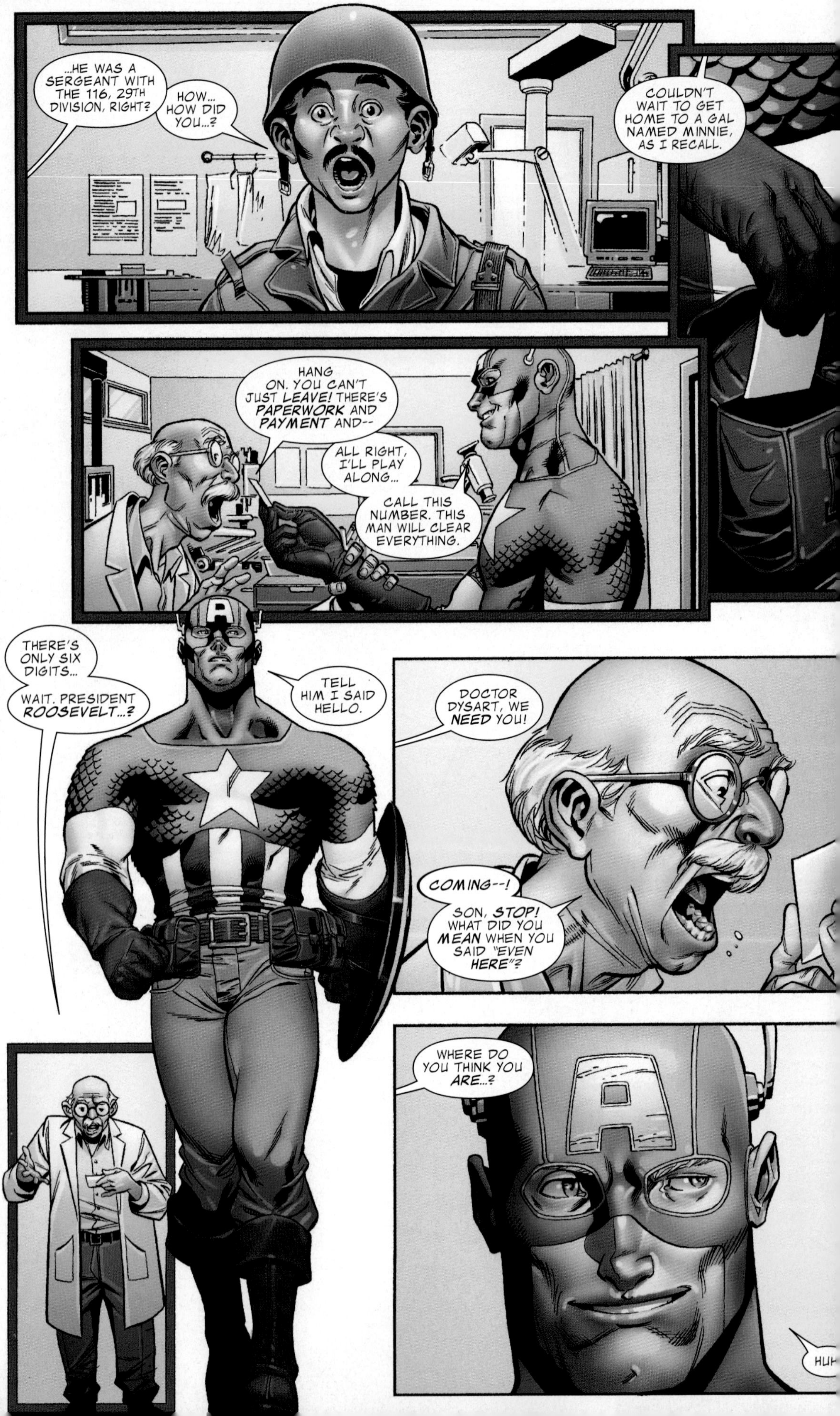
...HE WAS A SERGEANT WITH THE 116, 29TH DIVISION, RIGHT?
HOW... HOW DID YOU...?
COULDN'T WAIT TO GET HOME TO A GAL NAMED MINNIE, AS I RECALL.
HANG ON. YOU CAN'T JUST LEAVE! THERE'S PAPERWORK AND PAYMENT AND--
ALL RIGHT, I'LL PLAY ALONG...
CALL THIS NUMBER. THIS MAN WILL CLEAR EVERYTHING.
THERE'S ONLY SIX DIGITS...
WAIT. PRESIDENT ROOSEVELT...?
TELL HIM I SAID HELLO.
DOCTOR DYSART, WE NEED YOU!
COMING--!
SON, STOP! WHAT DID YOU MEAN WHEN YOU SAID "EVEN HERE"?
WHERE DO YOU THINK YOU ARE...?

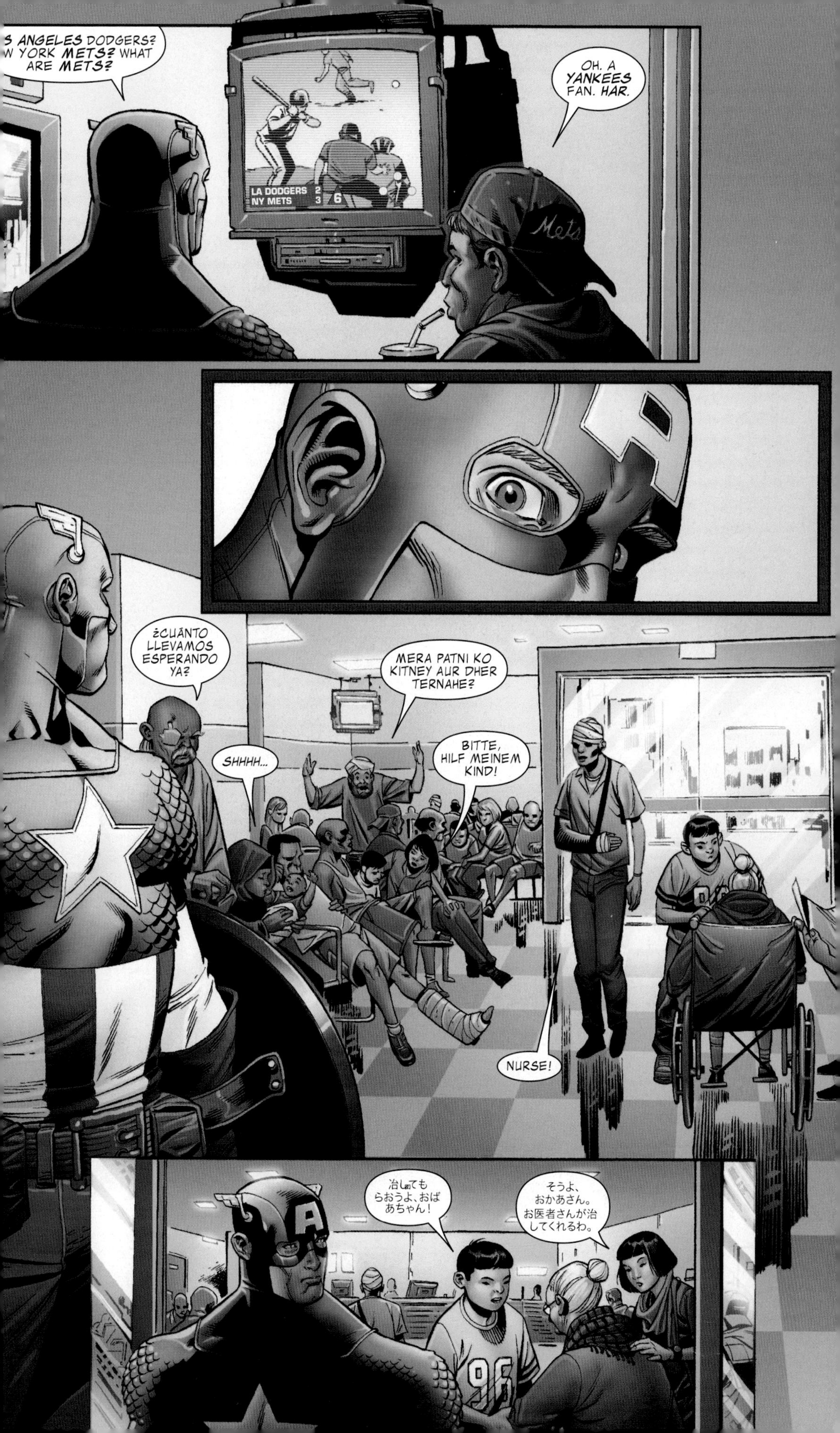

S ANGELES DODGERS? W YORK METS? WHAT ARE METS?
LA DODGERS 2
NY METS 3
6
OH. A YANKEES FAN. HAR.
Mets
¿CUÁNTO LLEVAMOS ESPERANDO YA?
MERA PATNI KO KITNEY AUR DHER TERNAHE?
SHHHH...
BITTE, HILF MEINEM KIND!
NURSE!
治してもらおうよ、おばあちゃん！
そうよ、おかあさん。お医者さんが治してくれるわ。
96

FROM: CAPTAIN AMERICA
TO: GEN. SIMON, ARMY INTELLIGENCE
RECON REPORT, CONT'D

EVEN THE **LOCALS** SPEAK A FOREIGN LANGUAGE.

"LAPTOP." "JUMP THE SHARK." "TEXTING." JUST SOME OF TH[E] TERMS I'VE OVERHEARD IN THE LAST THREE MINUTES.

I DON'T HAVE ANY MOR[E] LUCK TELEPHONING **MILITARY COMMAND** THAN I DO FINDING THE [...]

I DIDN'T KNOW IT WAS **HALLOWEEN!**

WHAT'S WITH THE **FLAG,** BUDDY?

HOW DOES THE HUMAN MIN[D] COME **UP** WITH A WORLD L[IKE] THIS? WHENEVER I FEEL L[...] I'M GETTING MY **BEARING[S]**

--SOMETHING KNOCKS ME **SIDEWAYS** AGAIN.

HEY, CAP!

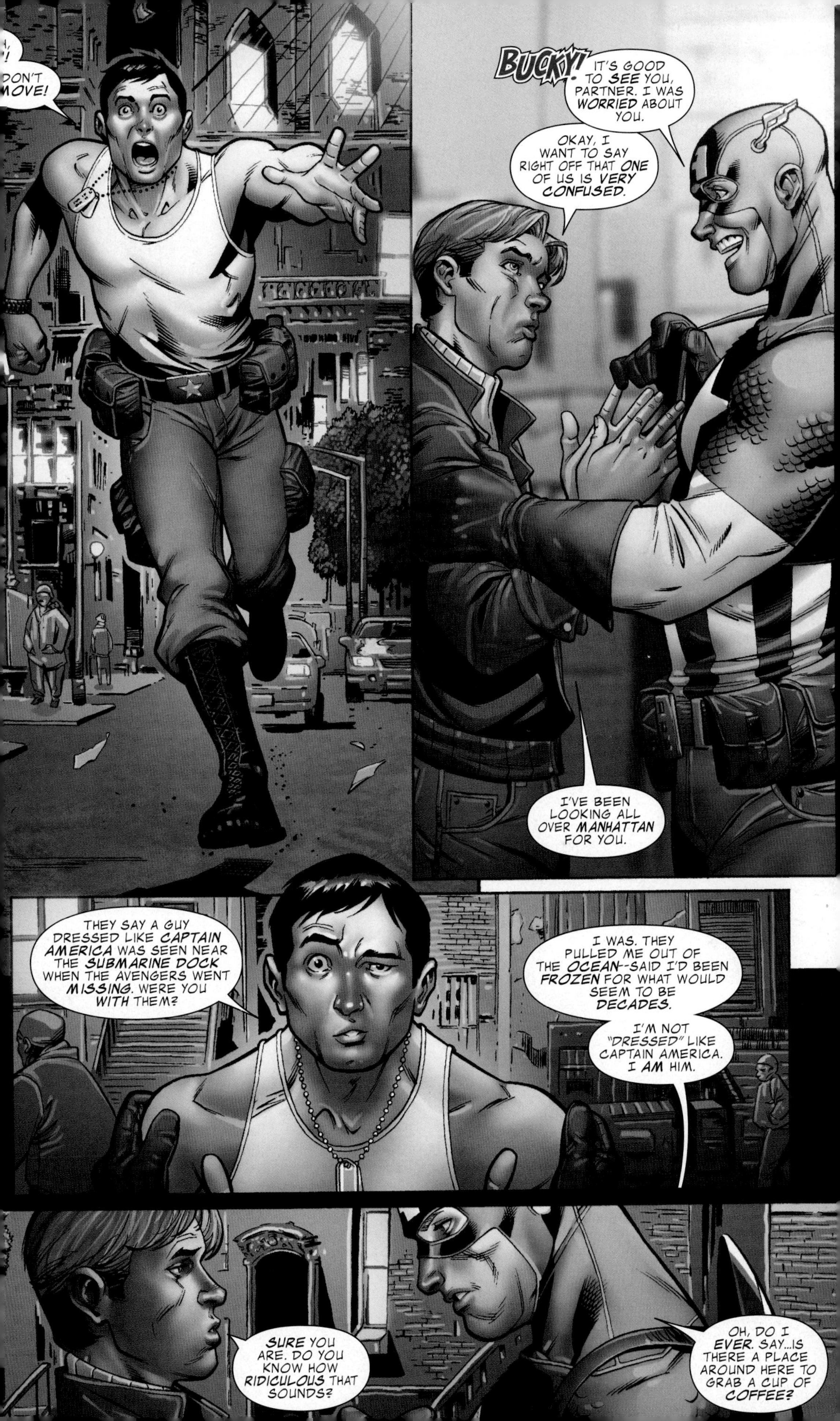
DON'T MOVE!
BUCKY!
IT'S GOOD TO SEE YOU, PARTNER. I WAS WORRIED ABOUT YOU.
OKAY, I WANT TO SAY RIGHT OFF THAT ONE OF US IS VERY CONFUSED.
I'VE BEEN LOOKING ALL OVER MANHATTAN FOR YOU.
THEY SAY A GUY DRESSED LIKE CAPTAIN AMERICA WAS SEEN NEAR THE SUBMARINE DOCK WHEN THE AVENGERS WENT MISSING. WERE YOU WITH THEM?
I WAS. THEY PULLED ME OUT OF THE OCEAN--SAID I'D BEEN FROZEN FOR WHAT WOULD SEEM TO BE DECADES.
I'M NOT "DRESSED" LIKE CAPTAIN AMERICA. I AM HIM.
SURE YOU ARE. DO YOU KNOW HOW RIDICULOUS THAT SOUNDS?
OH, DO I EVER. SAY...IS THERE A PLACE AROUND HERE TO GRAB A CUP OF COFFEE?

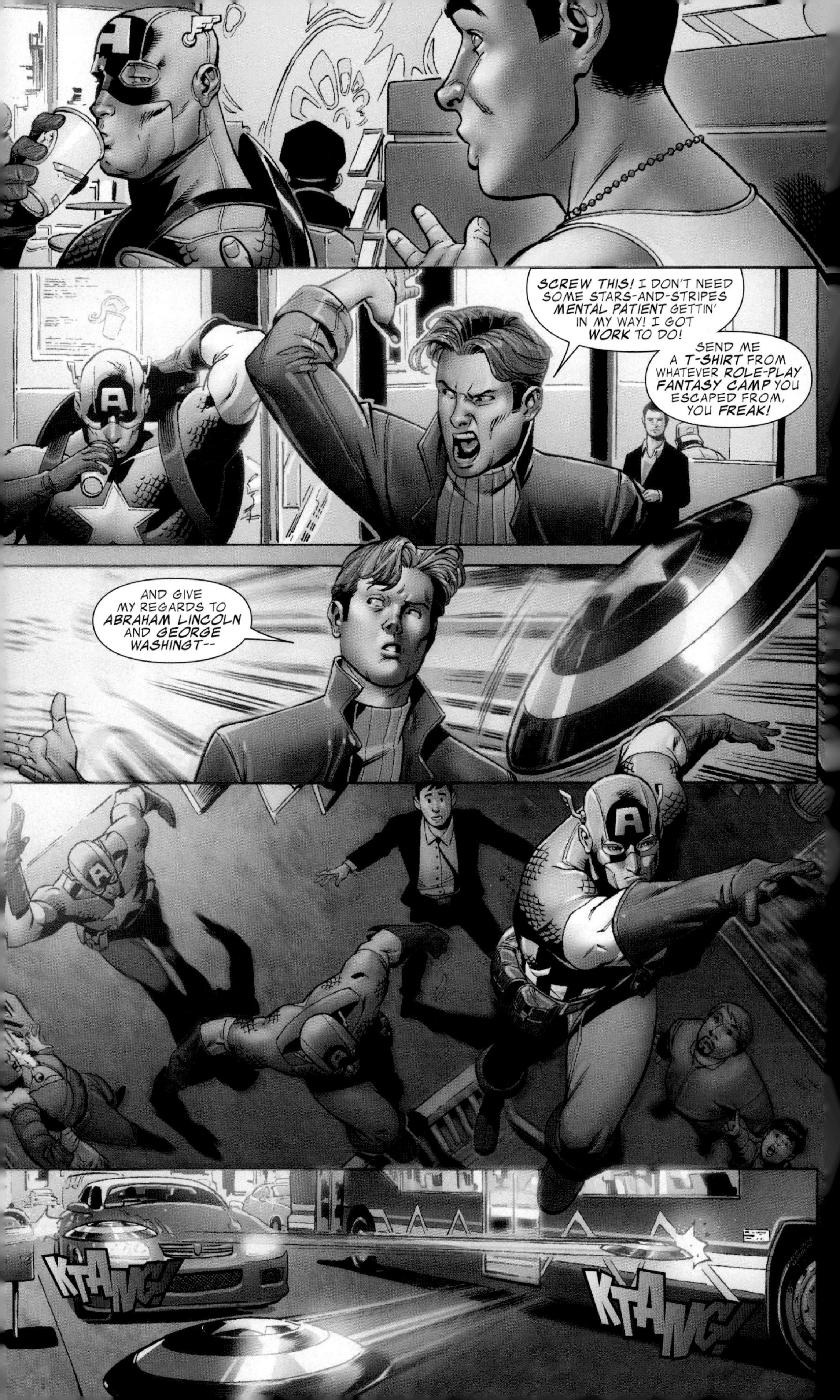
SCREW THIS! I DON'T NEED SOME STARS-AND-STRIPES MENTAL PATIENT GETTIN' IN MY WAY! I GOT WORK TO DO!
SEND ME A T-SHIRT FROM WHATEVER ROLE-PLAY FANTASY CAMP YOU ESCAPED FROM, YOU FREAK!
AND GIVE MY REGARDS TO ABRAHAM LINCOLN AND GEORGE WASHINGT--
KTANG!
KTANG!

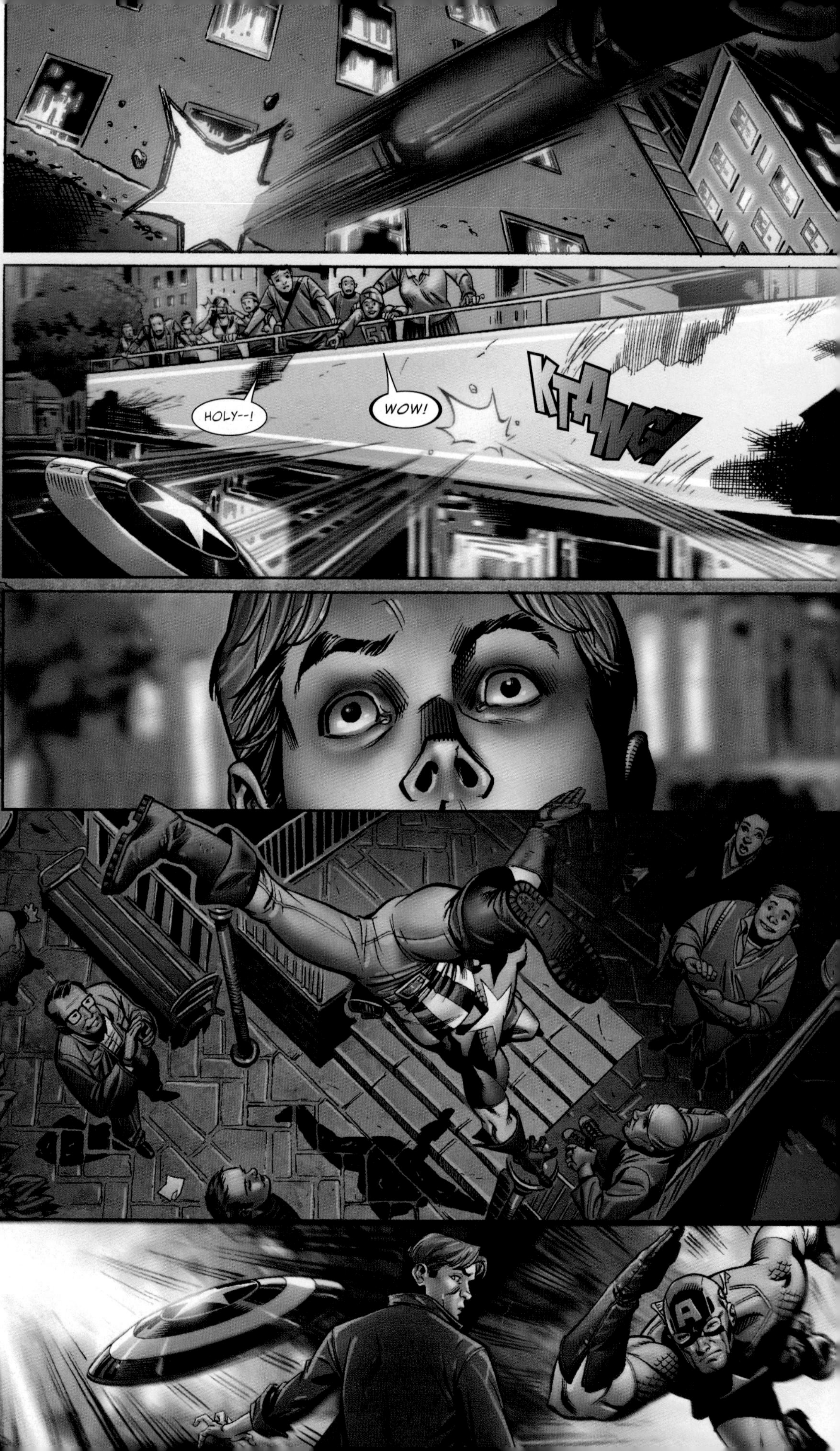
HOLY--!
WOW!
KTANG!

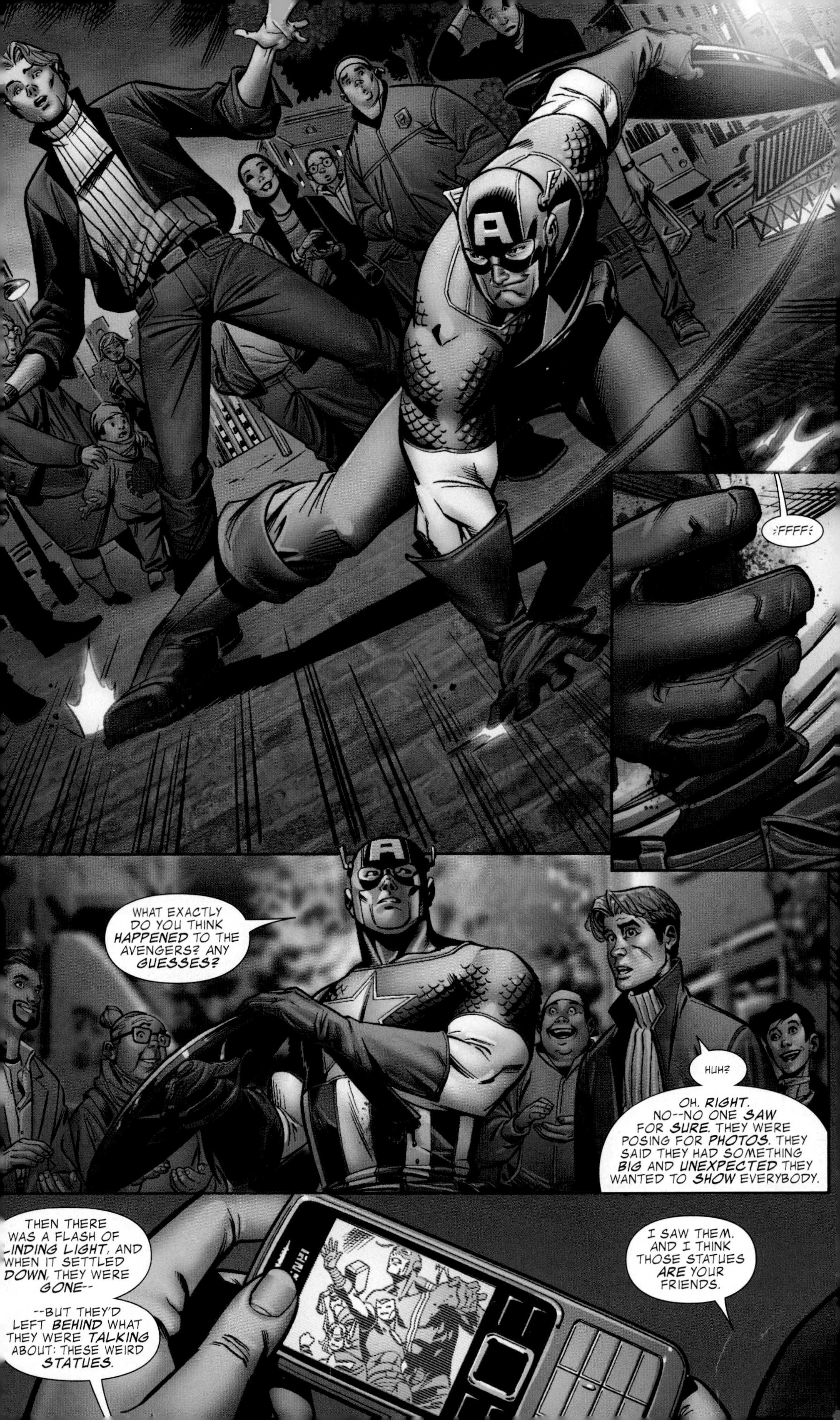

:FFFF:
WHAT EXACTLY DO YOU THINK HAPPENED TO THE AVENGERS? ANY GUESSES?
HUH?
OH. RIGHT. NO--NO ONE SAW FOR SURE. THEY WERE POSING FOR PHOTOS. THEY SAID THEY HAD SOMETHING BIG AND UNEXPECTED THEY WANTED TO SHOW EVERYBODY.
THEN THERE WAS A FLASH OF LINDING LIGHT, AND WHEN IT SETTLED DOWN, THEY WERE GONE--
--BUT THEY'D LEFT BEHIND WHAT THEY WERE TALKING ABOUT: THESE WEIRD STATUES.
I SAW THEM. AND I THINK THOSE STATUES ARE YOUR FRIENDS.

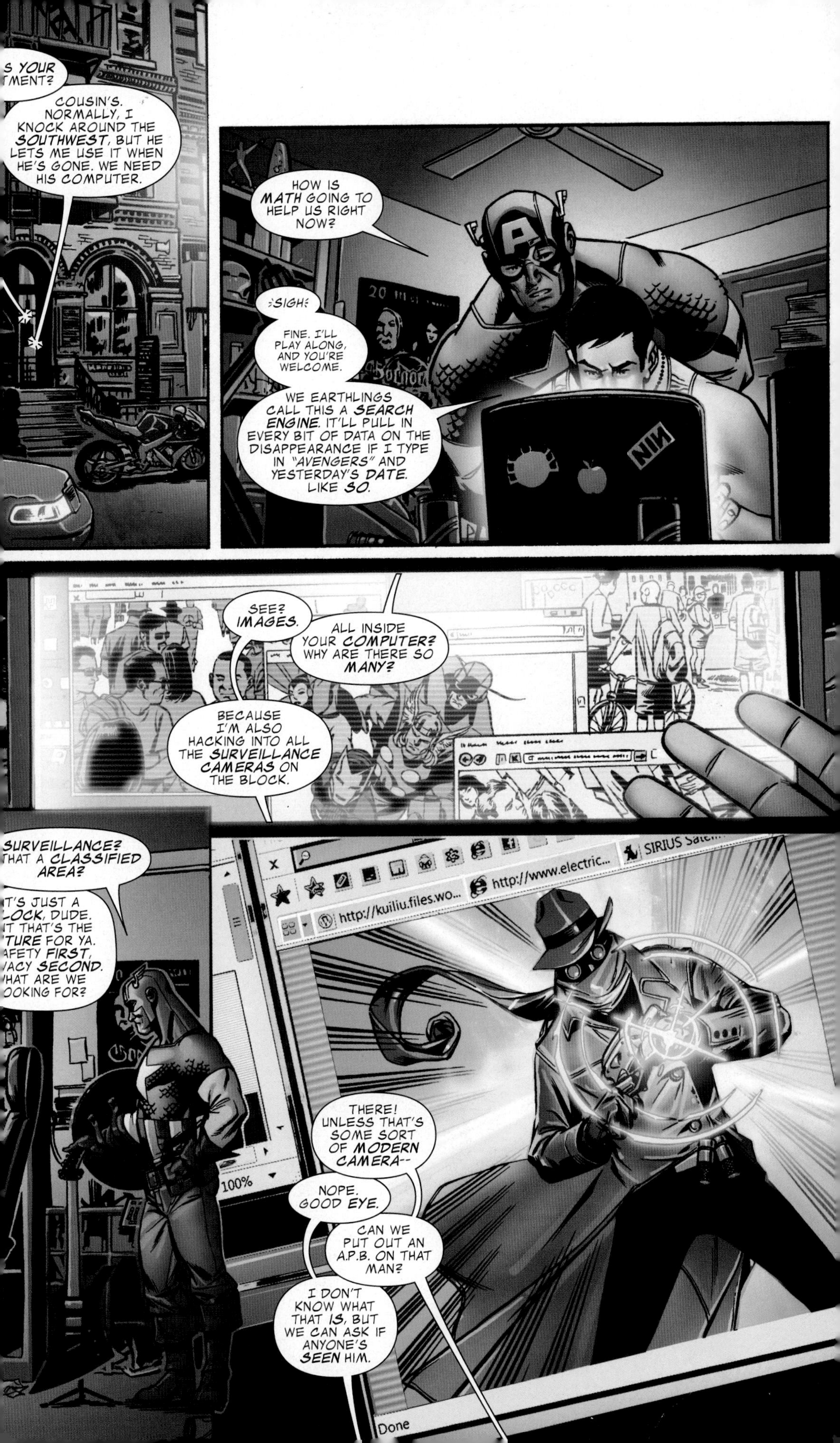
S YOUR
TMENT?
COUSIN'S. NORMALLY, I KNOCK AROUND THE SOUTHWEST, BUT HE LETS ME USE IT WHEN HE'S GONE. WE NEED HIS COMPUTER.
HOW IS MATH GOING TO HELP US RIGHT NOW?
SIGH
FINE. I'LL PLAY ALONG, AND YOU'RE WELCOME.
WE EARTHLINGS CALL THIS A SEARCH ENGINE. IT'LL PULL IN EVERY BIT OF DATA ON THE DISAPPEARANCE IF I TYPE IN "AVENGERS" AND YESTERDAY'S DATE. LIKE SO.
SEE? IMAGES.
ALL INSIDE YOUR COMPUTER? WHY ARE THERE SO MANY?
BECAUSE I'M ALSO HACKING INTO ALL THE SURVEILLANCE CAMERAS ON THE BLOCK.
SURVEILLANCE? THAT A CLASSIFIED AREA?
T'S JUST A LOCK, DUDE. T THAT'S THE TURE FOR YA. AFETY FIRST, VACY SECOND. HAT ARE WE OOKING FOR?
SIRIUS Sate...
http://www.electric...
http://kuiliu.files.wo...
THERE! UNLESS THAT'S SOME SORT OF MODERN CAMERA--
NOPE. GOOD EYE.
CAN WE PUT OUT AN A.P.B. ON THAT MAN?
I DON'T KNOW WHAT THAT IS, BUT WE CAN ASK IF ANYONE'S SEEN HIM.
100%
Done

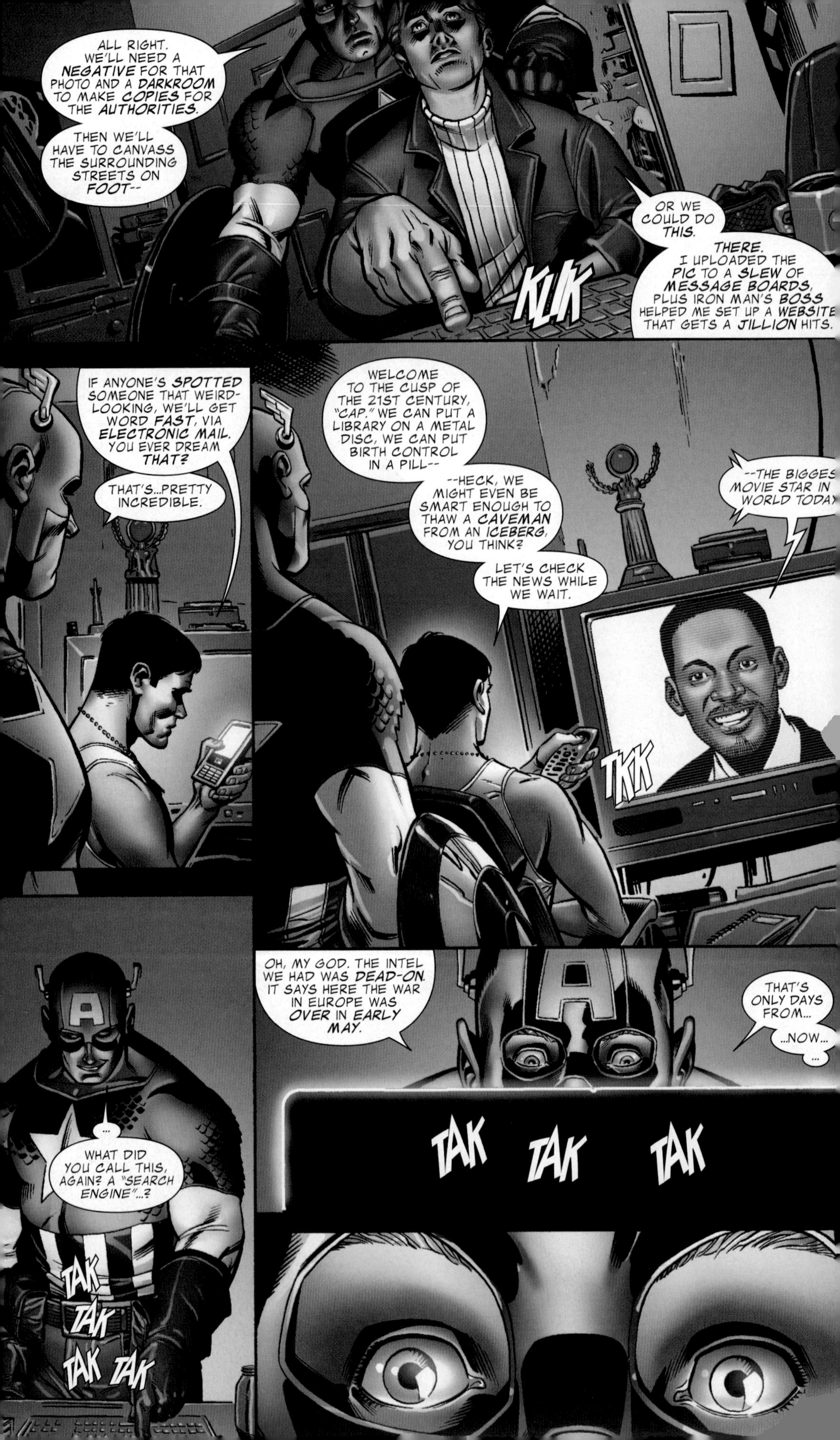

ALL RIGHT. WE'LL NEED A NEGATIVE FOR THAT PHOTO AND A DARKROOM TO MAKE COPIES FOR THE AUTHORITIES.
THEN WE'LL HAVE TO CANVASS THE SURROUNDING STREETS ON FOOT--
OR WE COULD DO THIS.
KLIK
THERE. I UPLOADED THE PIC TO A SLEW OF MESSAGE BOARDS, PLUS IRON MAN'S BOSS HELPED ME SET UP A WEBSITE THAT GETS A JILLION HITS.
IF ANYONE'S SPOTTED SOMEONE THAT WEIRD-LOOKING, WE'LL GET WORD FAST, VIA ELECTRONIC MAIL. YOU EVER DREAM THAT?
THAT'S...PRETTY INCREDIBLE.
WELCOME TO THE CUSP OF THE 21ST CENTURY, "CAP." WE CAN PUT A LIBRARY ON A METAL DISC, WE CAN PUT BIRTH CONTROL IN A PILL--
--HECK, WE MIGHT EVEN BE SMART ENOUGH TO THAW A CAVEMAN FROM AN ICEBERG, YOU THINK?
LET'S CHECK THE NEWS WHILE WE WAIT.
--THE BIGGES MOVIE STAR IN WORLD TODAY
TKK
...
WHAT DID YOU CALL THIS, AGAIN? A "SEARCH ENGINE"...?
TAK TAK TAK TAK
OH, MY GOD. THE INTEL WE HAD WAS DEAD-ON. IT SAYS HERE THE WAR IN EUROPE WAS OVER IN EARLY MAY.
THAT'S ONLY DAYS FROM...
...NOW...
...
TAK TAK TAK

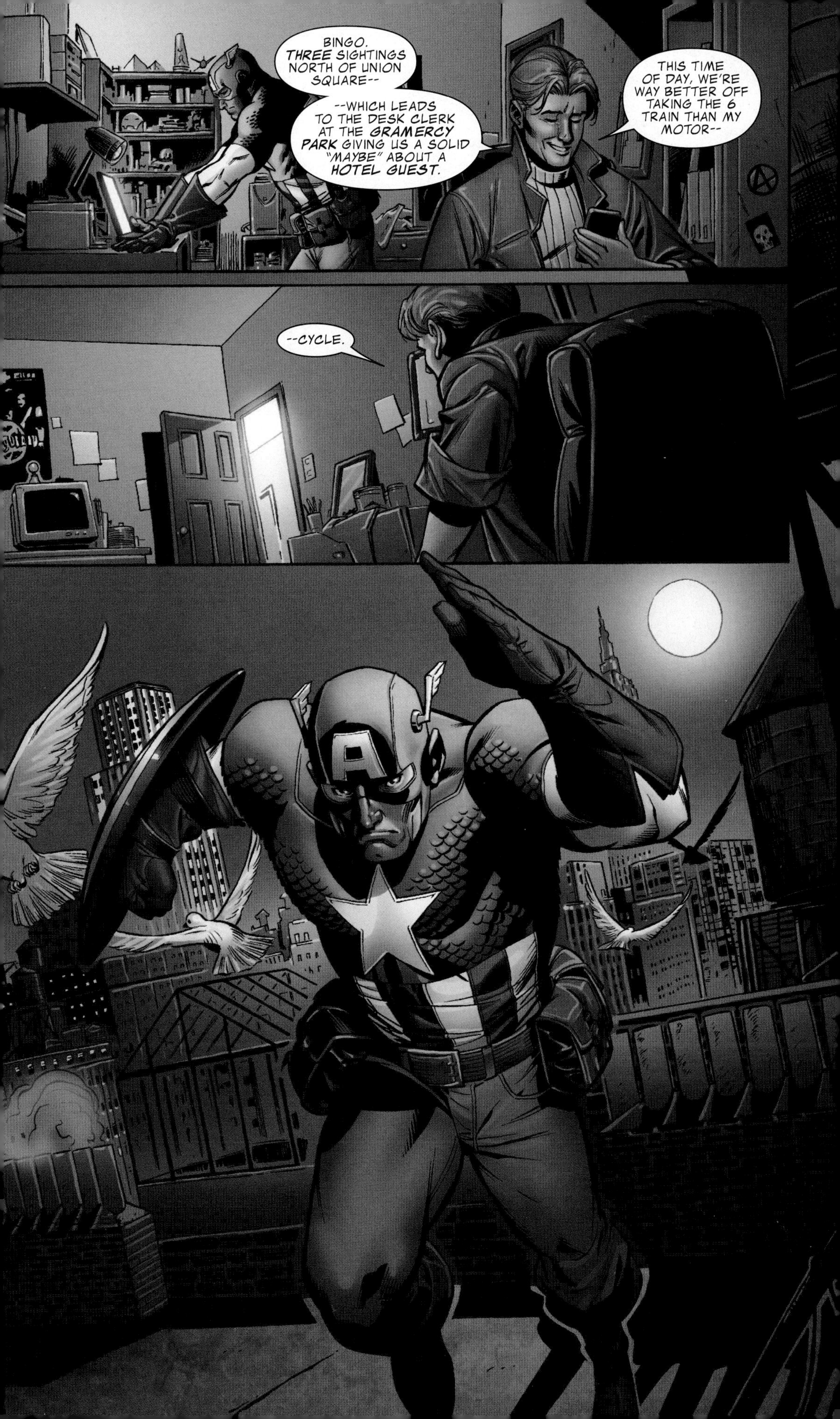
BINGO. THREE SIGHTINGS NORTH OF UNION SQUARE--
--WHICH LEADS TO THE DESK CLERK AT THE GRAMERCY PARK GIVING US A SOLID "MAYBE" ABOUT A HOTEL GUEST.
THIS TIME OF DAY, WE'RE WAY BETTER OFF TAKING THE 6 TRAIN THAN MY MOTOR--
--CYCLE.

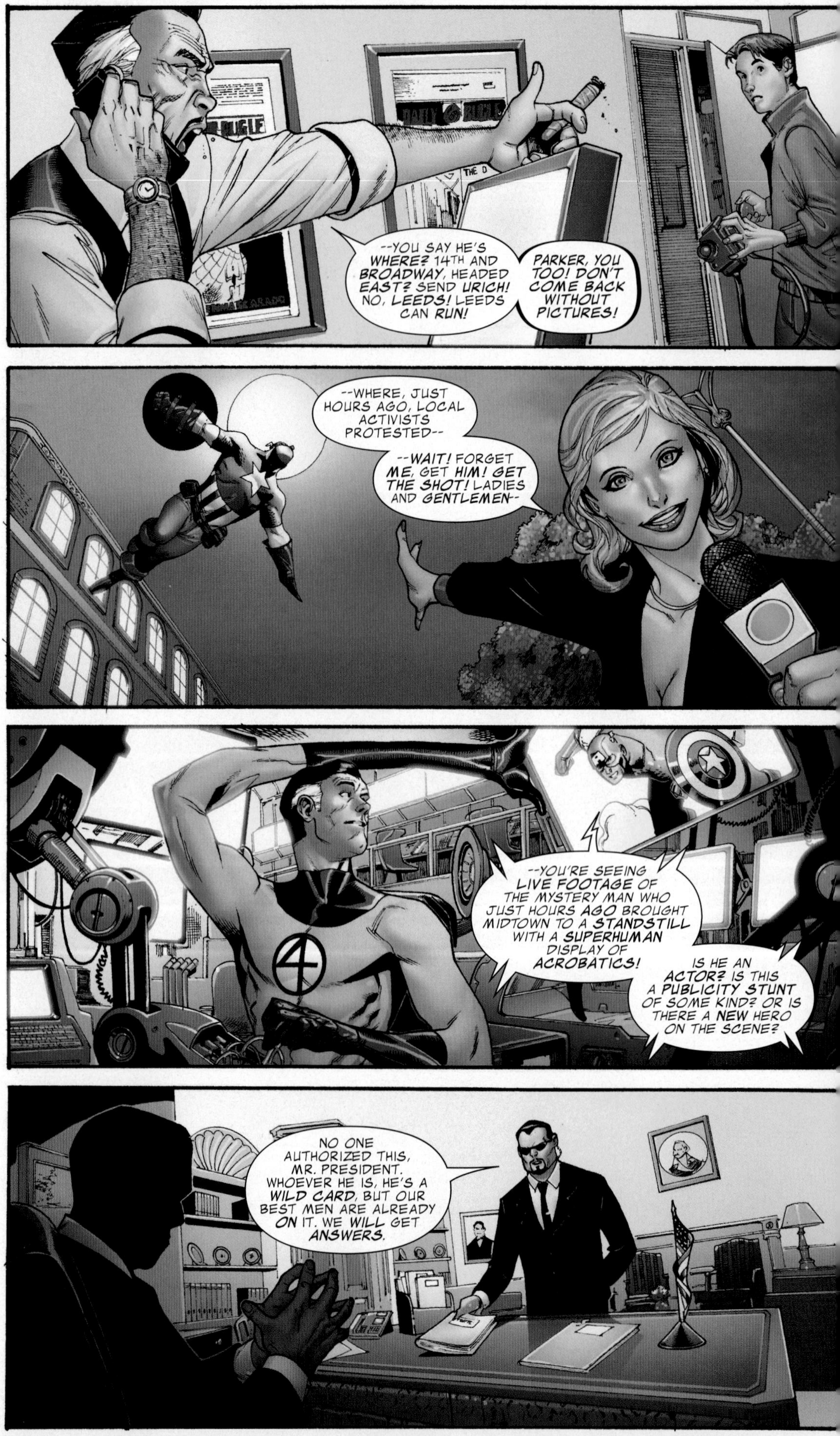
--YOU SAY HE'S WHERE? 14TH AND BROADWAY, HEADED EAST? SEND URICH! NO, LEEDS! LEEDS CAN RUN!
PARKER, YOU TOO! DON'T COME BACK WITHOUT PICTURES!
--WHERE, JUST HOURS AGO, LOCAL ACTIVISTS PROTESTED--
--WAIT! FORGET ME, GET HIM! GET THE SHOT! LADIES AND GENTLEMEN--
--YOU'RE SEEING LIVE FOOTAGE OF THE MYSTERY MAN WHO JUST HOURS AGO BROUGHT MIDTOWN TO A STANDSTILL WITH A SUPERHUMAN DISPLAY OF ACROBATICS!
IS HE AN ACTOR? IS THIS A PUBLICITY STUNT OF SOME KIND? OR IS THERE A NEW HERO ON THE SCENE?
NO ONE AUTHORIZED THIS, MR. PRESIDENT. WHOEVER HE IS, HE'S A WILD CARD, BUT OUR BEST MEN ARE ALREADY ON IT. WE WILL GET ANSWERS.

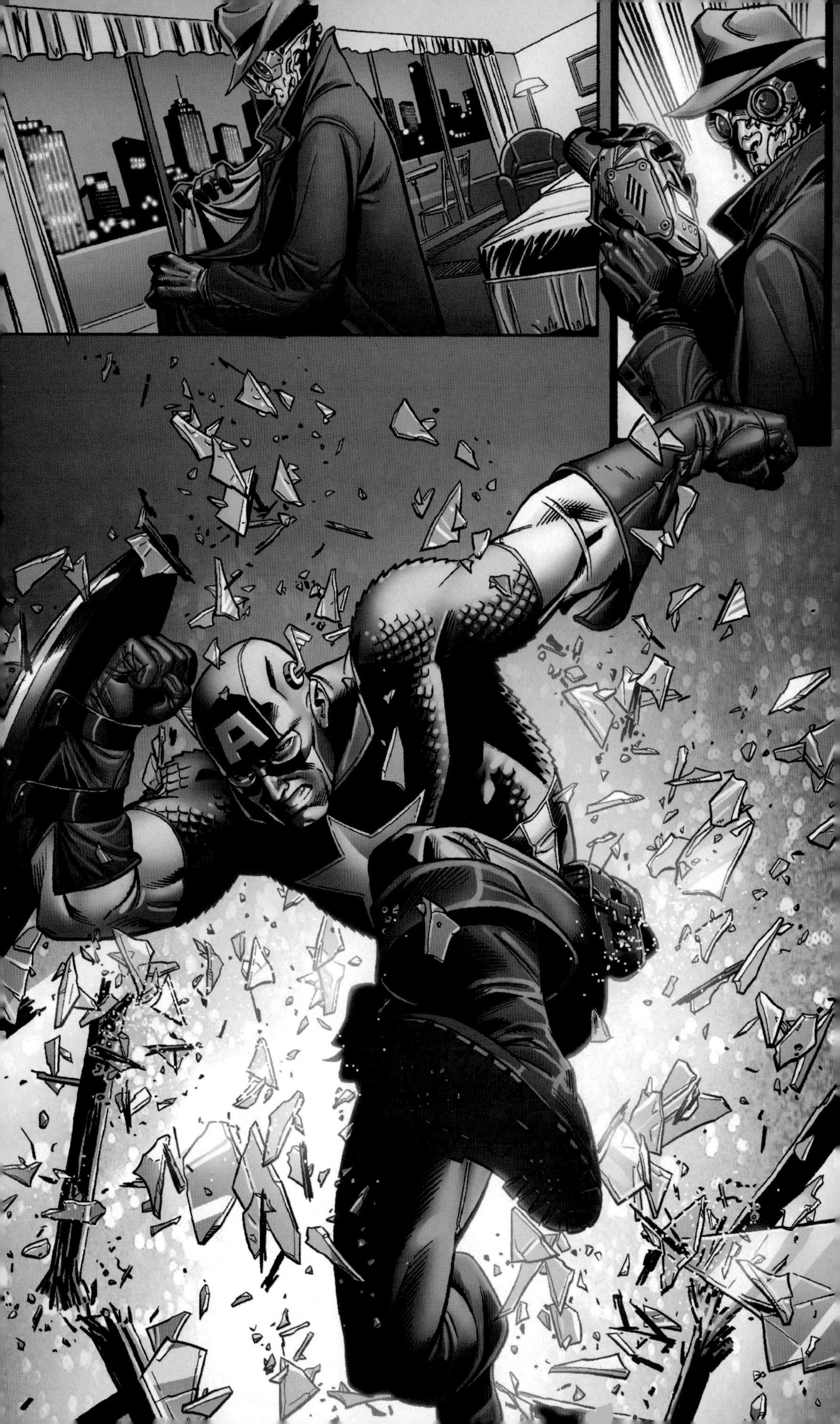

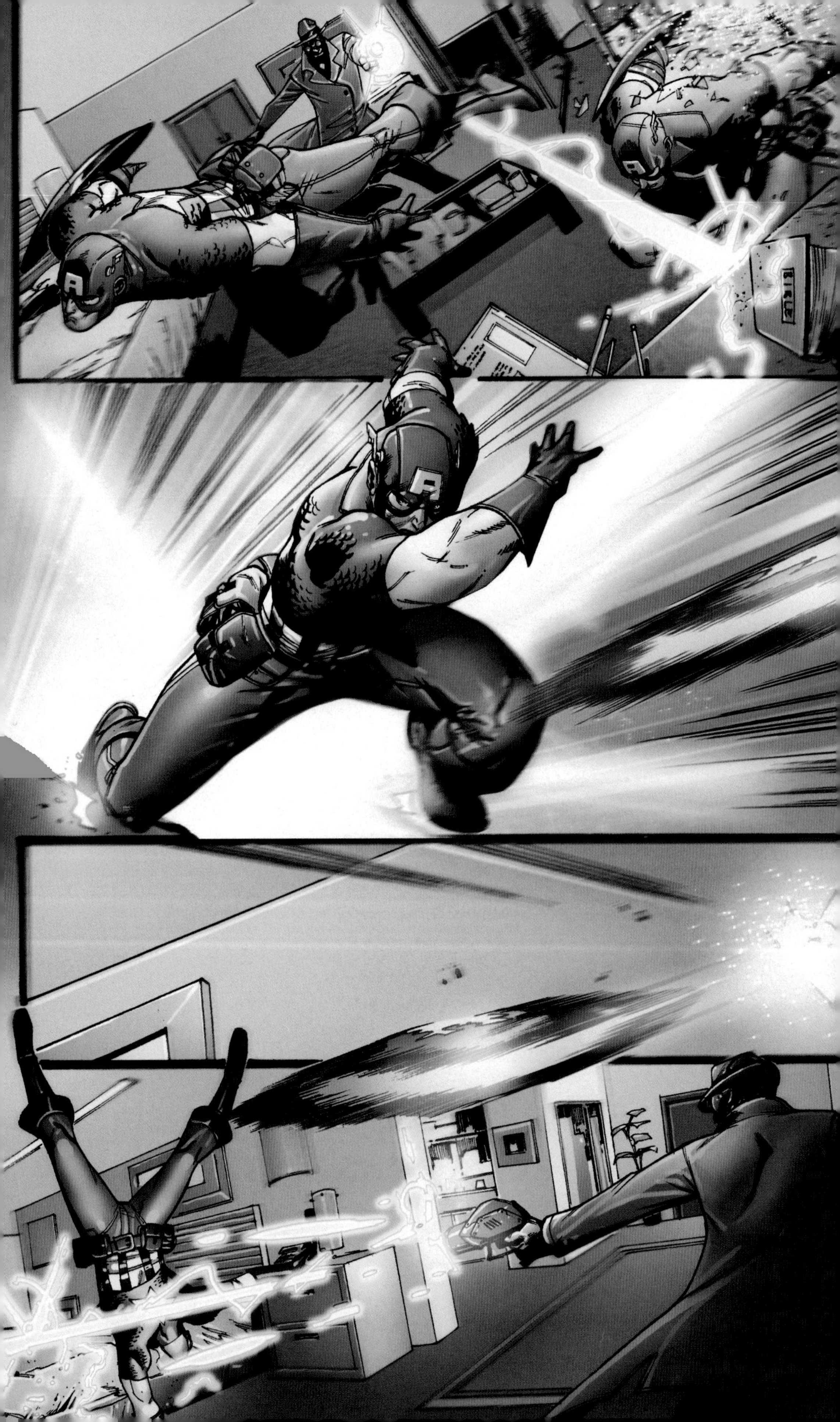

WHO ARE YOU? **TALK!**

SMIZE NICCIEM

SMIZE NICCIEM I EEE **REVERSE.** NO **HURT.** *WEEXIM* CAN **REVERSE** RAY--!

HEH. YOU'RE A **MAN FROM MARS.** OF COURSE YOU'RE A MAN FROM MARS!

HAHAHAHAHAHAHAHAHAHAHAHAHA

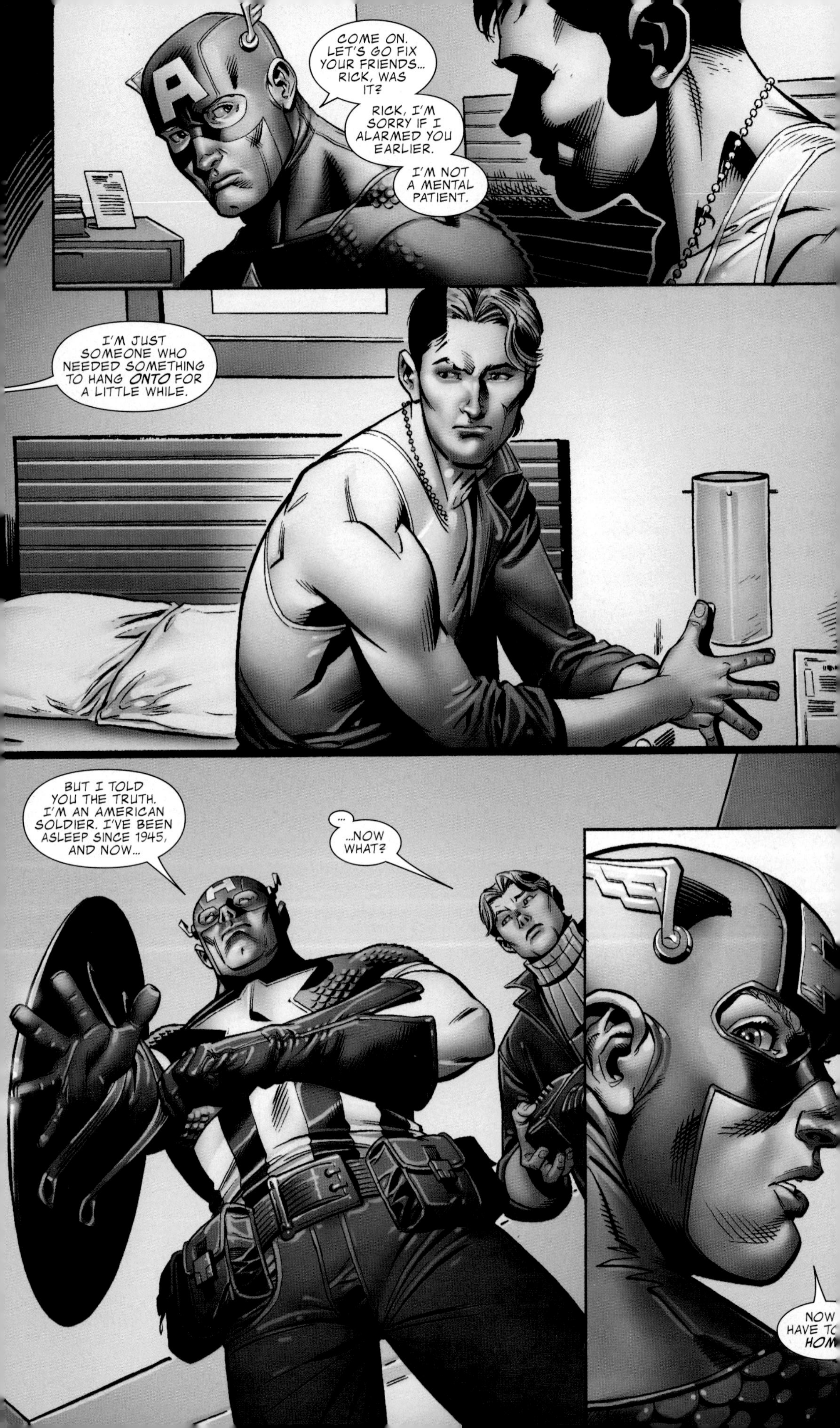
COME ON. LET'S GO FIX YOUR FRIENDS... RICK, WAS IT?
RICK, I'M SORRY IF I ALARMED YOU EARLIER.
I'M NOT A MENTAL PATIENT.
I'M JUST SOMEONE WHO NEEDED SOMETHING TO HANG ONTO FOR A LITTLE WHILE.
BUT I TOLD YOU THE TRUTH. I'M AN AMERICAN SOLDIER. I'VE BEEN ASLEEP SINCE 1945, AND NOW...
...
...NOW WHAT?

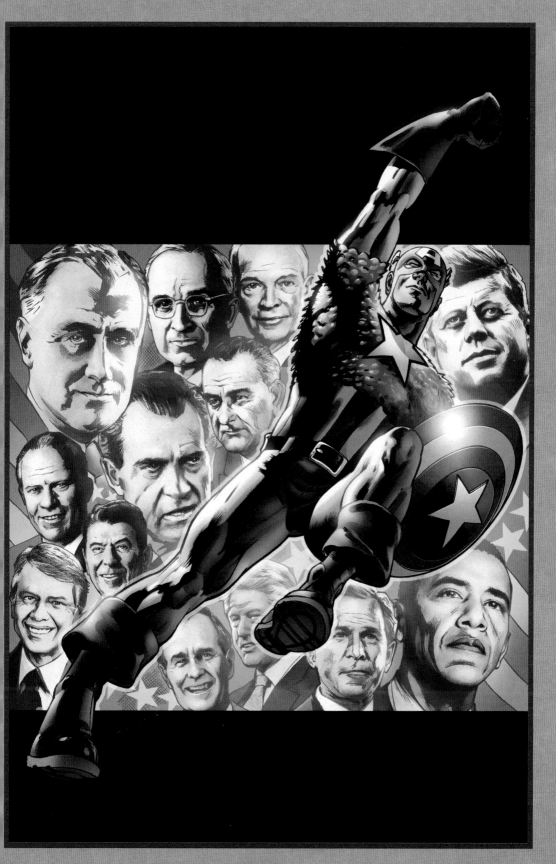

[3]

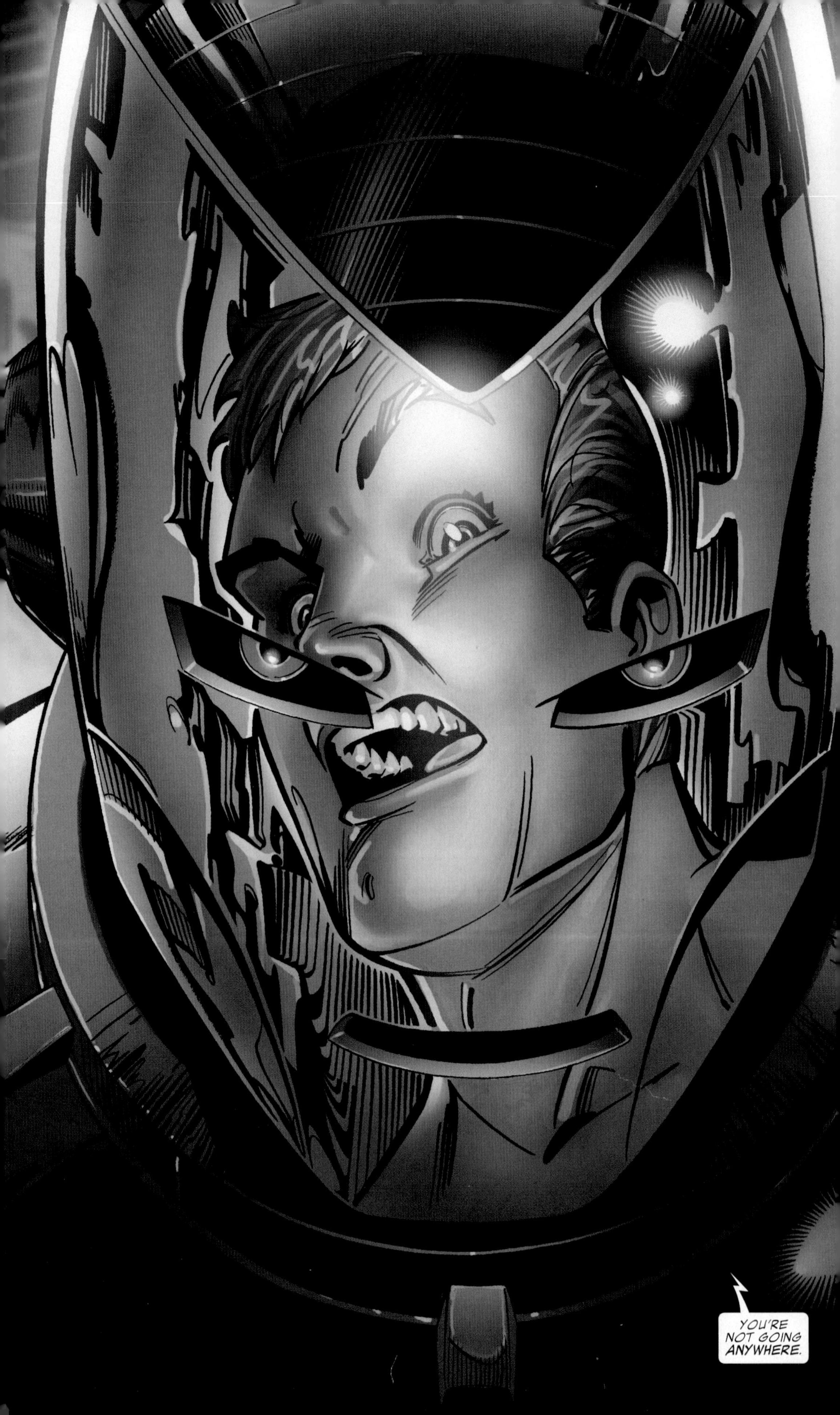
YOU'RE NOT GOING ANYWHERE.

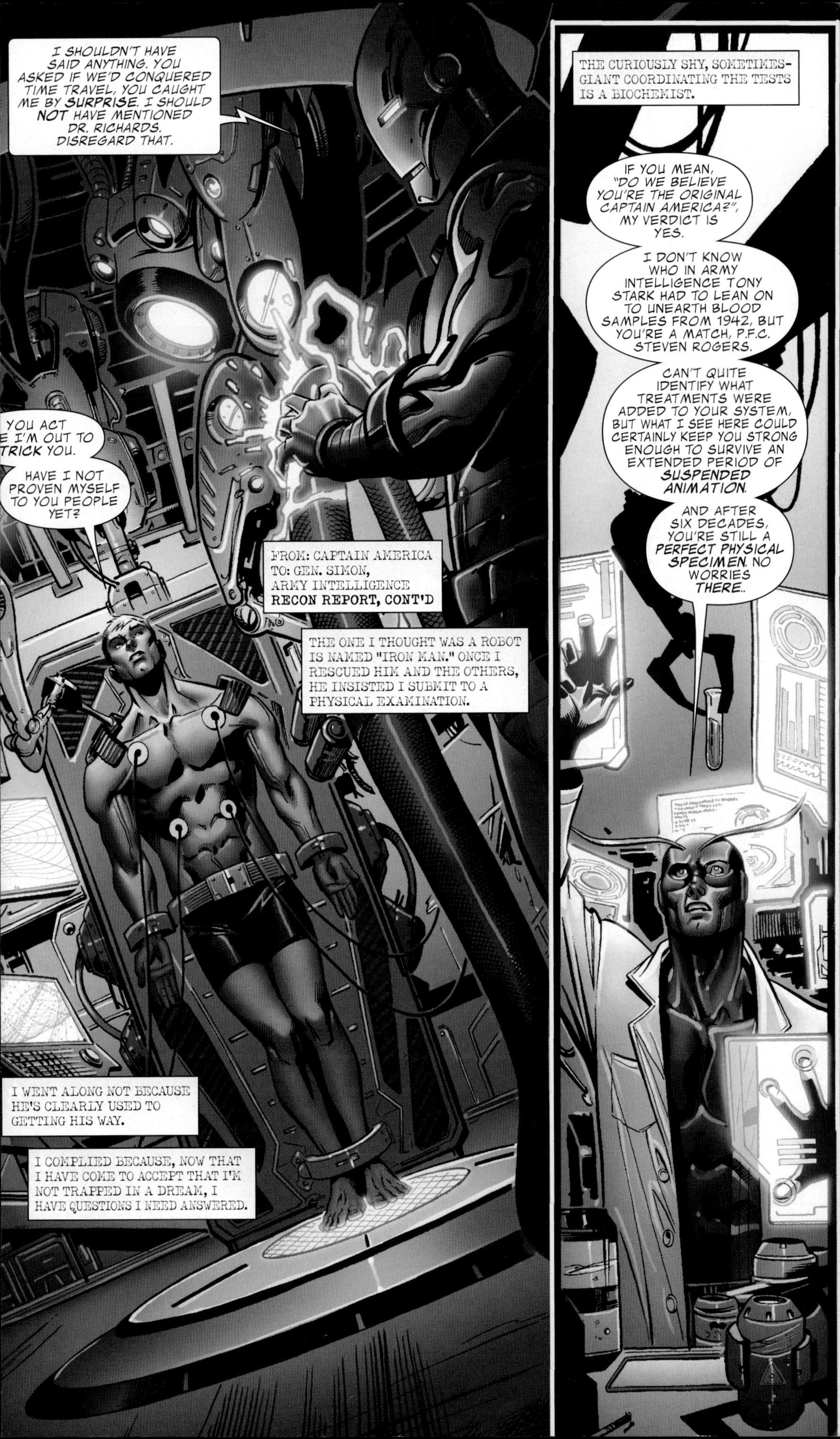

I SHOULDN'T HAVE SAID ANYTHING. YOU ASKED IF WE'D CONQUERED TIME TRAVEL, YOU CAUGHT ME BY SURPRISE. I SHOULD NOT HAVE MENTIONED DR. RICHARDS. DISREGARD THAT.
YOU ACT E I'M OUT TO TRICK YOU.
HAVE I NOT PROVEN MYSELF TO YOU PEOPLE YET?
FROM: CAPTAIN AMERICA TO: GEN. SIMON, ARMY INTELLIGENCE RECON REPORT, CONT'D
THE ONE I THOUGHT WAS A ROBOT IS NAMED "IRON MAN." ONCE I RESCUED HIM AND THE OTHERS, HE INSISTED I SUBMIT TO A PHYSICAL EXAMINATION.
I WENT ALONG NOT BECAUSE HE'S CLEARLY USED TO GETTING HIS WAY.
I COMPLIED BECAUSE, NOW THAT I HAVE COME TO ACCEPT THAT I'M NOT TRAPPED IN A DREAM, I HAVE QUESTIONS I NEED ANSWERED.
THE CURIOUSLY SHY, SOMETIMES-GIANT COORDINATING THE TESTS IS A BIOCHEMIST.
IF YOU MEAN, "DO WE BELIEVE YOU'RE THE ORIGINAL CAPTAIN AMERICA?", MY VERDICT IS YES.
I DON'T KNOW WHO IN ARMY INTELLIGENCE TONY STARK HAD TO LEAN ON TO UNEARTH BLOOD SAMPLES FROM 1942, BUT YOU'RE A MATCH, P.F.C. STEVEN ROGERS.
CAN'T QUITE IDENTIFY WHAT TREATMENTS WERE ADDED TO YOUR SYSTEM, BUT WHAT I SEE HERE COULD CERTAINLY KEEP YOU STRONG ENOUGH TO SURVIVE AN EXTENDED PERIOD OF SUSPENDED ANIMATION.
AND AFTER SIX DECADES, YOU'RE STILL A PERFECT PHYSICAL SPECIMEN. NO WORRIES THERE..

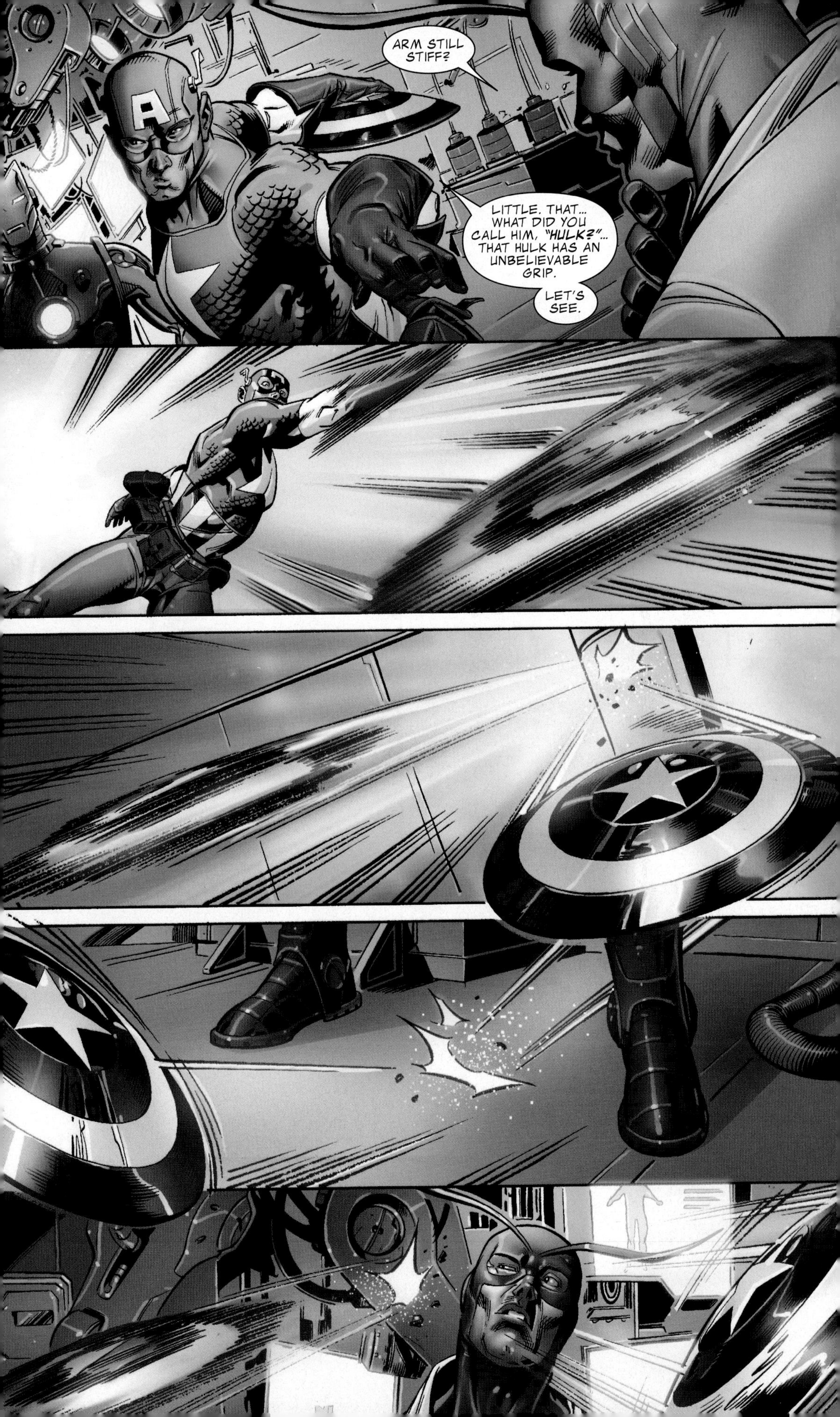
ARM STILL STIFF?
LITTLE. THAT... WHAT DID YOU CALL HIM, "HULK?"... THAT HULK HAS AN UNBELIEVABLE GRIP.
LET'S SEE.

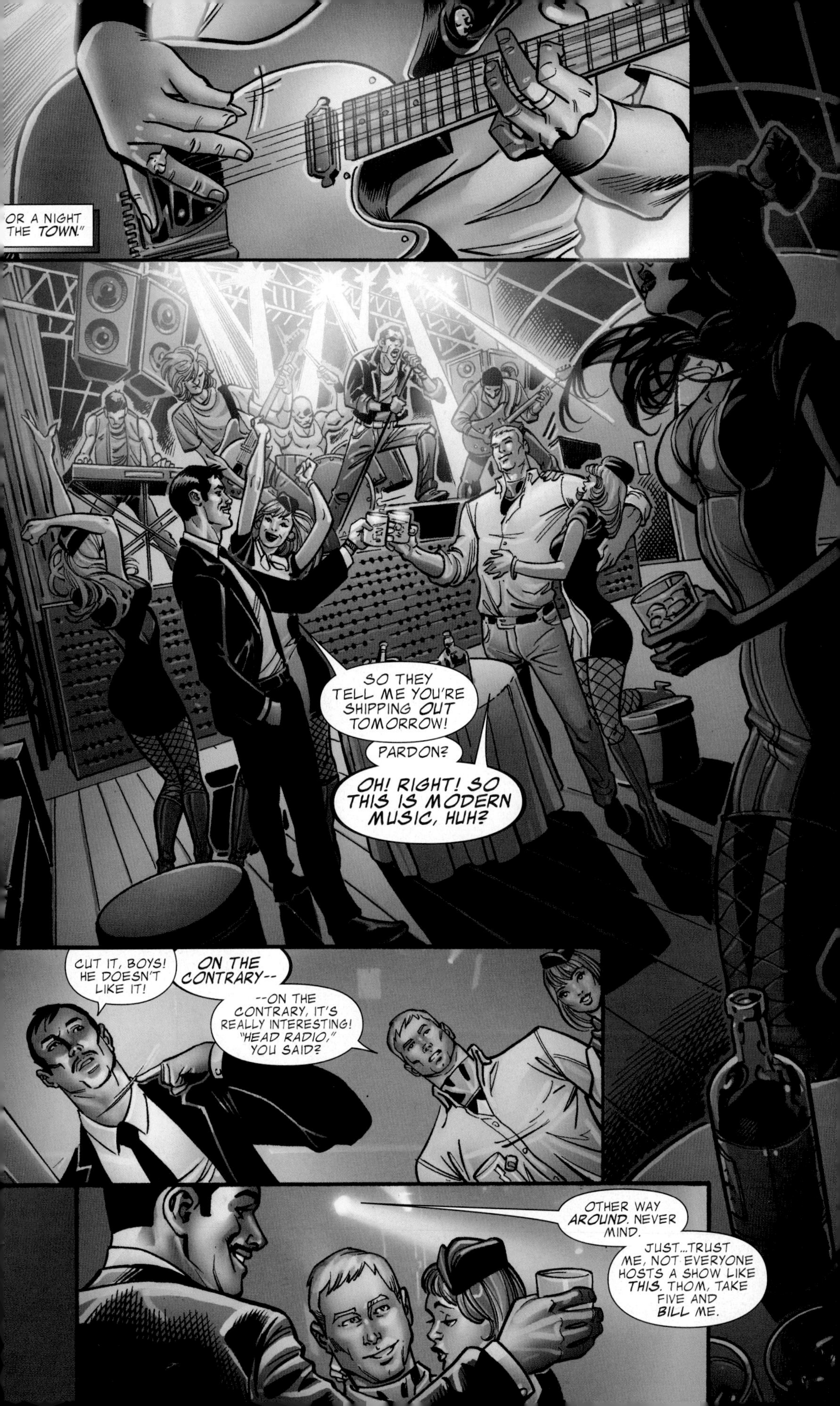
OR A NIGHT
THE TOWN."
SO THEY TELL ME YOU'RE SHIPPING OUT TOMORROW!
PARDON?
OH! RIGHT! SO THIS IS MODERN MUSIC, HUH?
CUT IT, BOYS! HE DOESN'T LIKE IT!
ON THE CONTRARY--
--ON THE CONTRARY, IT'S REALLY INTERESTING! "HEAD RADIO," YOU SAID?
OTHER WAY AROUND. NEVER MIND.
JUST...TRUST ME, NOT EVERYONE HOSTS A SHOW LIKE THIS. THOM, TAKE FIVE AND BILL ME.

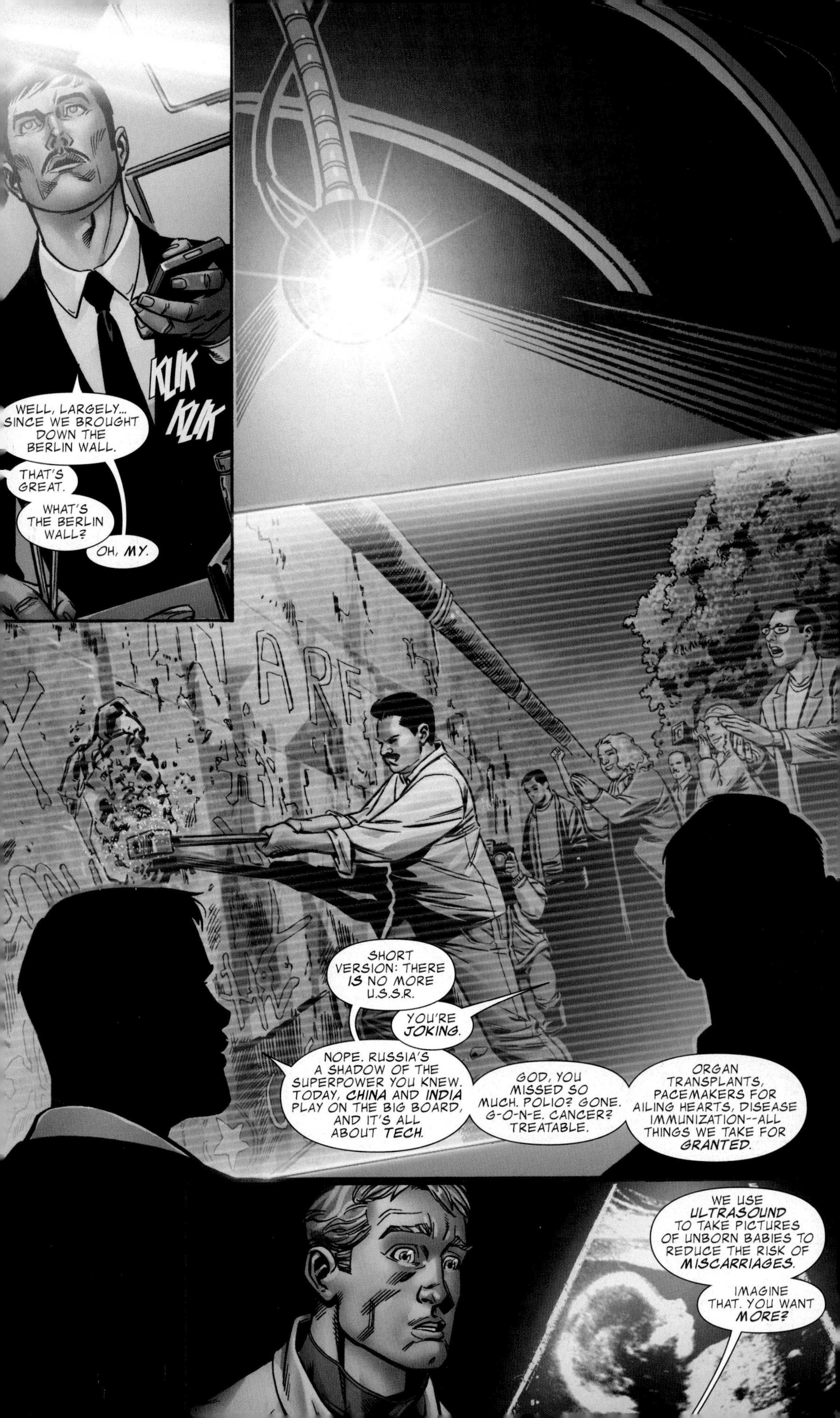
KLIK
KLIK
WELL, LARGELY... SINCE WE BROUGHT DOWN THE BERLIN WALL.
THAT'S GREAT.
WHAT'S THE BERLIN WALL?
OH, MY.
SHORT VERSION: THERE IS NO MORE U.S.S.R.
YOU'RE JOKING.
NOPE. RUSSIA'S A SHADOW OF THE SUPERPOWER YOU KNEW. TODAY, CHINA AND INDIA PLAY ON THE BIG BOARD, AND IT'S ALL ABOUT TECH.
GOD, YOU MISSED SO MUCH. POLIO? GONE. G-O-N-E. CANCER? TREATABLE.
ORGAN TRANSPLANTS, PACEMAKERS FOR AILING HEARTS, DISEASE IMMUNIZATION--ALL THINGS WE TAKE FOR GRANTED.
WE USE ULTRASOUND TO TAKE PICTURES OF UNBORN BABIES TO REDUCE THE RISK OF MISCARRIAGES.
IMAGINE THAT. YOU WANT MORE?

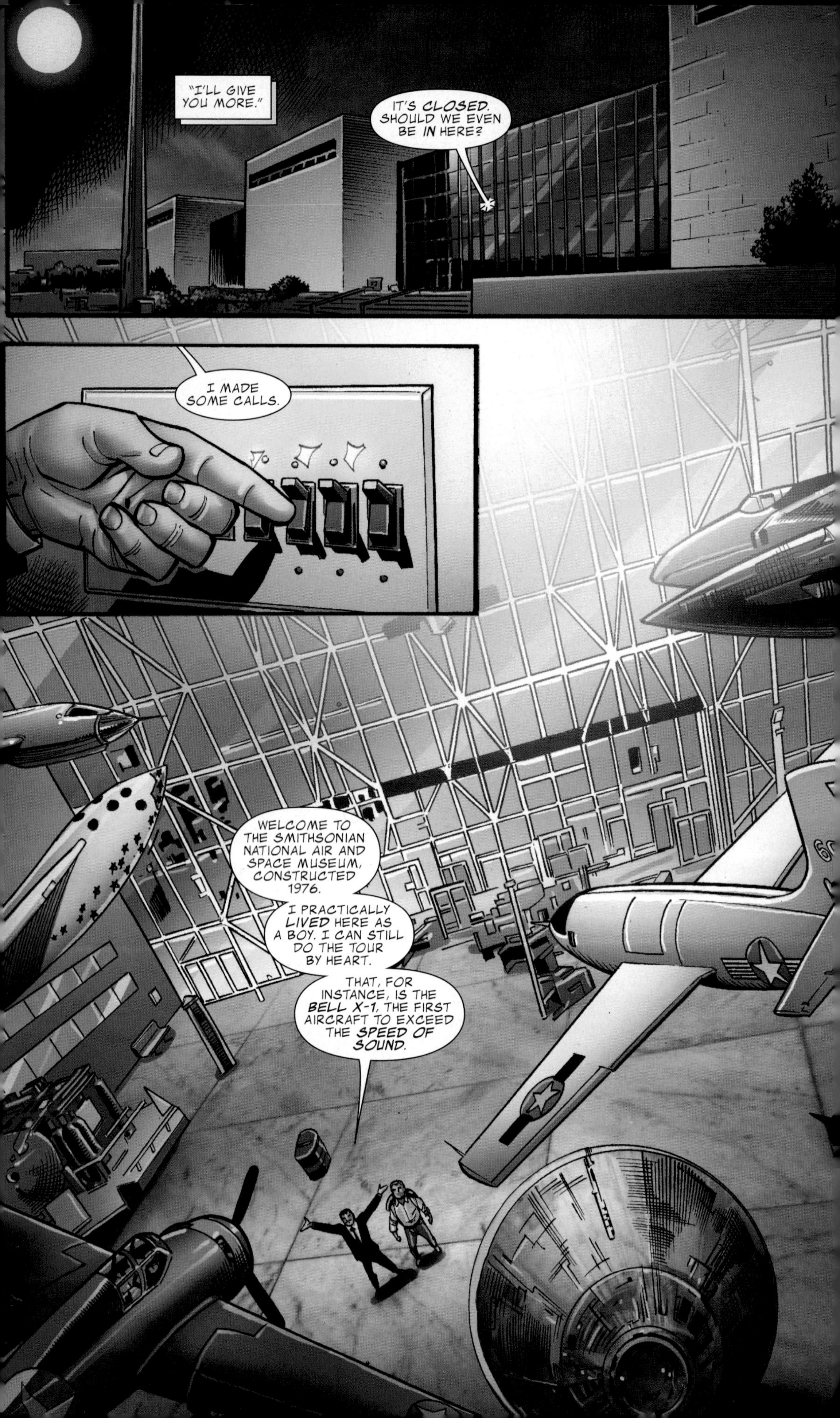
"I'LL GIVE YOU MORE."
IT'S CLOSED. SHOULD WE EVEN BE IN HERE?
I MADE SOME CALLS.
WELCOME TO THE SMITHSONIAN NATIONAL AIR AND SPACE MUSEUM, CONSTRUCTED 1976.
I PRACTICALLY LIVED HERE AS A BOY. I CAN STILL DO THE TOUR BY HEART.
THAT, FOR INSTANCE, IS THE BELL X-1, THE FIRST AIRCRAFT TO EXCEED THE SPEED OF SOUND.

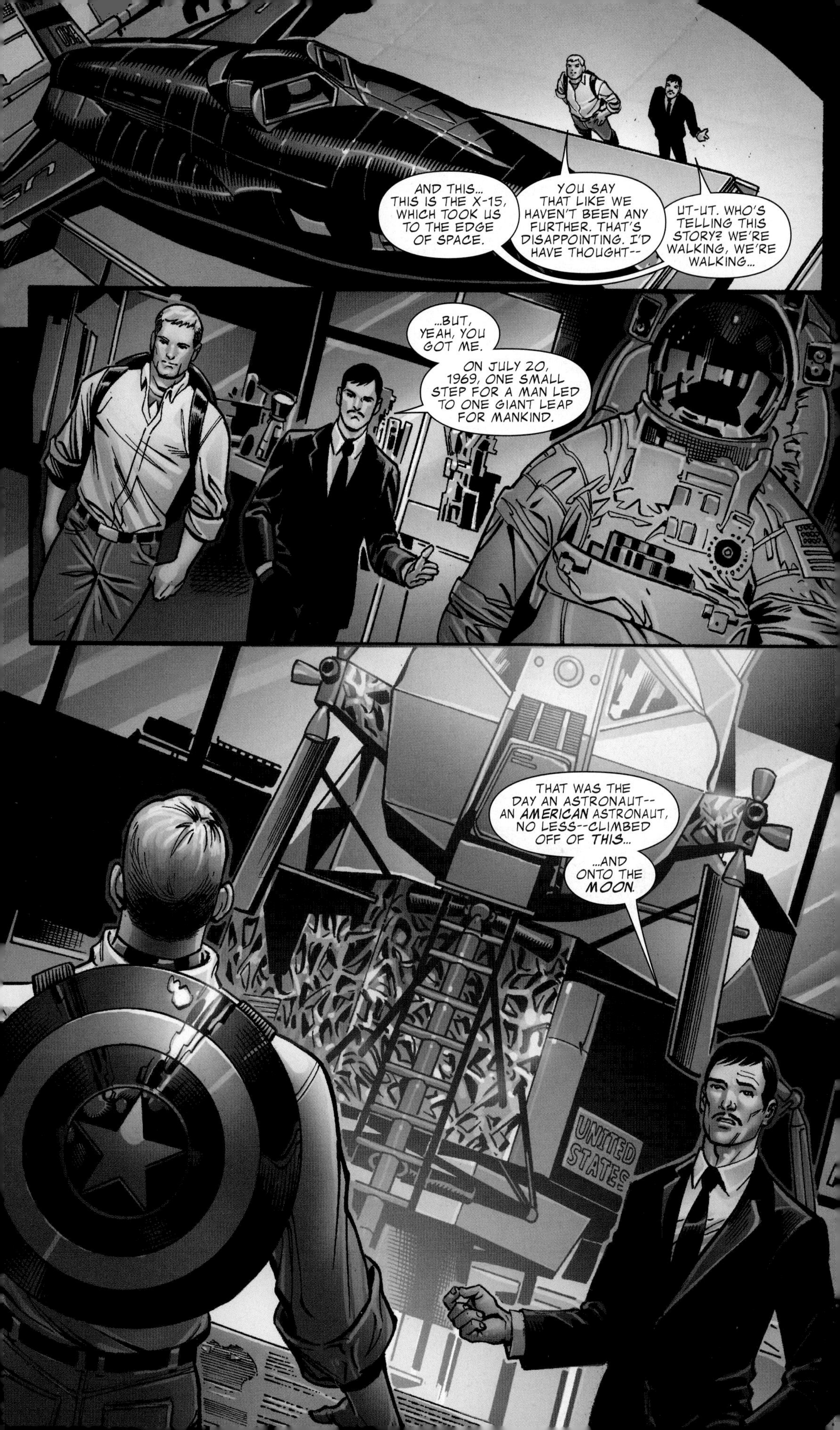
AND THIS... THIS IS THE X-15, WHICH TOOK US TO THE EDGE OF SPACE.
YOU SAY THAT LIKE WE HAVEN'T BEEN ANY FURTHER. THAT'S DISAPPOINTING. I'D HAVE THOUGHT--
UT-UT. WHO'S TELLING THIS STORY? WE'RE WALKING, WE'RE WALKING...
...BUT, YEAH, YOU GOT ME.
ON JULY 20, 1969, ONE SMALL STEP FOR A MAN LED TO ONE GIANT LEAP FOR MANKIND.
THAT WAS THE DAY AN ASTRONAUT-- AN AMERICAN ASTRONAUT, NO LESS--CLIMBED OFF OF THIS...
...AND ONTO THE MOON.
UNITED STATES

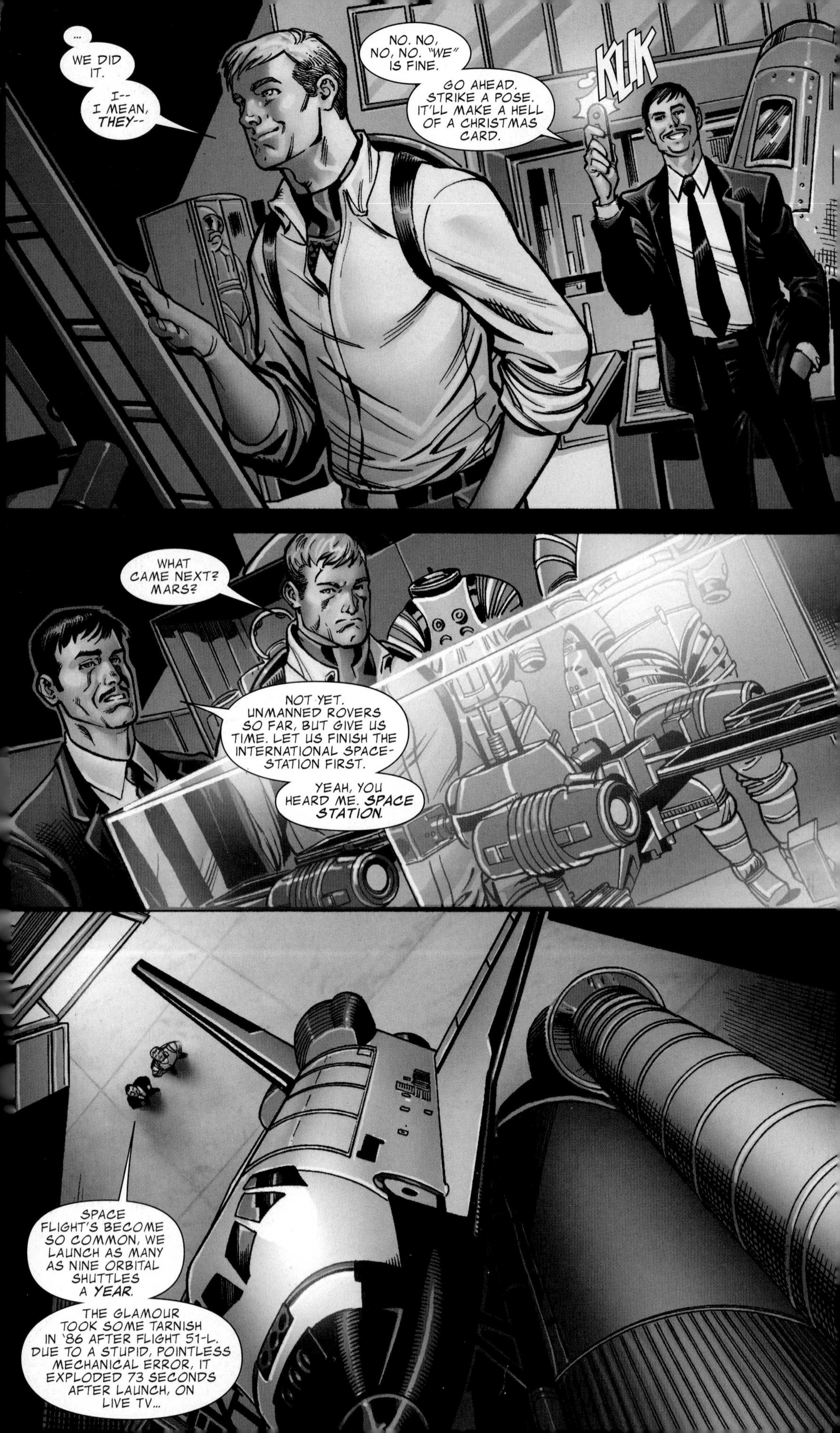
...
WE DID IT.
I-- I MEAN, THEY--
NO. NO, NO, NO. "WE" IS FINE.
GO AHEAD. STRIKE A POSE. IT'LL MAKE A HELL OF A CHRISTMAS CARD.
KLIK
WHAT CAME NEXT? MARS?
NOT YET. UNMANNED ROVERS SO FAR, BUT GIVE US TIME. LET US FINISH THE INTERNATIONAL SPACE-STATION FIRST.
YEAH, YOU HEARD ME. SPACE STATION.
SPACE FLIGHT'S BECOME SO COMMON, WE LAUNCH AS MANY AS NINE ORBITAL SHUTTLES A YEAR.
THE GLAMOUR TOOK SOME TARNISH IN '86 AFTER FLIGHT 51-L. DUE TO A STUPID, POINTLESS MECHANICAL ERROR, IT EXPLODED 73 SECONDS AFTER LAUNCH, ON LIVE TV...

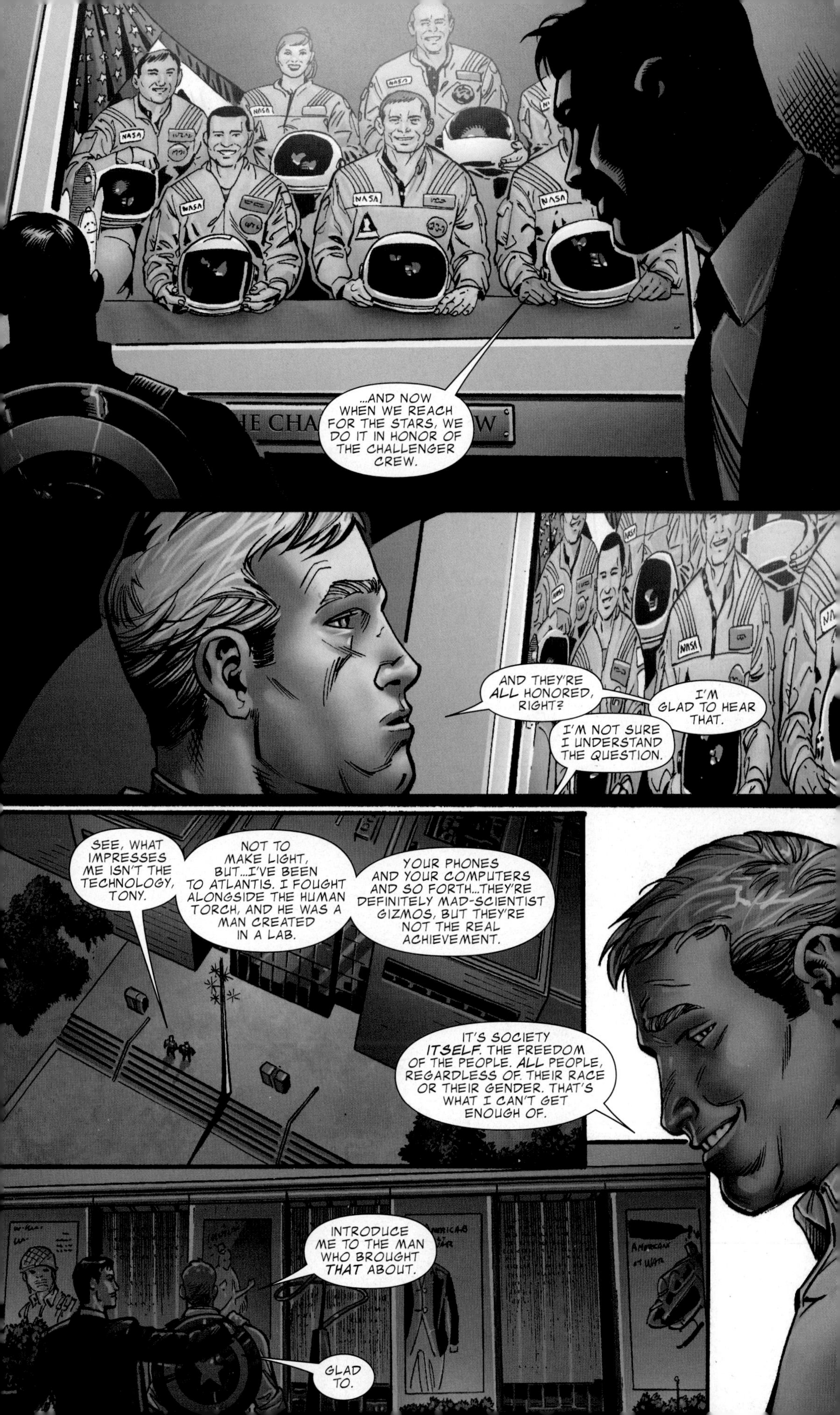
...AND NOW WHEN WE REACH FOR THE STARS, WE DO IT IN HONOR OF THE CHALLENGER CREW.
AND THEY'RE ALL HONORED, RIGHT?
I'M NOT SURE I UNDERSTAND THE QUESTION.
I'M GLAD TO HEAR THAT.
SEE, WHAT IMPRESSES ME ISN'T THE TECHNOLOGY, TONY.
NOT TO MAKE LIGHT, BUT...I'VE BEEN TO ATLANTIS. I FOUGHT ALONGSIDE THE HUMAN TORCH, AND HE WAS A MAN CREATED IN A LAB.
YOUR PHONES AND YOUR COMPUTERS AND SO FORTH...THEY'RE DEFINITELY MAD-SCIENTIST GIZMOS, BUT THEY'RE NOT THE REAL ACHIEVEMENT.
IT'S SOCIETY ITSELF. THE FREEDOM OF THE PEOPLE. ALL PEOPLE, REGARDLESS OF THEIR RACE OR THEIR GENDER. THAT'S WHAT I CAN'T GET ENOUGH OF.
INTRODUCE ME TO THE MAN WHO BROUGHT THAT ABOUT.
GLAD TO.

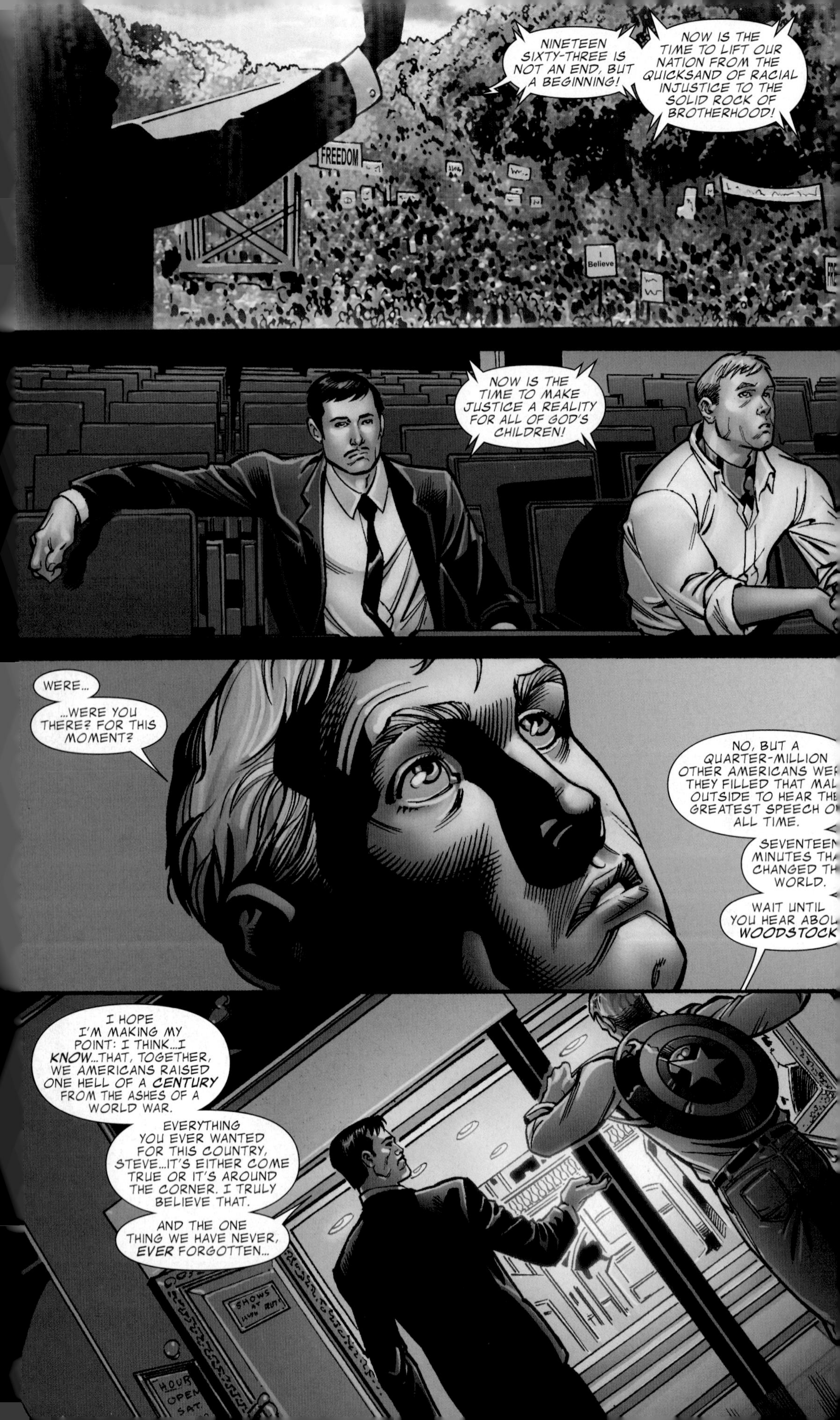
NINETEEN SIXTY-THREE IS NOT AN END, BUT A BEGINNING!
NOW IS THE TIME TO LIFT OUR NATION FROM THE QUICKSAND OF RACIAL INJUSTICE TO THE SOLID ROCK OF BROTHERHOOD!
FREEDOM
I Believe
NOW IS THE TIME TO MAKE JUSTICE A REALITY FOR ALL OF GOD'S CHILDREN!
WERE...
...WERE YOU THERE? FOR THIS MOMENT?
NO, BUT A QUARTER-MILLION OTHER AMERICANS WER THEY FILLED THAT MAL OUTSIDE TO HEAR THE GREATEST SPEECH O ALL TIME.
SEVENTEEN MINUTES TH CHANGED TH WORLD.
WAIT UNTIL YOU HEAR ABO WOODSTOCK
I HOPE I'M MAKING MY POINT: I THINK...I *KNOW*...THAT, TOGETHER, WE AMERICANS RAISED ONE HELL OF A *CENTURY* FROM THE ASHES OF A WORLD WAR.
EVERYTHING YOU EVER WANTED FOR THIS COUNTRY, STEVE...IT'S EITHER COME TRUE OR IT'S AROUND THE CORNER. I TRULY BELIEVE THAT.
AND THE ONE THING WE HAVE NEVER, *EVER* FORGOTTEN...

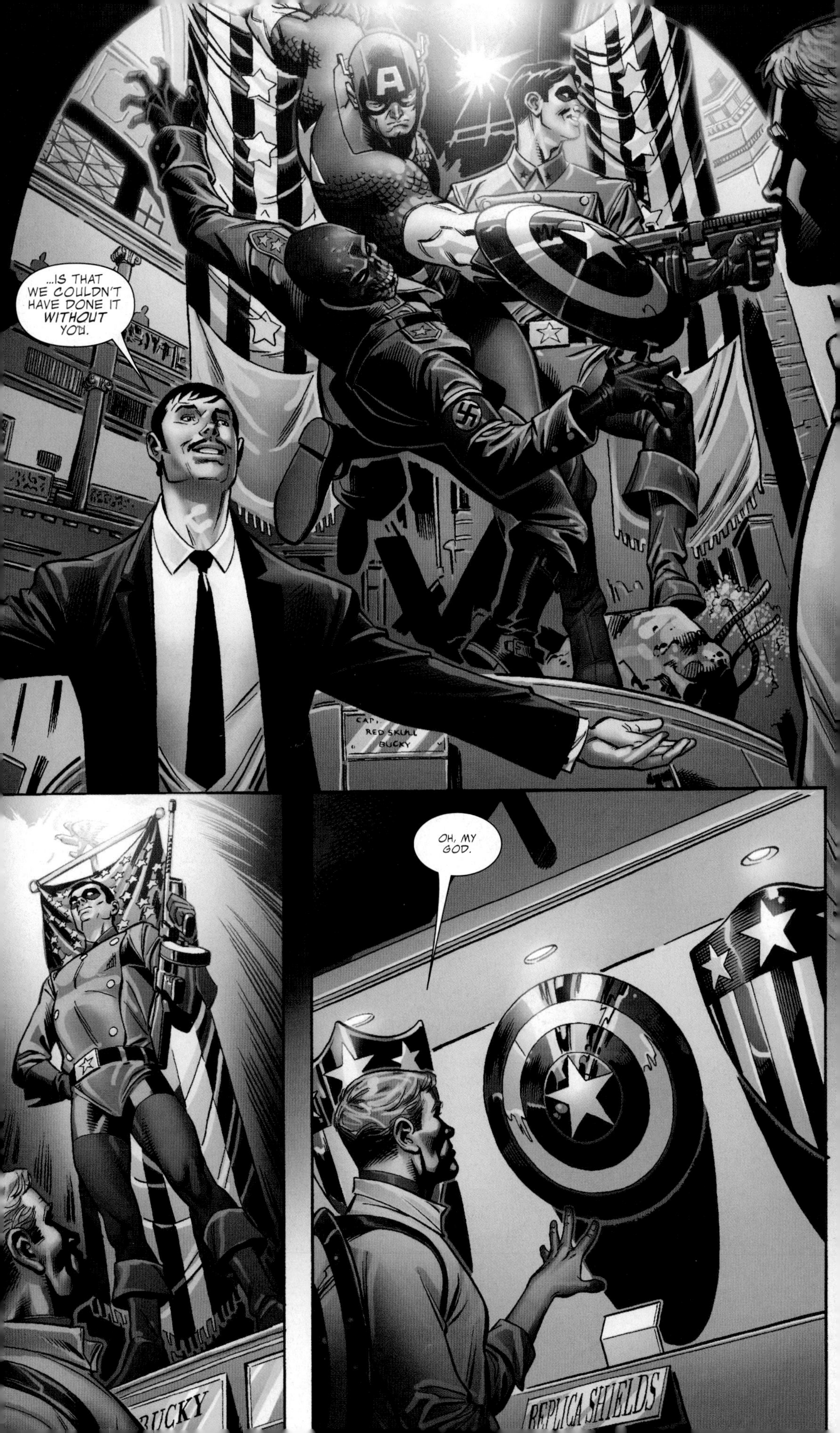
...IS THAT WE COULDN'T HAVE DONE IT WITHOUT YOU.
CAP. RED SKULL BUCKY
OH, MY GOD.
BUCKY
REPLICA SHIELDS

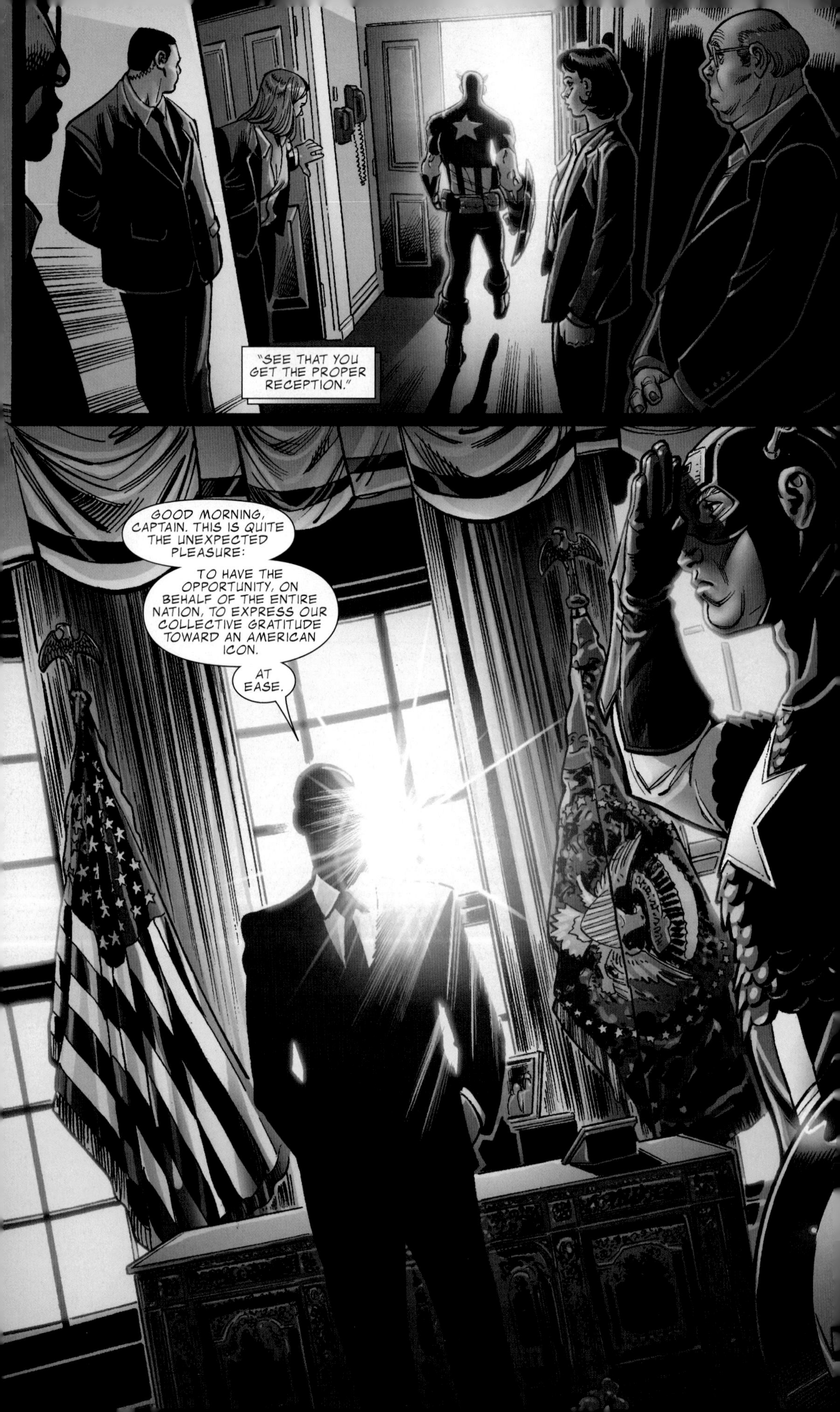
"SEE THAT YOU GET THE PROPER RECEPTION."
GOOD MORNING, CAPTAIN. THIS IS QUITE THE UNEXPECTED PLEASURE:
TO HAVE THE OPPORTUNITY, ON BEHALF OF THE ENTIRE NATION, TO EXPRESS OUR COLLECTIVE GRATITUDE TOWARD AN AMERICAN ICON.
AT EASE.

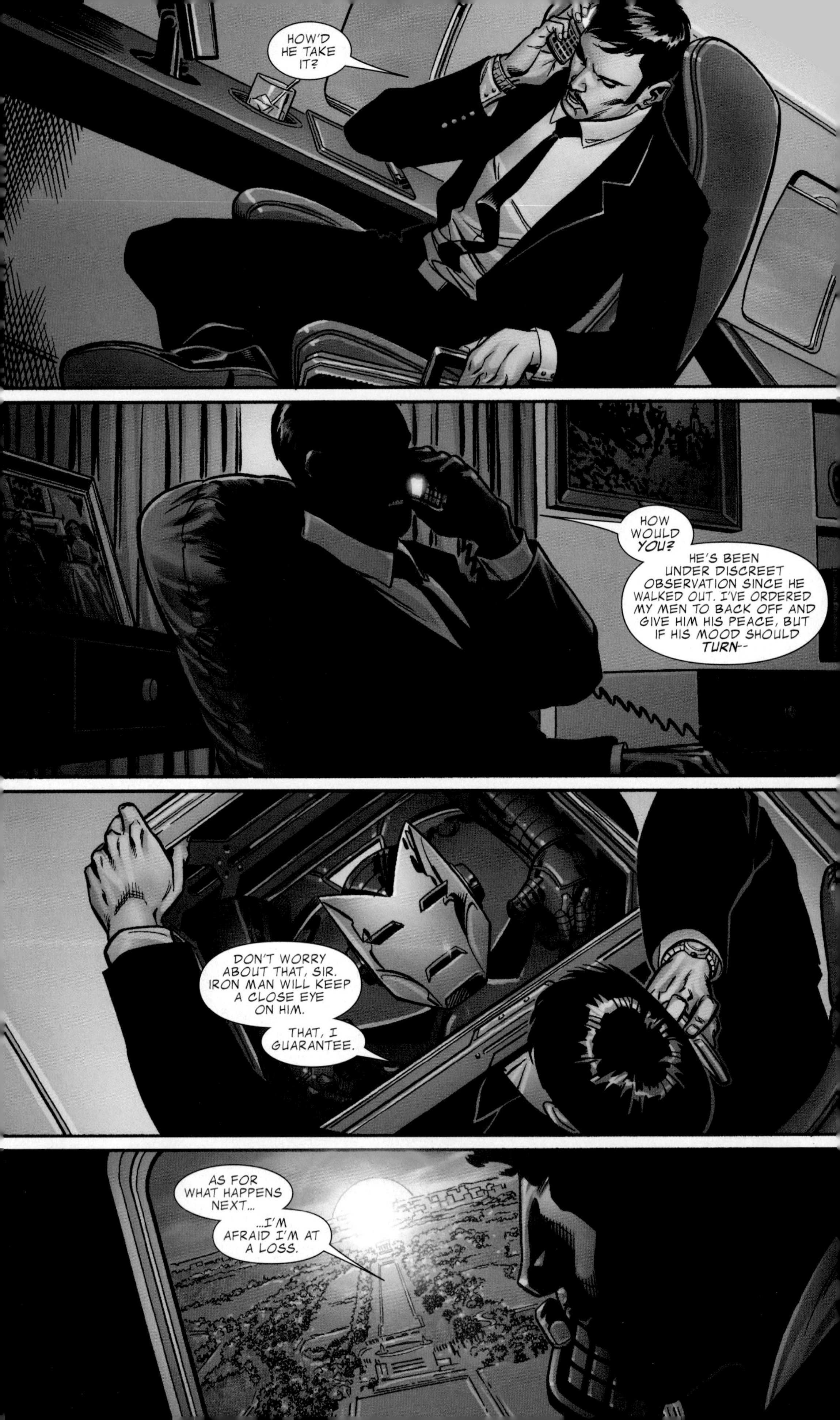
HOW'D HE TAKE IT?
HOW WOULD *YOU?*
HE'S BEEN UNDER DISCREET OBSERVATION SINCE HE WALKED OUT. I'VE ORDERED MY MEN TO BACK OFF AND GIVE HIM HIS PEACE, BUT IF HIS MOOD SHOULD *TURN*--
DON'T WORRY ABOUT THAT, SIR. IRON MAN WILL KEEP A CLOSE EYE ON HIM.
THAT, I GUARANTEE.
AS FOR WHAT HAPPENS NEXT...
...I'M AFRAID I'M AT A LOSS.

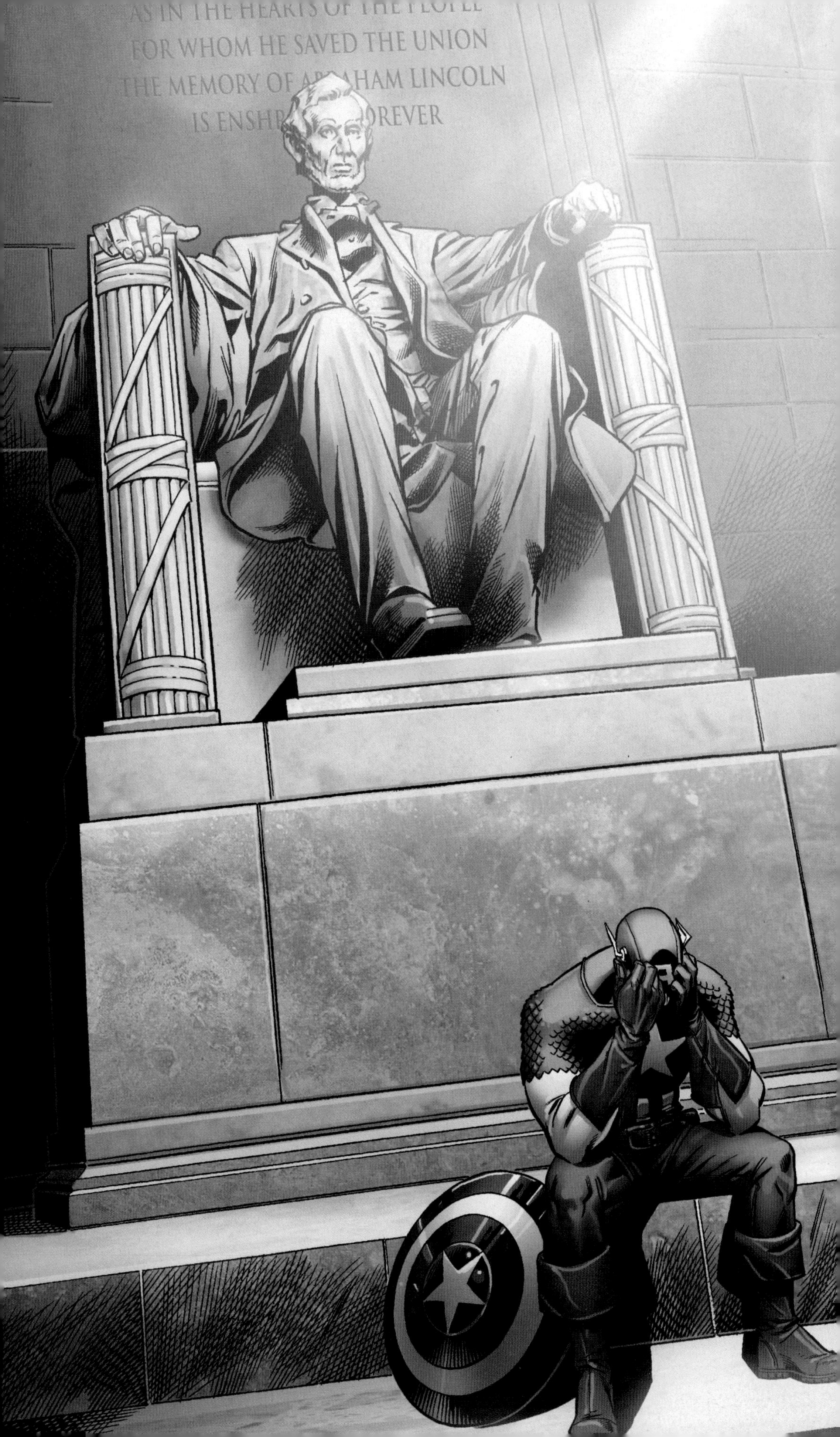
FOR WHOM HE SAVED THE UNION

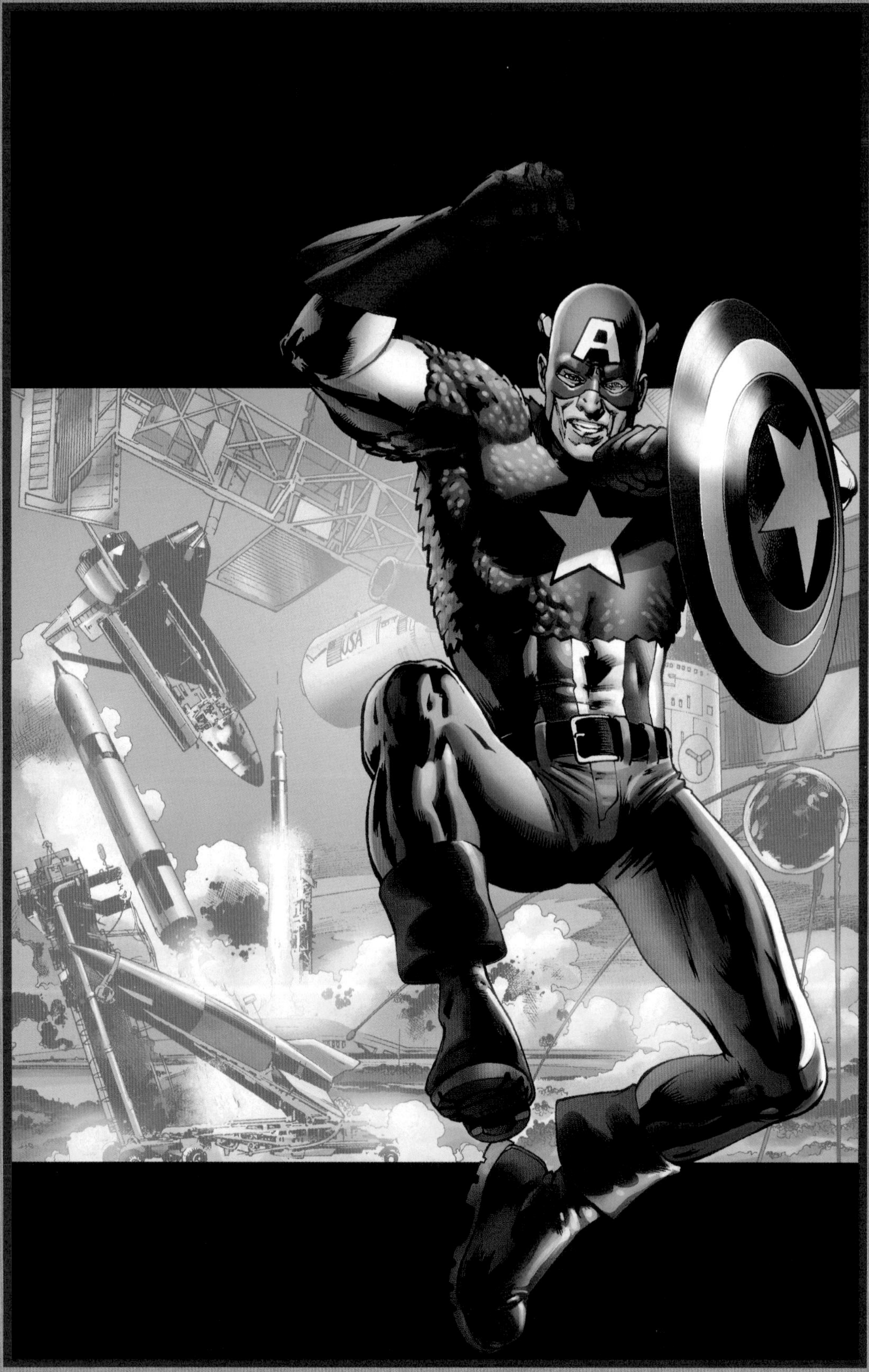
USA

[4]

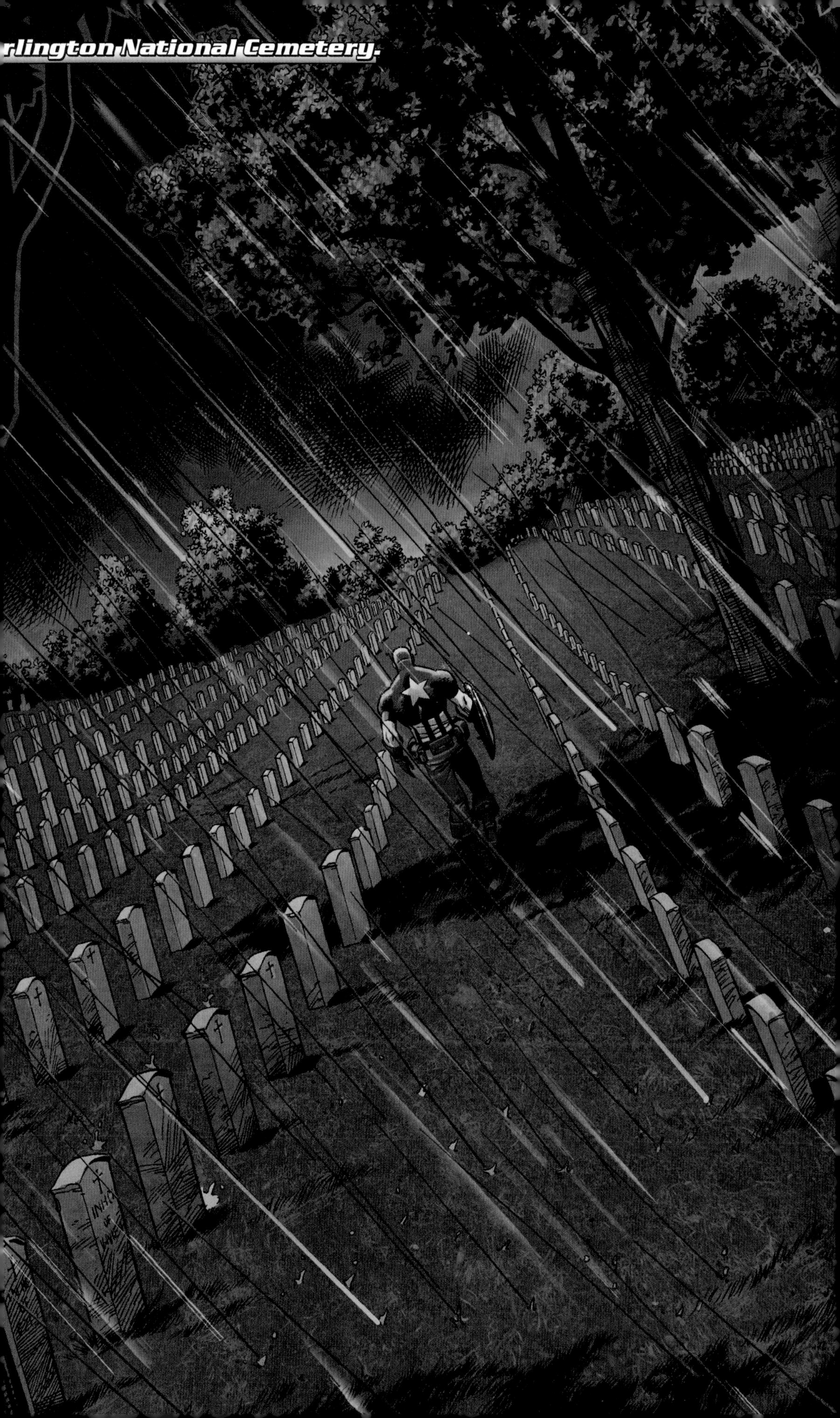
rlington National Cemetery.

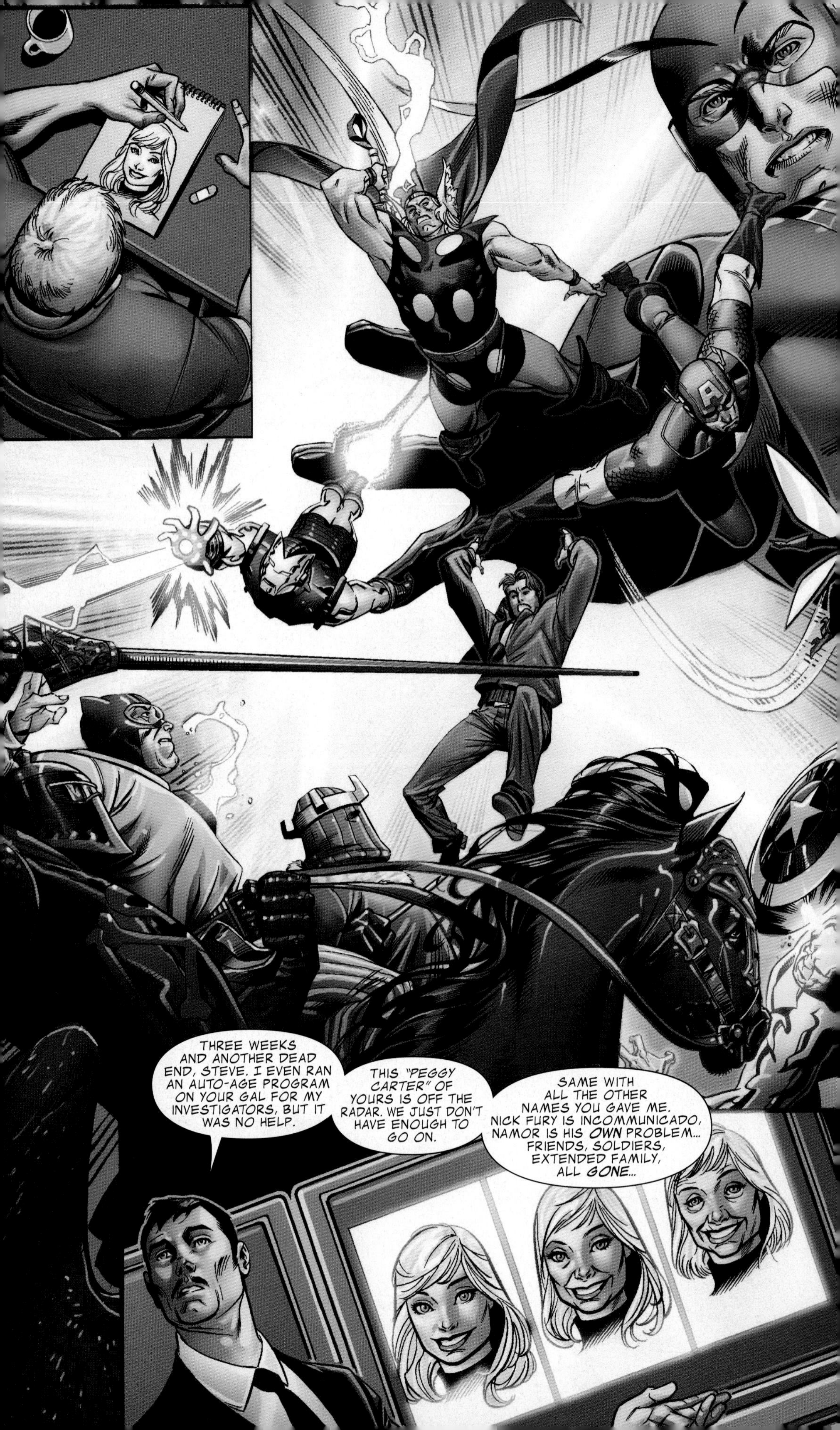
THREE WEEKS AND ANOTHER DEAD END, STEVE. I EVEN RAN AN AUTO-AGE PROGRAM ON YOUR GAL FOR MY INVESTIGATORS, BUT IT WAS NO HELP.
THIS "PEGGY CARTER" OF YOURS IS OFF THE RADAR. WE JUST DON'T HAVE ENOUGH TO GO ON.
SAME WITH ALL THE OTHER NAMES YOU GAVE ME. NICK FURY IS INCOMMUNICADO, NAMOR IS HIS OWN PROBLEM... FRIENDS, SOLDIERS, EXTENDED FAMILY, ALL GONE...

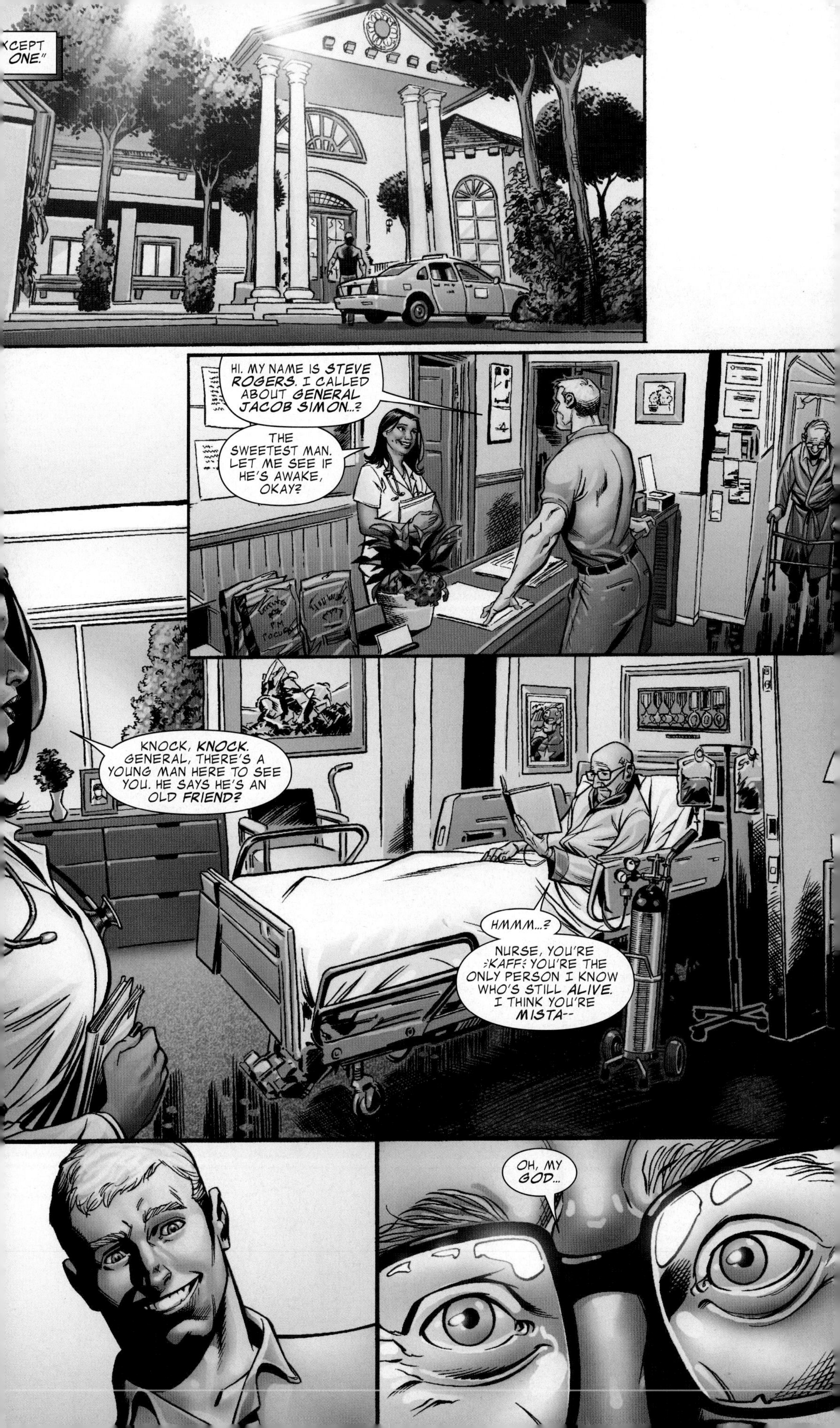
XCEPT ONE."
HI. MY NAME IS STEVE ROGERS. I CALLED ABOUT GENERAL JACOB SIMON...?
THE SWEETEST MAN. LET ME SEE IF HE'S AWAKE, OKAY?
KNOCK, KNOCK. GENERAL, THERE'S A YOUNG MAN HERE TO SEE YOU. HE SAYS HE'S AN OLD FRIEND?
HMMM...?
NURSE, YOU'RE *KAFF* YOU'RE THE ONLY PERSON I KNOW WHO'S STILL ALIVE. I THINK YOU'RE MISTA--
OH, MY GOD...

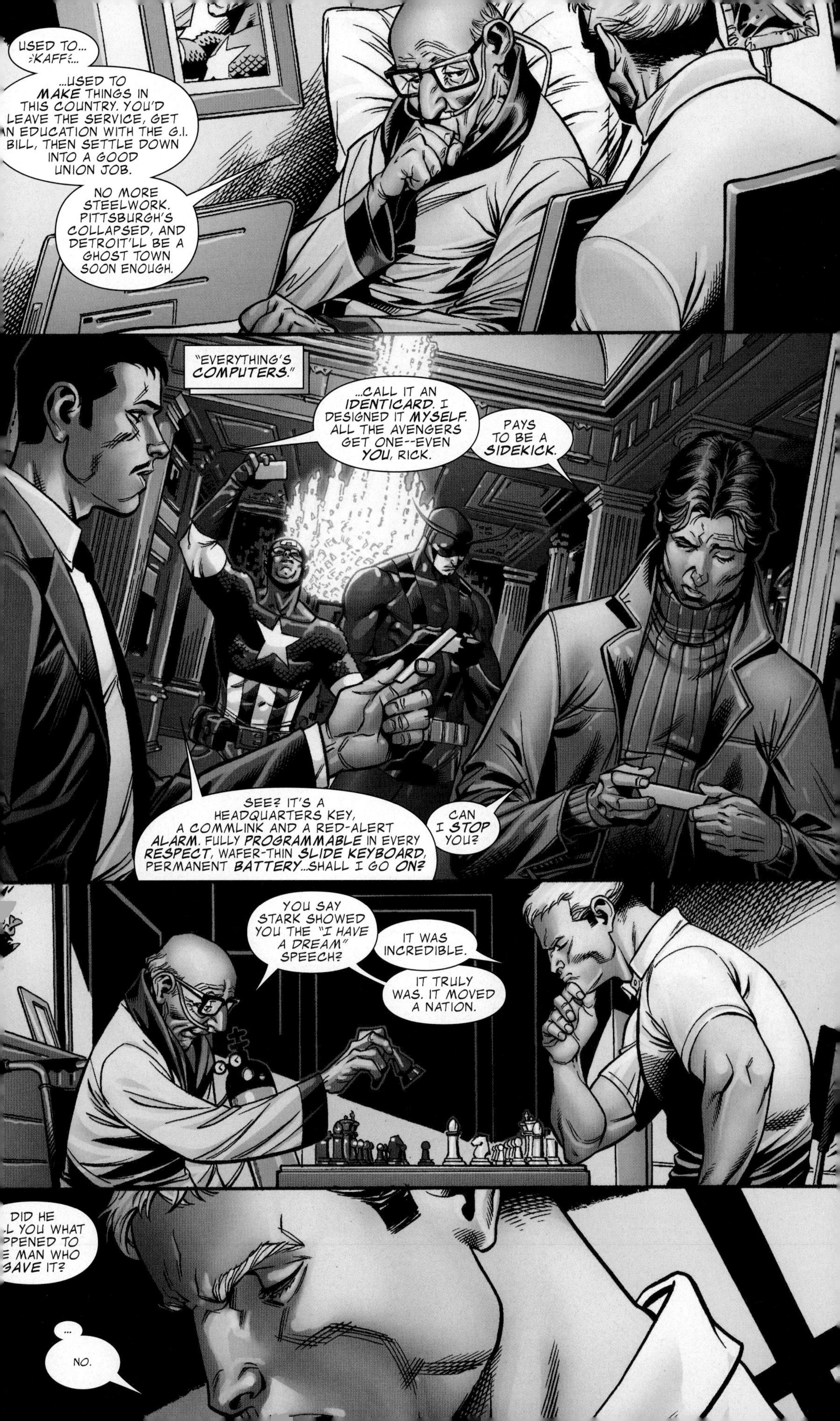
USED TO... ≈KAFF≈...
...USED TO MAKE THINGS IN THIS COUNTRY. YOU'D LEAVE THE SERVICE, GET N EDUCATION WITH THE G.I. BILL, THEN SETTLE DOWN INTO A GOOD UNION JOB.
NO MORE STEELWORK. PITTSBURGH'S COLLAPSED, AND DETROIT'LL BE A GHOST TOWN SOON ENOUGH.
"EVERYTHING'S COMPUTERS."
...CALL IT AN IDENTICARD. I DESIGNED IT MYSELF. ALL THE AVENGERS GET ONE--EVEN YOU, RICK.
PAYS TO BE A SIDEKICK.
SEE? IT'S A HEADQUARTERS KEY, A COMMLINK AND A RED-ALERT ALARM. FULLY PROGRAMMABLE IN EVERY RESPECT, WAFER-THIN SLIDE KEYBOARD, PERMANENT BATTERY...SHALL I GO ON?
CAN I STOP YOU?
YOU SAY STARK SHOWED YOU THE "I HAVE A DREAM" SPEECH?
IT WAS INCREDIBLE.
IT TRULY WAS. IT MOVED A NATION.
DID HE L YOU WHAT PPENED TO E MAN WHO GAVE IT?
... NO.

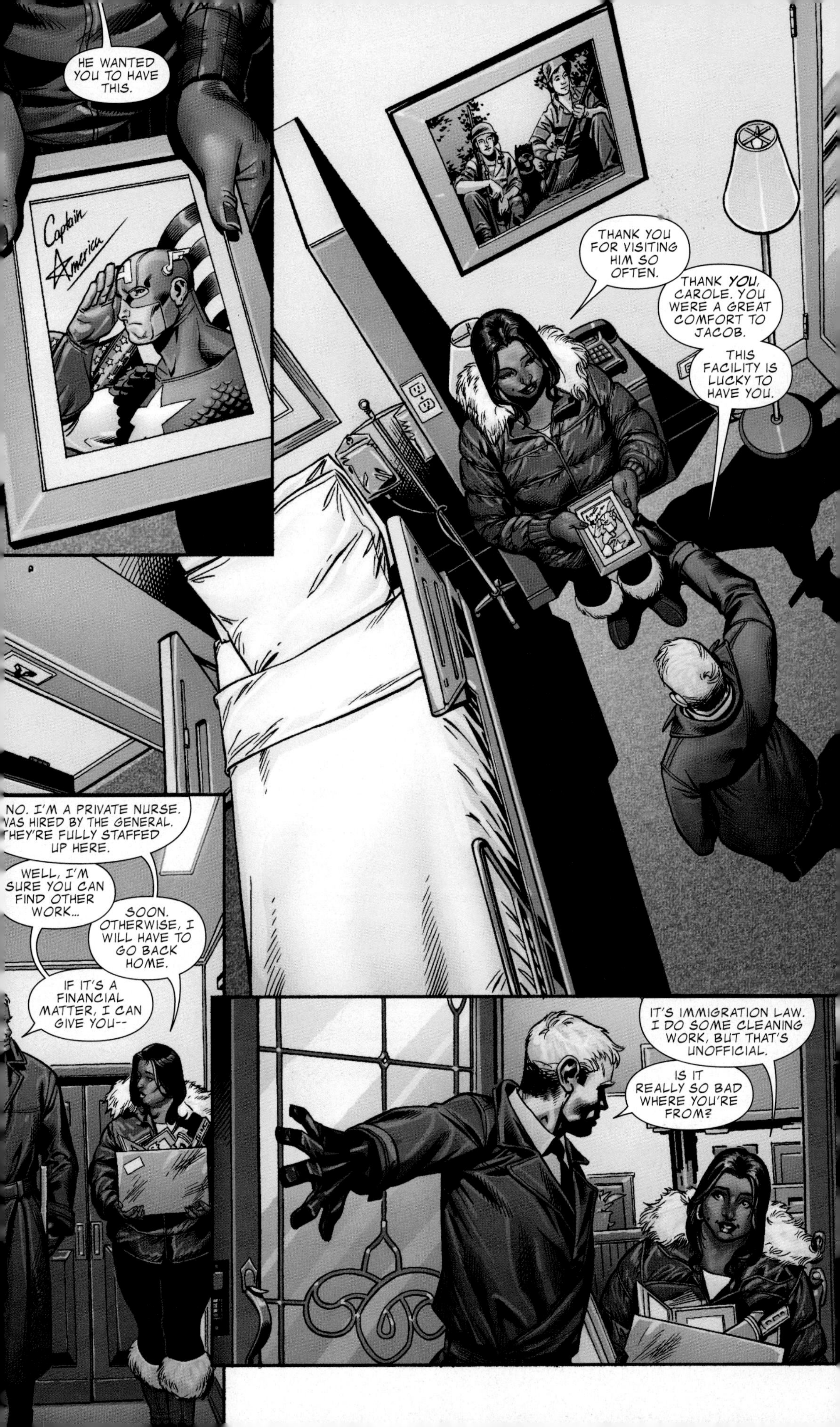
HE WANTED YOU TO HAVE THIS.
Captain America
THANK YOU FOR VISITING HIM SO OFTEN.
THANK YOU, CAROLE. YOU WERE A GREAT COMFORT TO JACOB.
THIS FACILITY IS LUCKY TO HAVE YOU.
NO. I'M A PRIVATE NURSE. WAS HIRED BY THE GENERAL. THEY'RE FULLY STAFFED UP HERE.
WELL, I'M SURE YOU CAN FIND OTHER WORK...
SOON. OTHERWISE, I WILL HAVE TO GO BACK HOME.
IF IT'S A FINANCIAL MATTER, I CAN GIVE YOU--
IT'S IMMIGRATION LAW. I DO SOME CLEANING WORK, BUT THAT'S UNOFFICIAL.
IS IT REALLY SO BAD WHERE YOU'RE FROM?

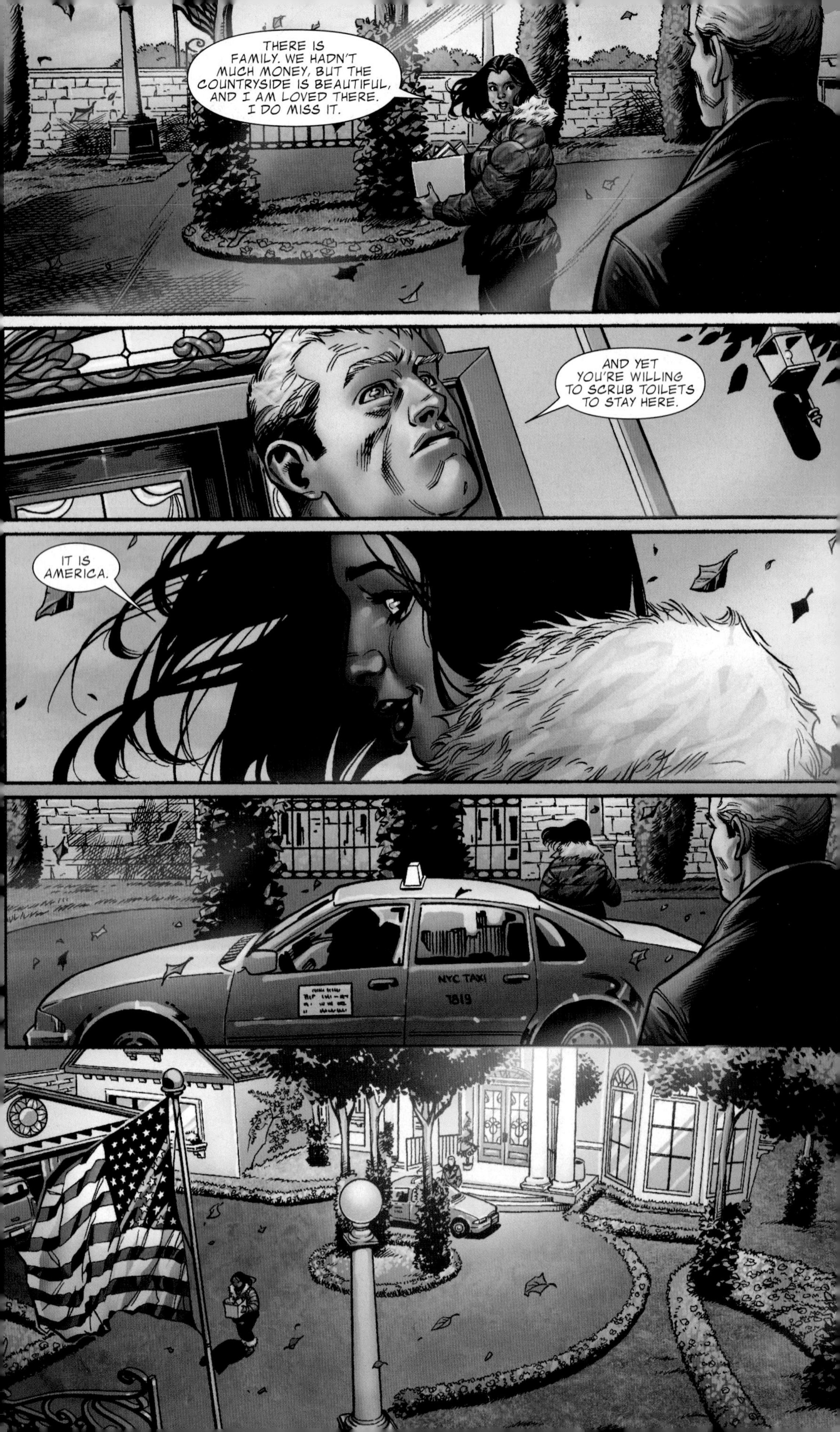
THERE IS FAMILY. WE HADN'T MUCH MONEY, BUT THE COUNTRYSIDE IS BEAUTIFUL, AND I AM LOVED THERE. I DO MISS IT.
AND YET YOU'RE WILLING TO SCRUB TOILETS TO STAY HERE.
IT IS AMERICA.
NYC TAXI
7819

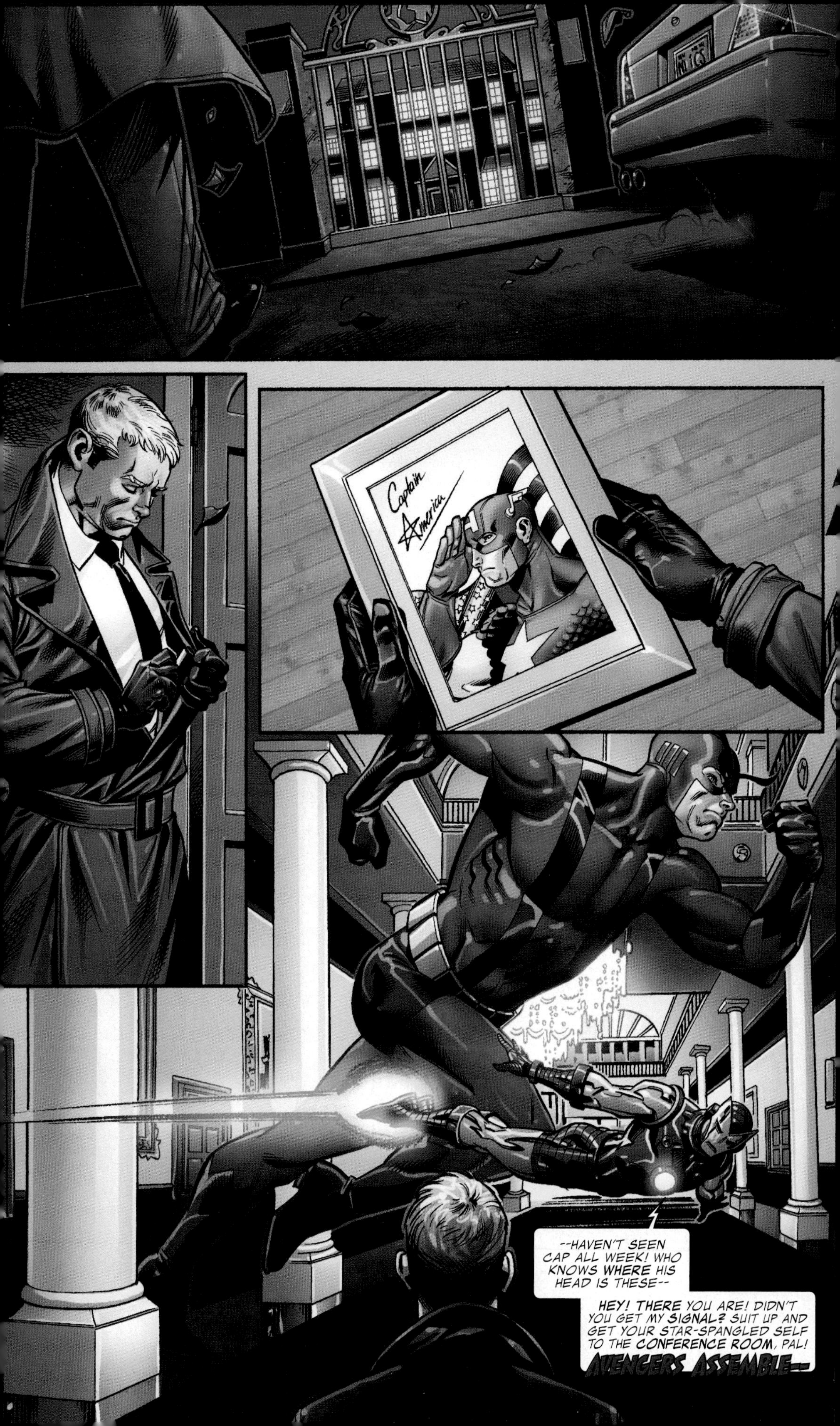
Captain America
--HAVEN'T SEEN CAP ALL WEEK! WHO KNOWS WHERE HIS HEAD IS THESE--
HEY! THERE YOU ARE! DIDN'T YOU GET MY SIGNAL? SUIT UP AND GET YOUR STAR-SPANGLED SELF TO THE CONFERENCE ROOM, PAL!
AVENGERS ASSEMBLE--

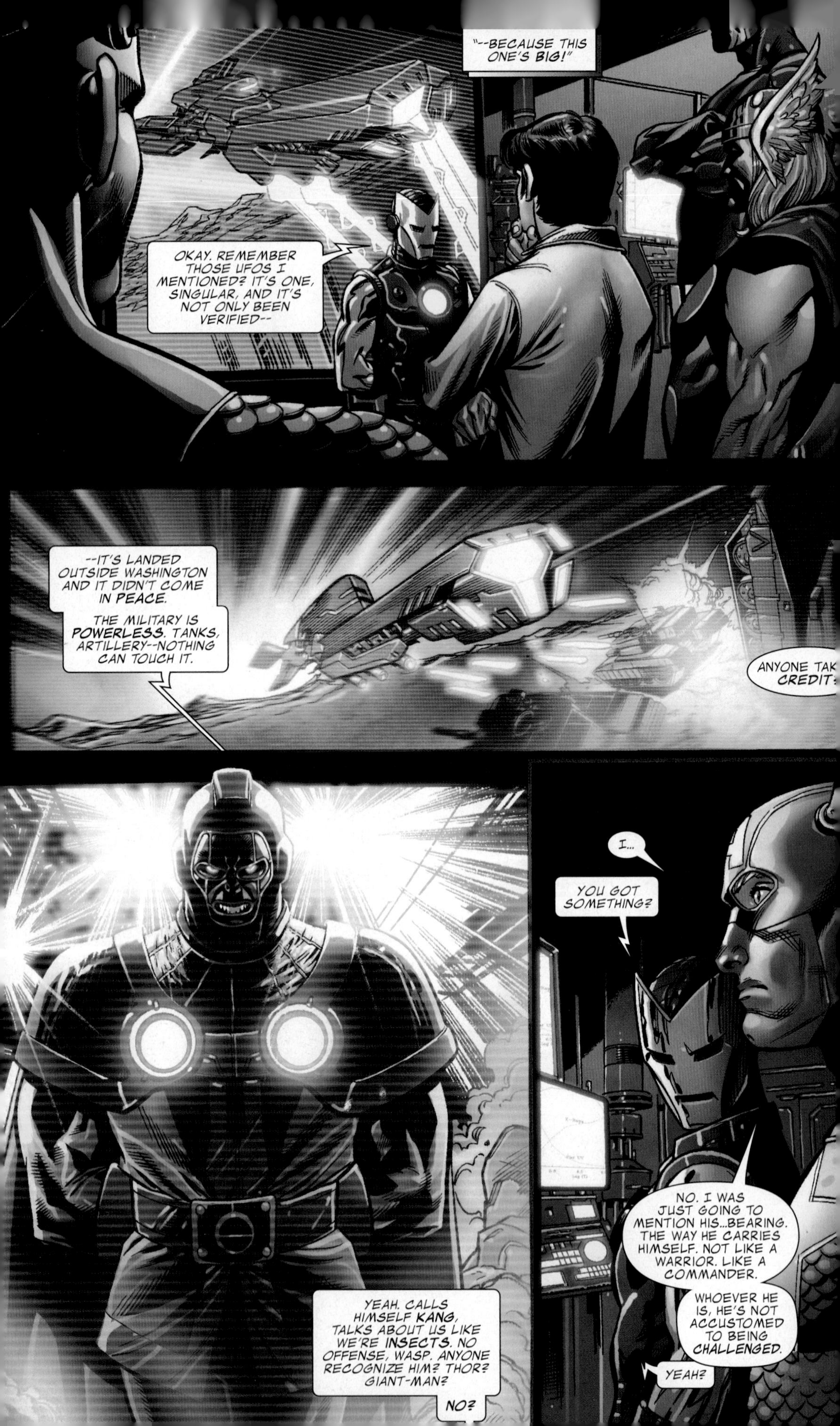
"--BECAUSE THIS ONE'S BIG!"
OKAY. REMEMBER THOSE UFOS I MENTIONED? IT'S ONE, SINGULAR, AND IT'S NOT ONLY BEEN VERIFIED--
--IT'S LANDED OUTSIDE WASHINGTON AND IT DIDN'T COME IN PEACE.
THE MILITARY IS POWERLESS. TANKS, ARTILLERY--NOTHING CAN TOUCH IT.
ANYONE TAK CREDIT
YEAH. CALLS HIMSELF KANG, TALKS ABOUT US LIKE WE'RE INSECTS. NO OFFENSE, WASP. ANYONE RECOGNIZE HIM? THOR? GIANT-MAN?
NO?
I...
YOU GOT SOMETHING?
NO. I WAS JUST GOING TO MENTION HIS...BEARING. THE WAY HE CARRIES HIMSELF. NOT LIKE A WARRIOR. LIKE A COMMANDER.
WHOEVER HE IS, HE'S NOT ACCUSTOMED TO BEING CHALLENGED.
YEAH?

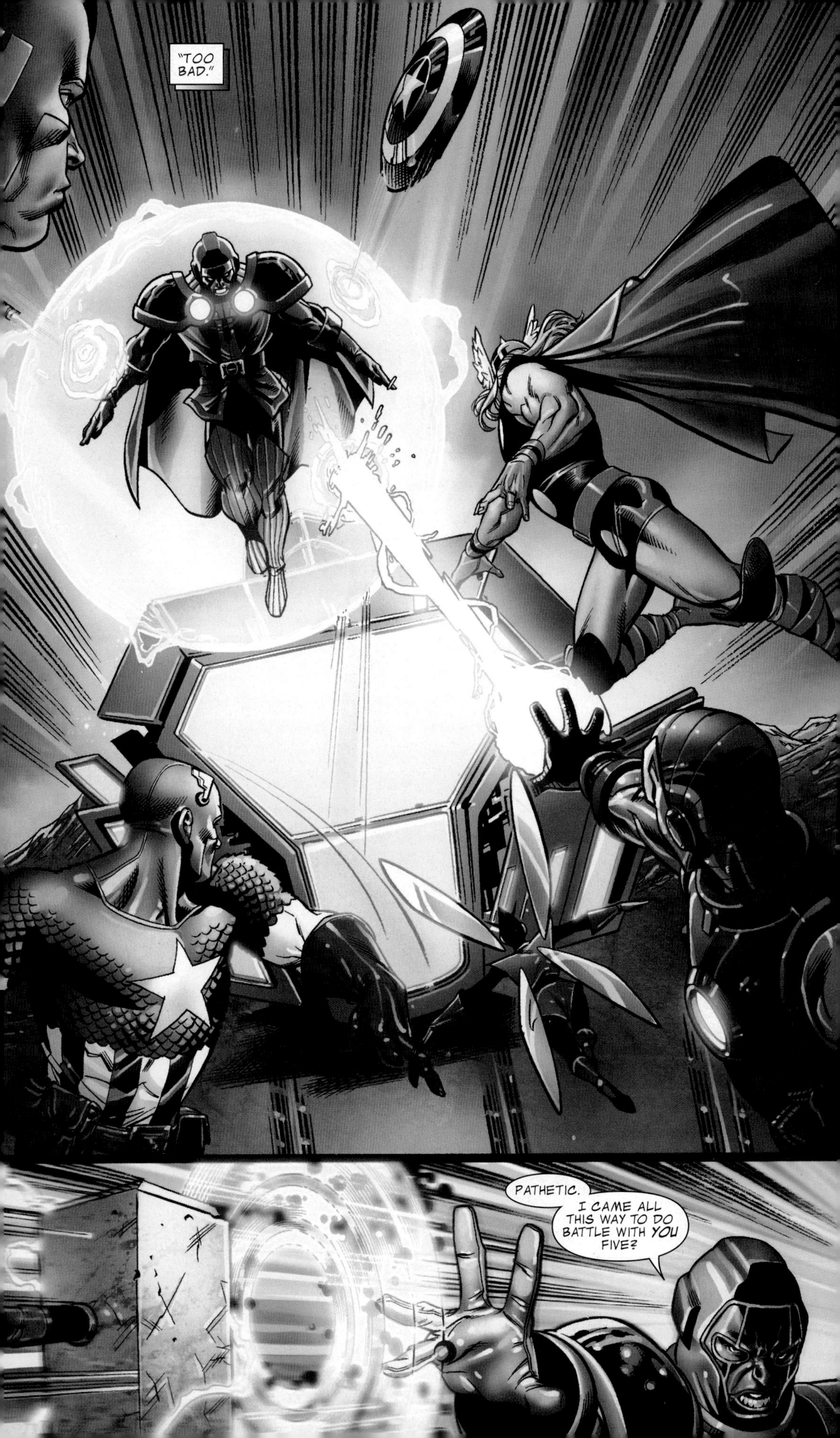
"TOO BAD."
PATHETIC.
I CAME ALL THIS WAY TO DO BATTLE WITH YOU FIVE?

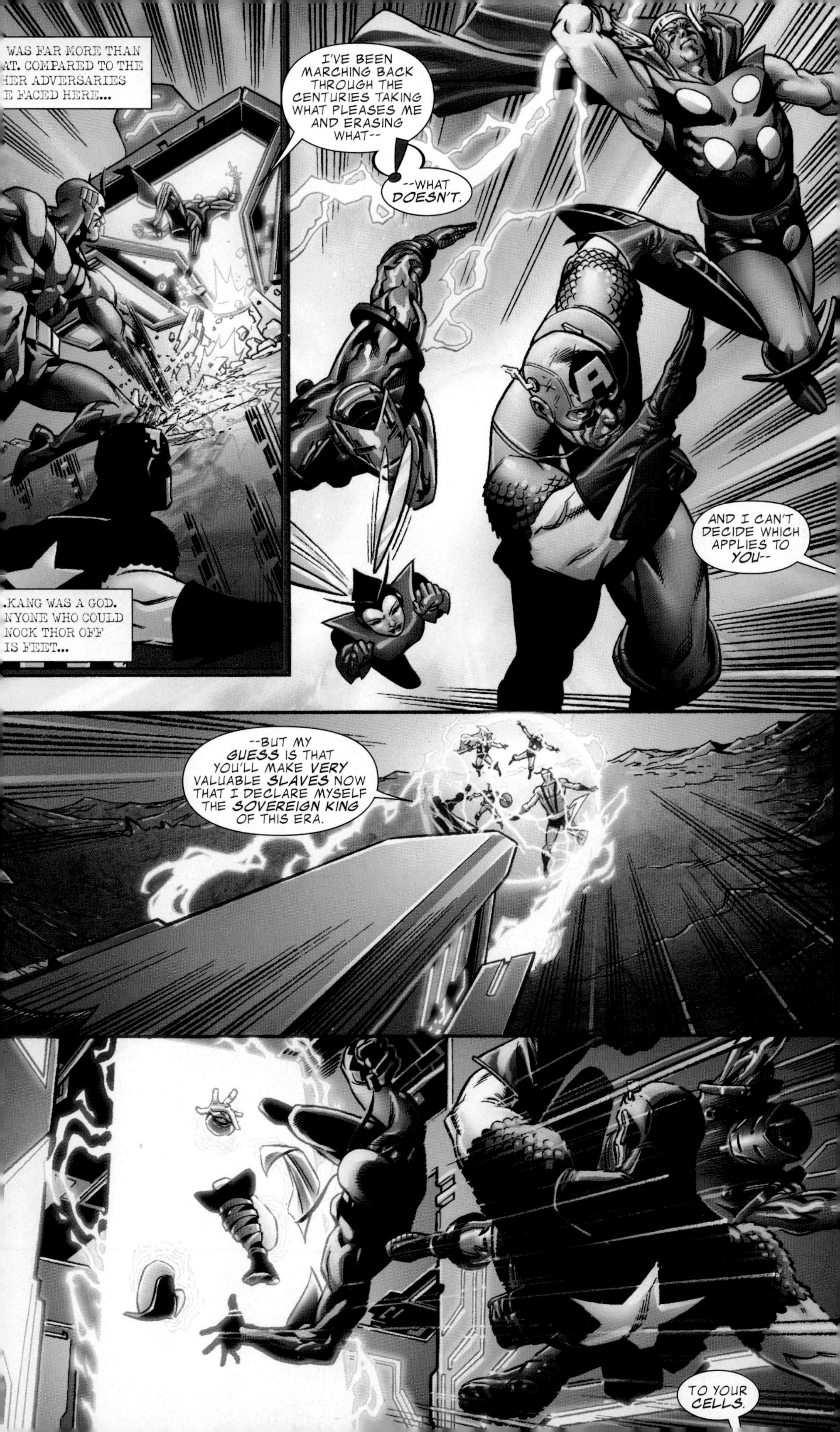
WAS FAR MORE THAN
AT. COMPARED TO THE
HER ADVERSARIES
E FACED HERE...
I'VE BEEN MARCHING BACK THROUGH THE CENTURIES TAKING WHAT PLEASES ME AND ERASING WHAT--
!
--WHAT DOESN'T.
.KANG WAS A GOD.
NYONE WHO COULD
NOCK THOR OFF
IS FEET...
AND I CAN'T DECIDE WHICH APPLIES TO YOU--
--BUT MY GUESS IS THAT YOU'LL MAKE VERY VALUABLE SLAVES NOW THAT I DECLARE MYSELF THE SOVEREIGN KING OF THIS ERA.
TO YOUR CELLS.

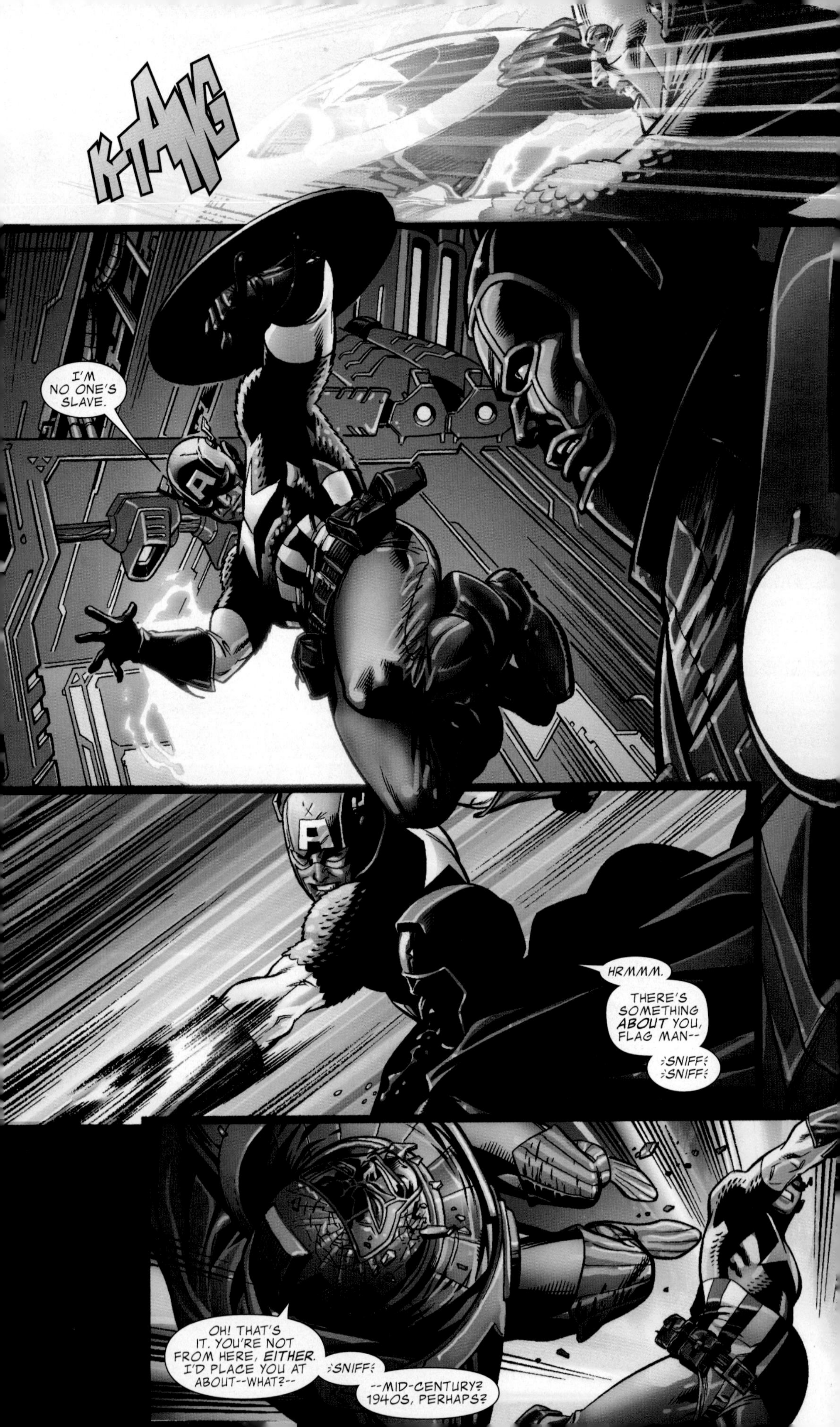
K-TANG
I'M NO ONE'S SLAVE.
HRMMM.
THERE'S SOMETHING ABOUT YOU, FLAG MAN--
:SNIFF: :SNIFF:
OH! THAT'S IT. YOU'RE NOT FROM HERE, EITHER. I'D PLACE YOU AT ABOUT--WHAT?--
:SNIFF:
--MID-CENTURY? 1940S, PERHAPS?

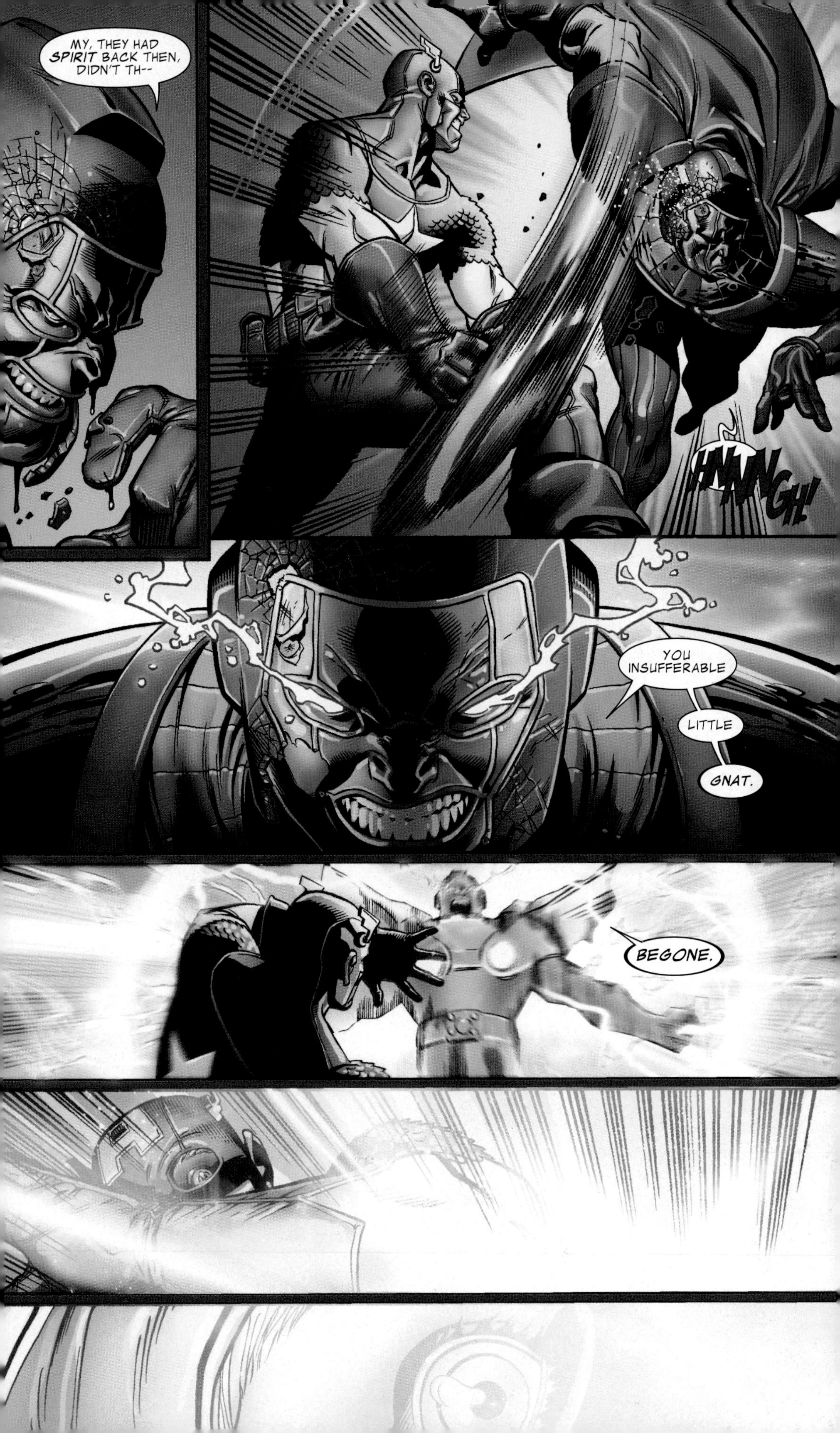
MY, THEY HAD SPIRIT BACK THEN, DIDN'T TH--
HNNNNGH!
YOU INSUFFERABLE
LITTLE
GNAT.
BEGONE.

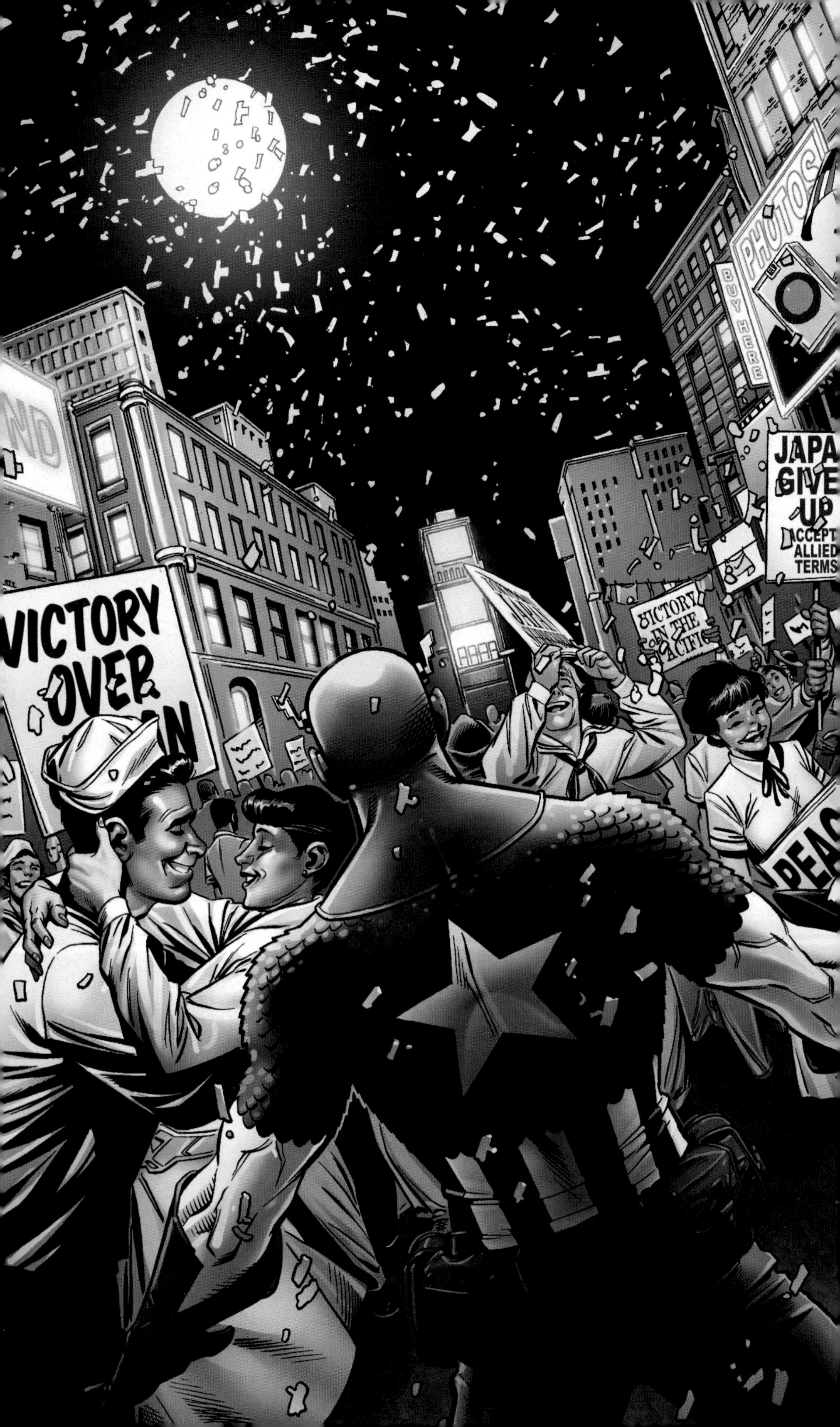
VICTORY
OVER
PHOTOS
BUY HERE
GIVE
UP
ACCEPT
ALLIED
TERMS
IN THE

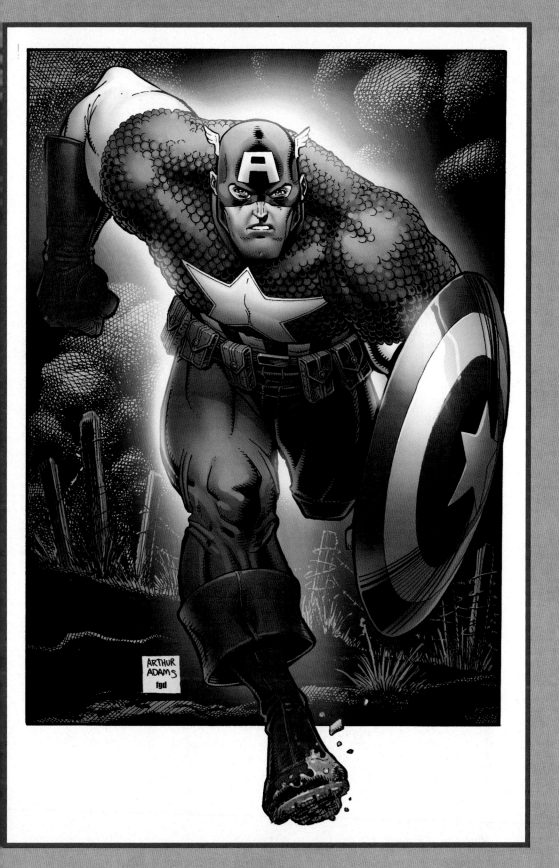

[1]
Variant by Artur Adams & Frank D'Armata

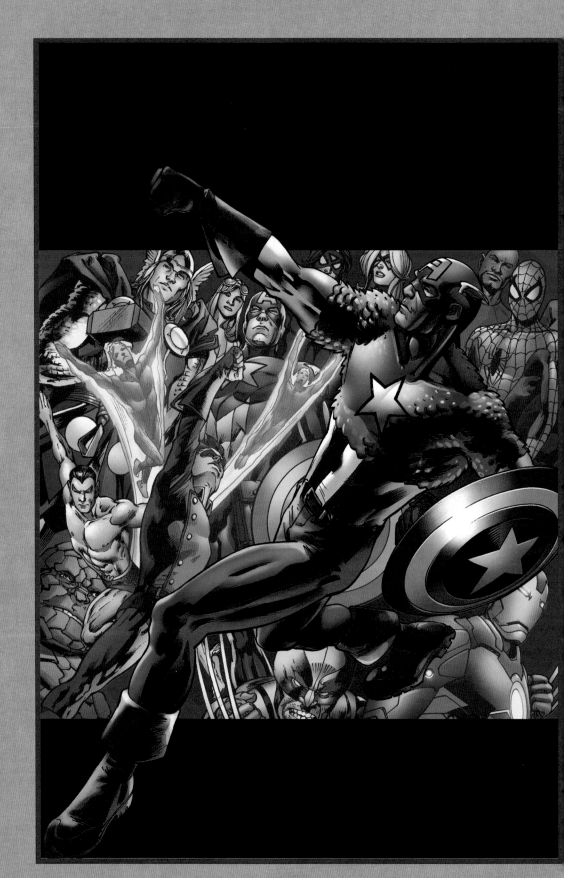

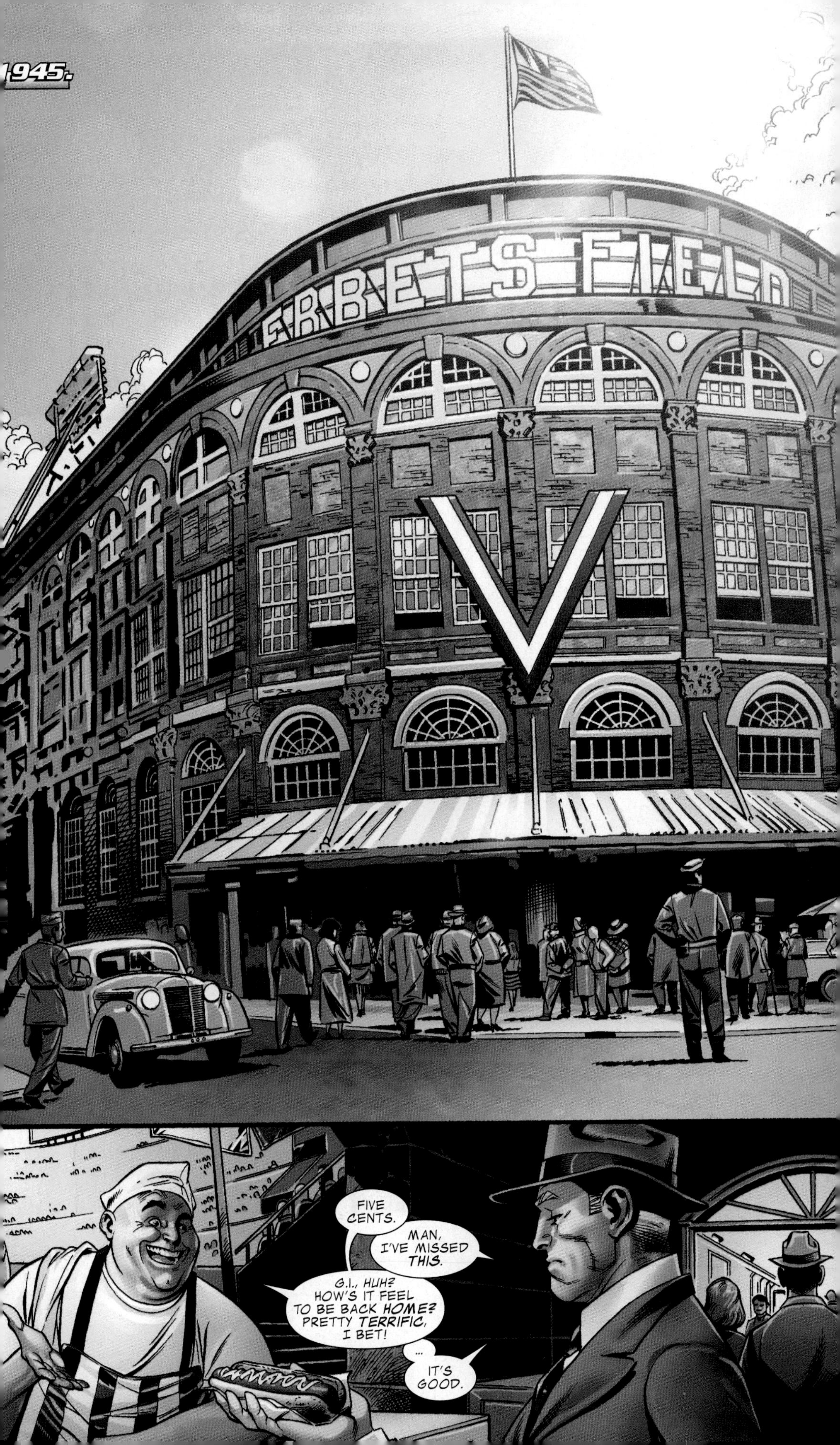
1945.
FIVE CENTS.
MAN, I'VE MISSED THIS.
G.I., HUH? HOW'S IT FEEL TO BE BACK HOME? PRETTY TERRIFIC, I BET!
...
IT'S GOOD.

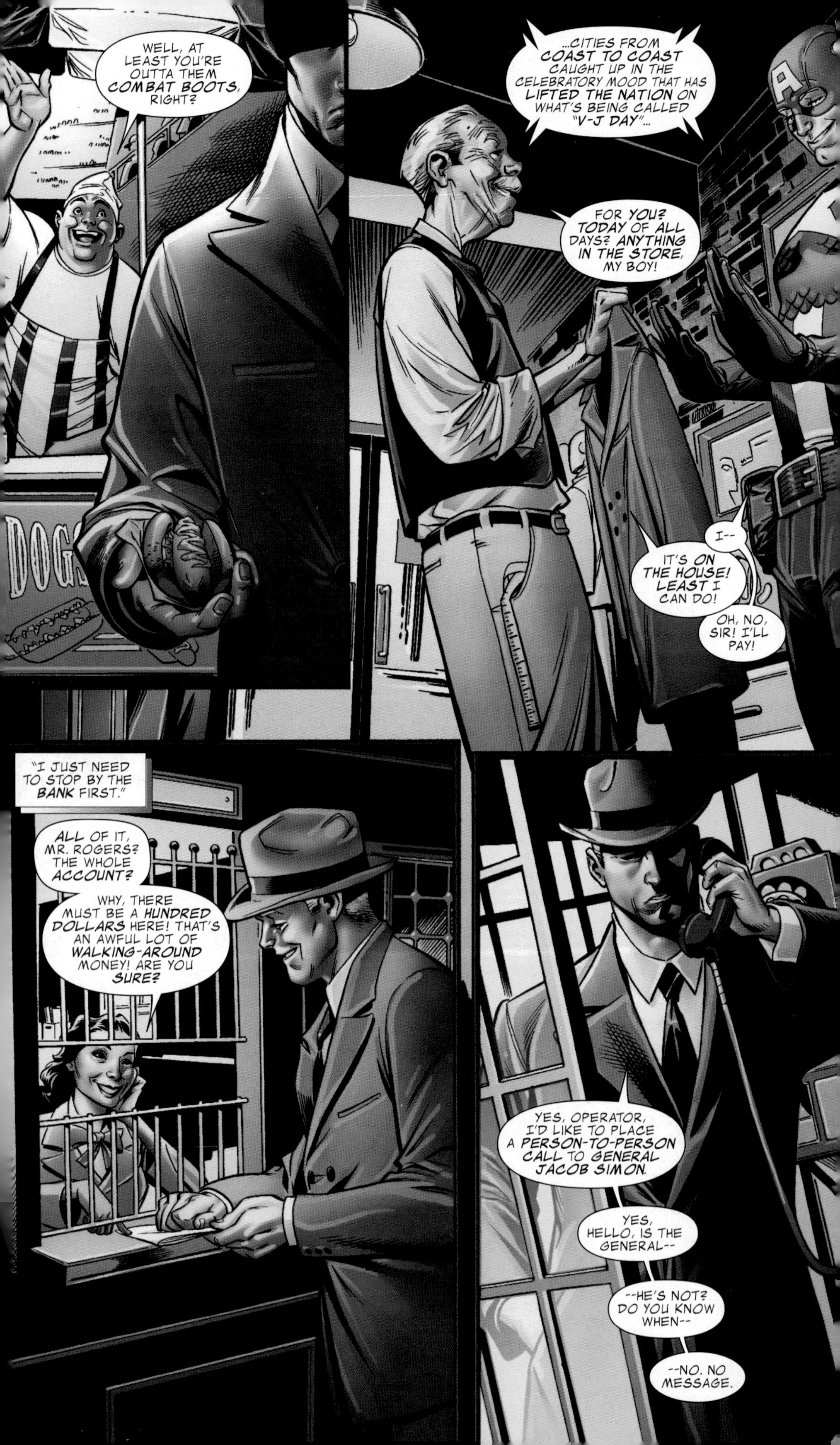
WELL, AT LEAST YOU'RE OUTTA THEM COMBAT BOOTS, RIGHT?
DOGS
...CITIES FROM COAST TO COAST CAUGHT UP IN THE CELEBRATORY MOOD THAT HAS LIFTED THE NATION ON WHAT'S BEING CALLED "V-J DAY"...
FOR YOU? TODAY OF ALL DAYS? ANYTHING IN THE STORE, MY BOY!
I--
IT'S ON THE HOUSE! LEAST I CAN DO!
OH, NO, SIR! I'LL PAY!
"I JUST NEED TO STOP BY THE BANK FIRST."
ALL OF IT, MR. ROGERS? THE WHOLE ACCOUNT?
WHY, THERE MUST BE A HUNDRED DOLLARS HERE! THAT'S AN AWFUL LOT OF WALKING-AROUND MONEY! ARE YOU SURE?
YES, OPERATOR, I'D LIKE TO PLACE A PERSON-TO-PERSON CALL TO GENERAL JACOB SIMON.
YES, HELLO, IS THE GENERAL--
--HE'S NOT? DO YOU KNOW WHEN--
--NO. NO MESSAGE.

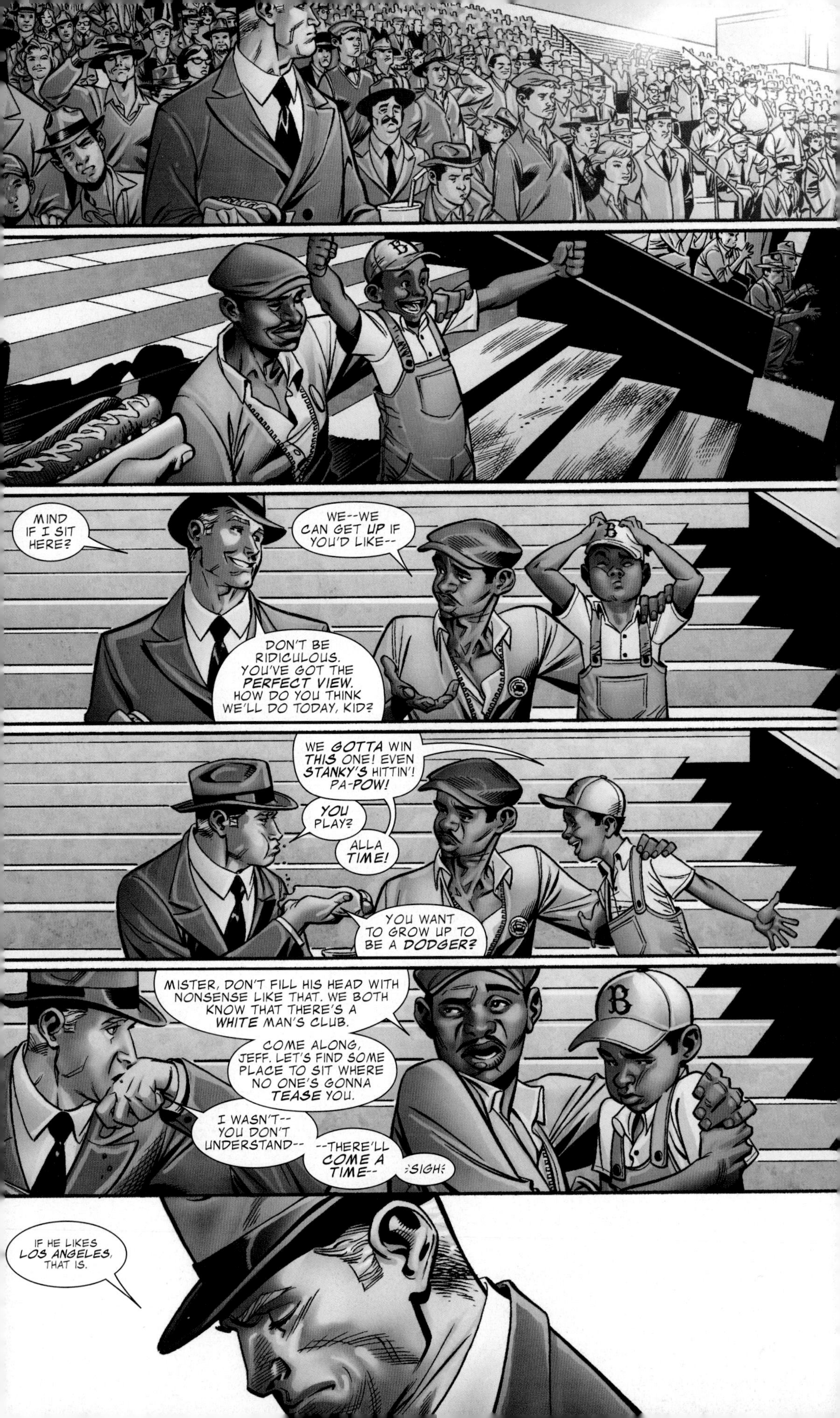
MIND IF I SIT HERE?
WE--WE CAN GET UP IF YOU'D LIKE--
DON'T BE RIDICULOUS. YOU'VE GOT THE PERFECT VIEW. HOW DO YOU THINK WE'LL DO TODAY, KID?
WE GOTTA WIN THIS ONE! EVEN STANKY'S HITTIN'! PA-POW!
YOU PLAY?
ALLA TIME!
YOU WANT TO GROW UP TO BE A DODGER?
MISTER, DON'T FILL HIS HEAD WITH NONSENSE LIKE THAT. WE BOTH KNOW THAT THERE'S A WHITE MAN'S CLUB.
COME ALONG, JEFF. LET'S FIND SOME PLACE TO SIT WHERE NO ONE'S GONNA TEASE YOU.
I WASN'T-- YOU DON'T UNDERSTAND--
--THERE'LL COME A TIME--
SIGH
IF HE LIKES LOS ANGELES, THAT IS.

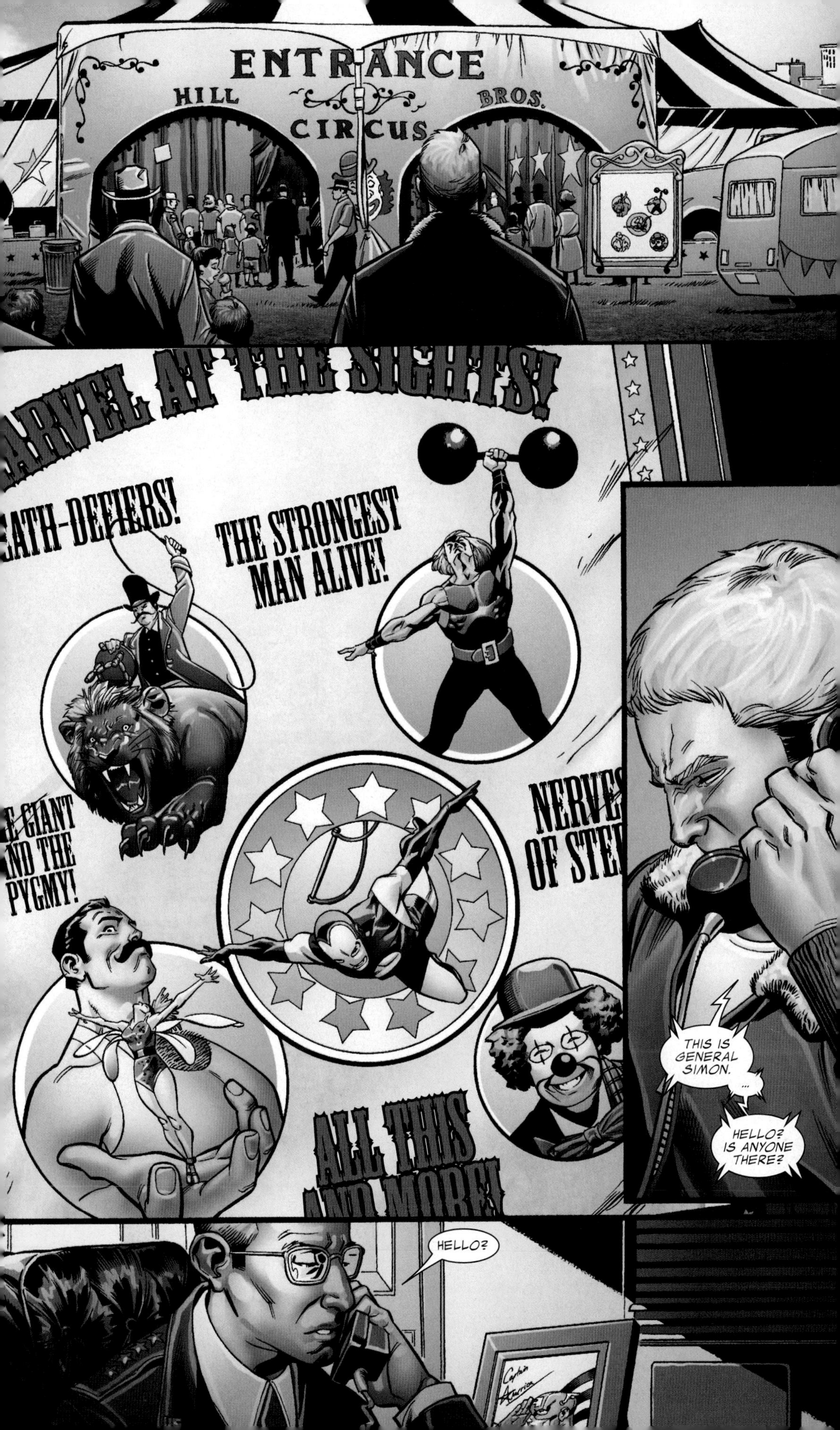
ENTRANCE
HILL BROS.
CIRCUS
ARVEL AT THE SIGHTS!
EATH-DEFIERS!
THE STRONGEST MAN ALIVE!
E GIANT
ND THE
PYGMY!
NERVES
OF STE
ALL THIS
THIS IS GENERAL SIMON.
...
HELLO? IS ANYONE THERE?
HELLO?
Captain America

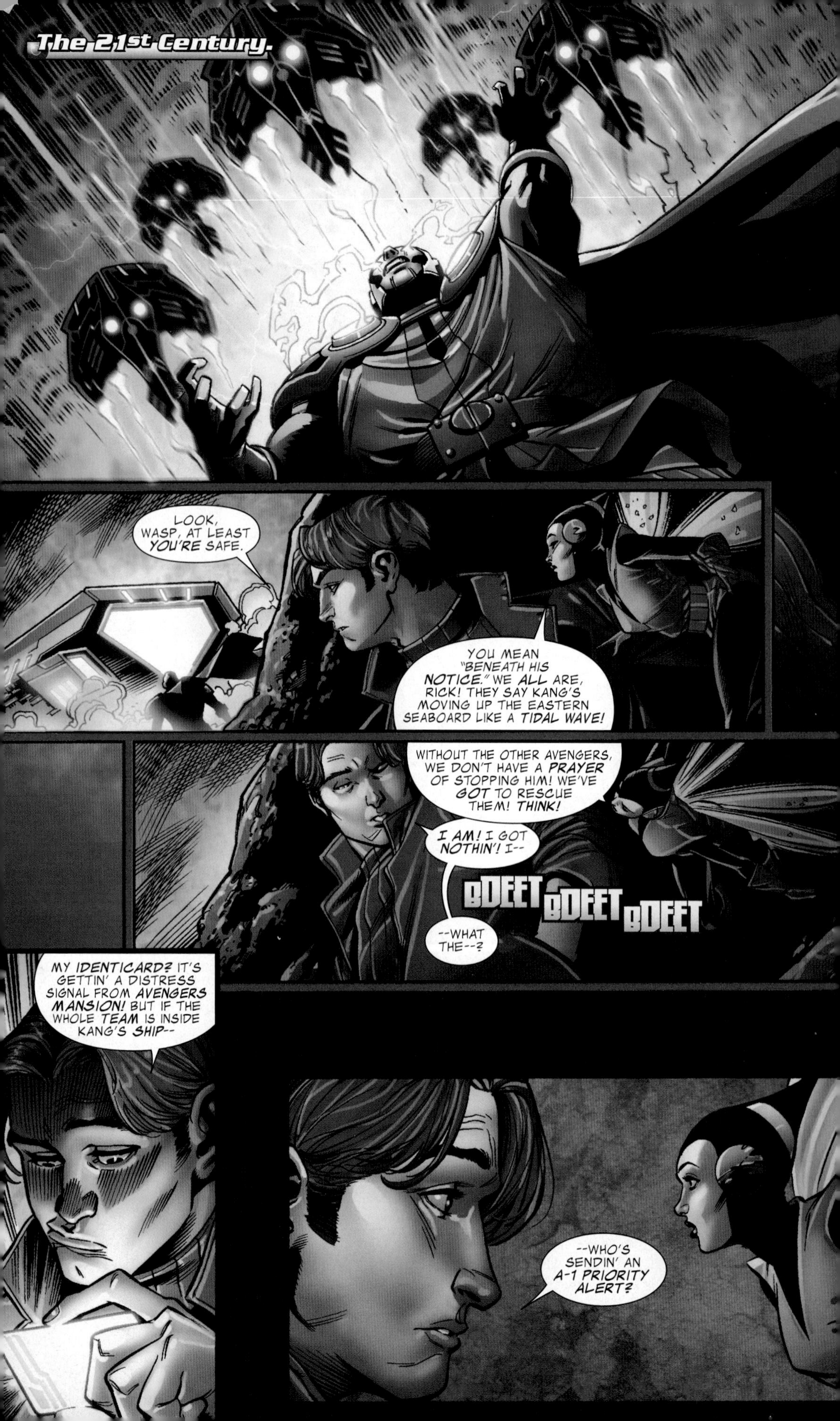
The 21st Century.
LOOK, WASP, AT LEAST YOU'RE SAFE.
YOU MEAN "BENEATH HIS NOTICE." WE ALL ARE, RICK! THEY SAY KANG'S MOVING UP THE EASTERN SEABOARD LIKE A TIDAL WAVE!
WITHOUT THE OTHER AVENGERS, WE DON'T HAVE A PRAYER OF STOPPING HIM! WE'VE GOT TO RESCUE THEM! THINK!
I AM! I GOT NOTHIN'! I--
BDEET BDEET BDEET
--WHAT THE--?
MY IDENTICARD? IT'S GETTIN' A DISTRESS SIGNAL FROM AVENGERS MANSION! BUT IF THE WHOLE TEAM IS INSIDE KANG'S SHIP--
--WHO'S SENDIN' AN A-1 PRIORITY ALERT?

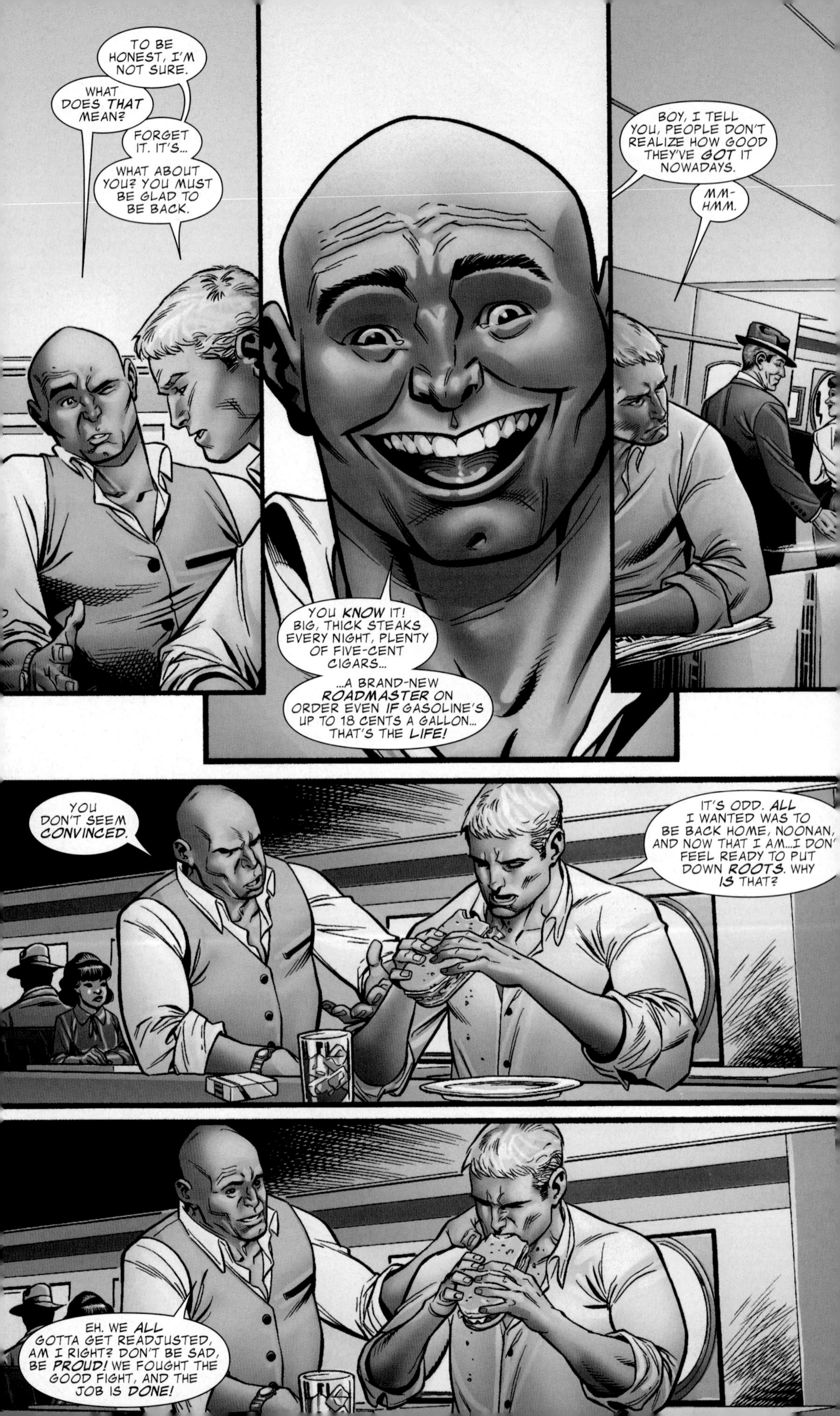
TO BE HONEST, I'M NOT SURE.
WHAT DOES THAT MEAN?
FORGET IT. IT'S...
WHAT ABOUT YOU? YOU MUST BE GLAD TO BE BACK.
YOU KNOW IT! BIG, THICK STEAKS EVERY NIGHT, PLENTY OF FIVE-CENT CIGARS...
...A BRAND-NEW ROADMASTER ON ORDER EVEN IF GASOLINE'S UP TO 18 CENTS A GALLON... THAT'S THE LIFE!
BOY, I TELL YOU, PEOPLE DON'T REALIZE HOW GOOD THEY'VE GOT IT NOWADAYS.
MM-HMM.
YOU DON'T SEEM CONVINCED.
IT'S ODD. ALL I WANTED WAS TO BE BACK HOME, NOONAN, AND NOW THAT I AM...I DON' FEEL READY TO PUT DOWN ROOTS. WHY IS THAT?
EH. WE ALL GOTTA GET READJUSTED, AM I RIGHT? DON'T BE SAD, BE PROUD! WE FOUGHT THE GOOD FIGHT, AND THE JOB IS DONE!

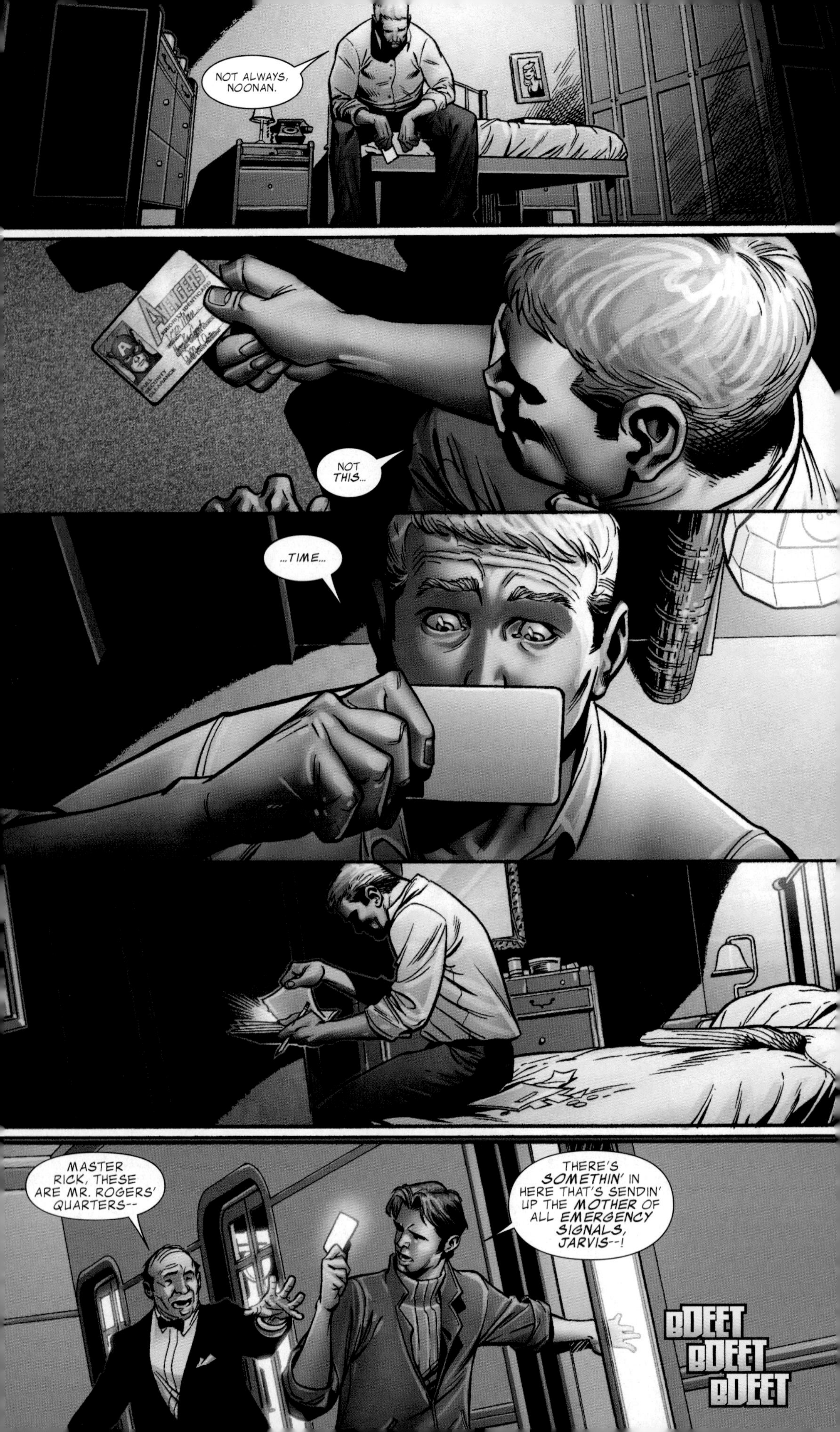
NOT ALWAYS, NOONAN.
NOT THIS...
...TIME...
MASTER RICK, THESE ARE MR. ROGERS' QUARTERS--
THERE'S SOMETHIN' IN HERE THAT'S SENDIN' UP THE MOTHER OF ALL EMERGENCY SIGNALS, JARVIS--!
BDEET BDEET BDEET

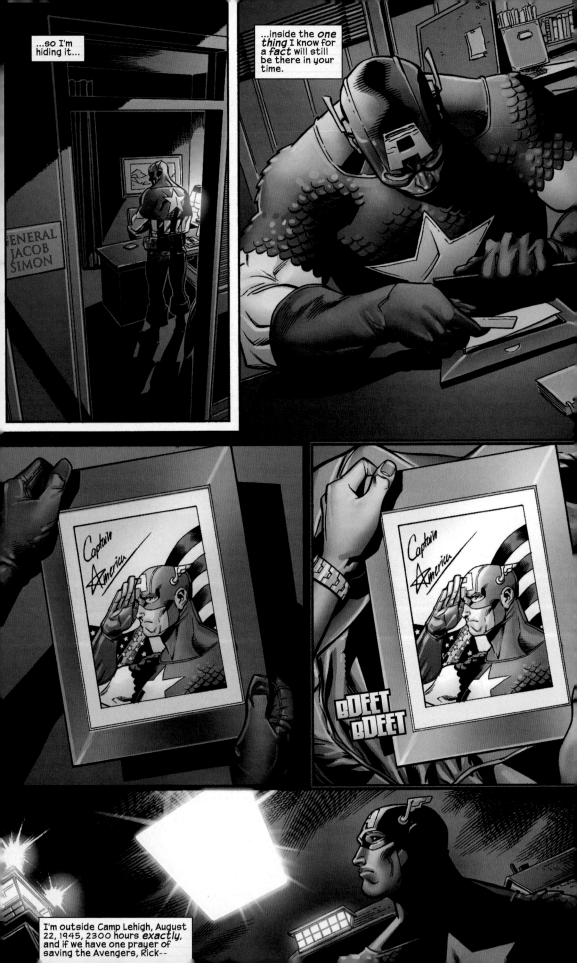

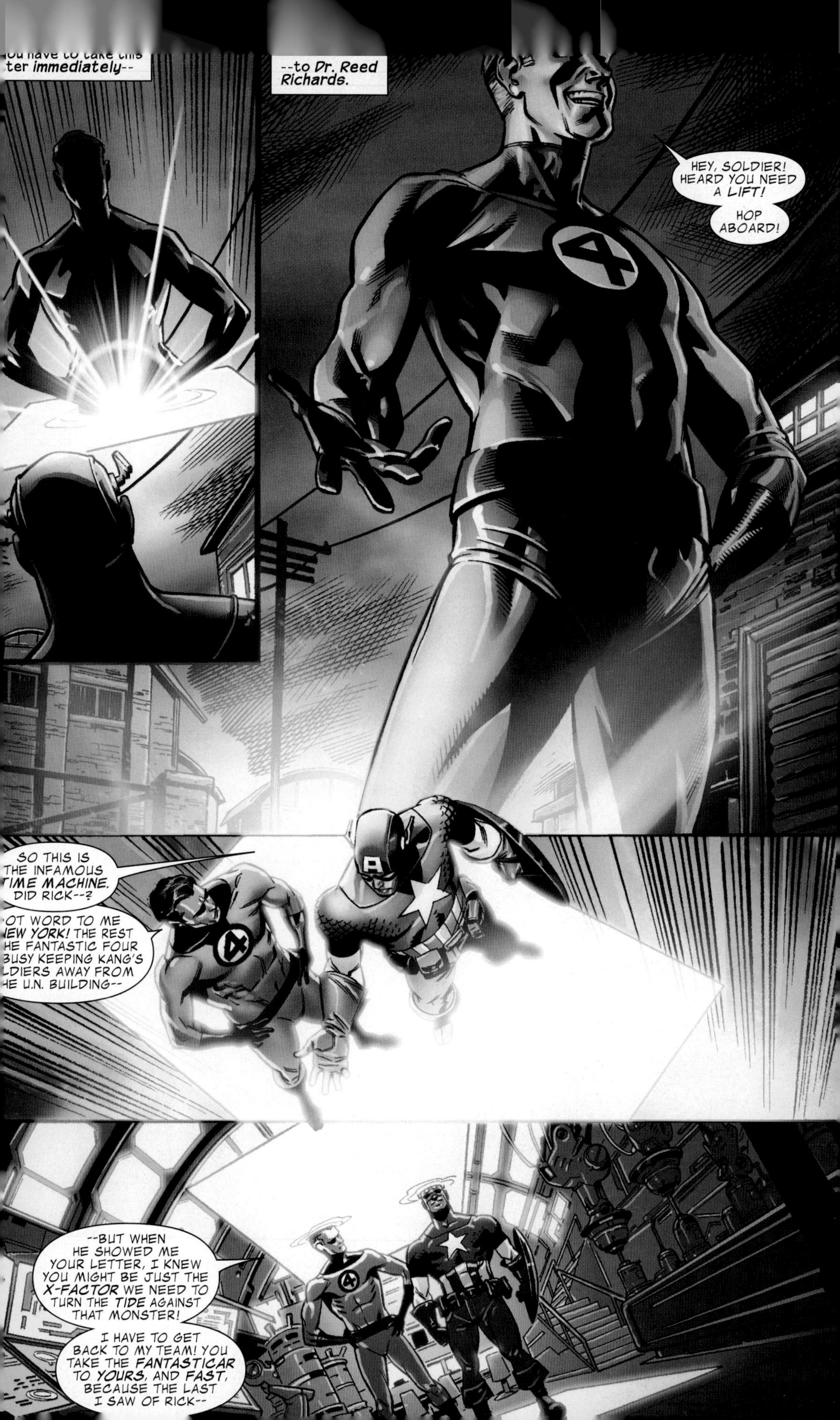
ou have to take this
ter immediately--
--to Dr. Reed Richards.
HEY, SOLDIER! HEARD YOU NEED A LIFT!
HOP ABOARD!
SO THIS IS THE INFAMOUS TIME MACHINE. DID RICK--?
OT WORD TO ME EW YORK! THE REST HE FANTASTIC FOUR BUSY KEEPING KANG'S LDIERS AWAY FROM HE U.N. BUILDING--
--BUT WHEN HE SHOWED ME YOUR LETTER, I KNEW YOU MIGHT BE JUST THE X-FACTOR WE NEED TO TURN THE TIDE AGAINST THAT MONSTER!
I HAVE TO GET BACK TO MY TEAM! YOU TAKE THE FANTASTICAR TO YOURS, AND FAST, BECAUSE THE LAST I SAW OF RICK--

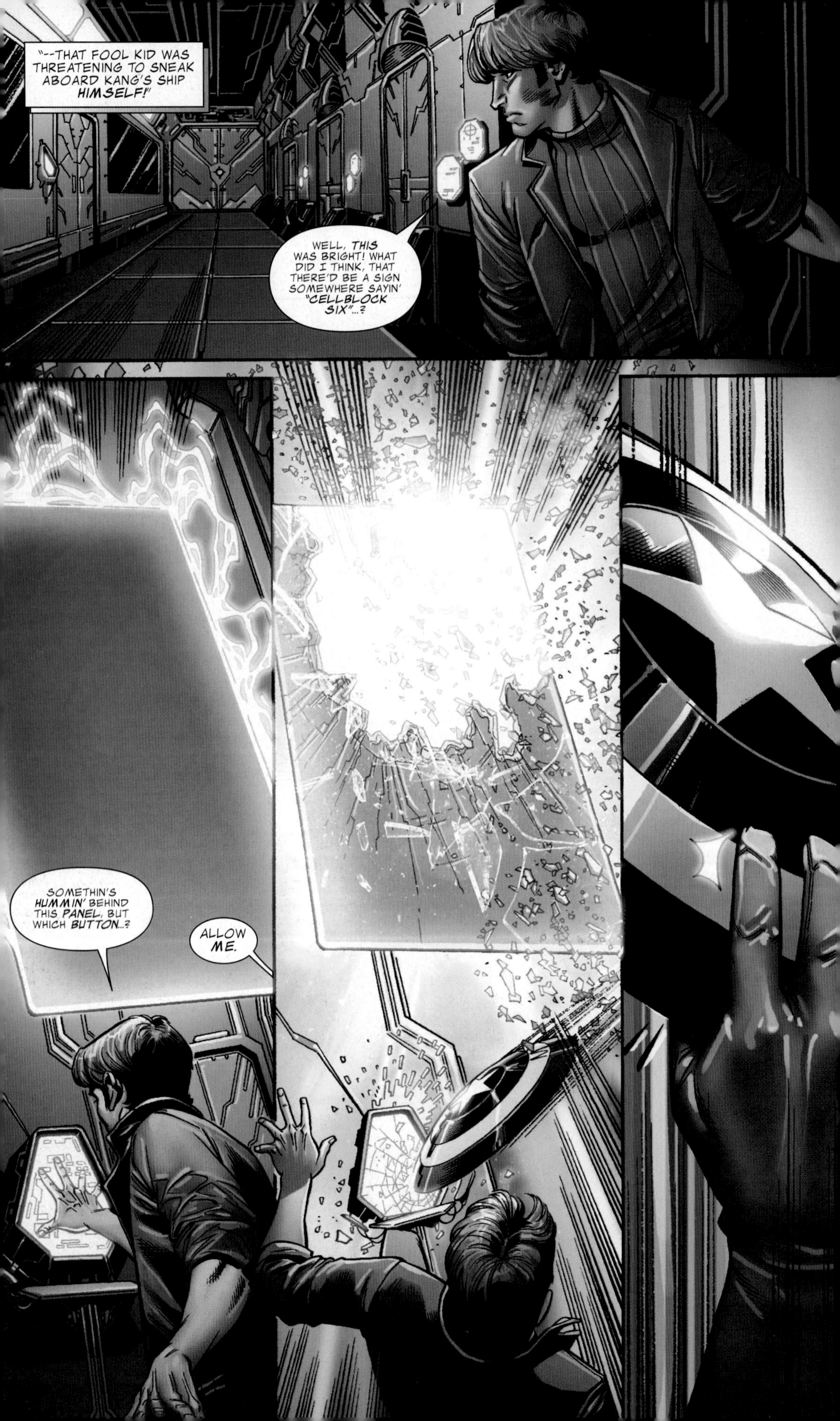
"--THAT FOOL KID WAS THREATENING TO SNEAK ABOARD KANG'S SHIP HIMSELF!"
WELL, THIS WAS BRIGHT! WHAT DID I THINK, THAT THERE'D BE A SIGN SOMEWHERE SAYIN' "CELLBLOCK SIX"...?
SOMETHIN'S HUMMIN' BEHIND THIS PANEL, BUT WHICH BUTTON...?
ALLOW ME.

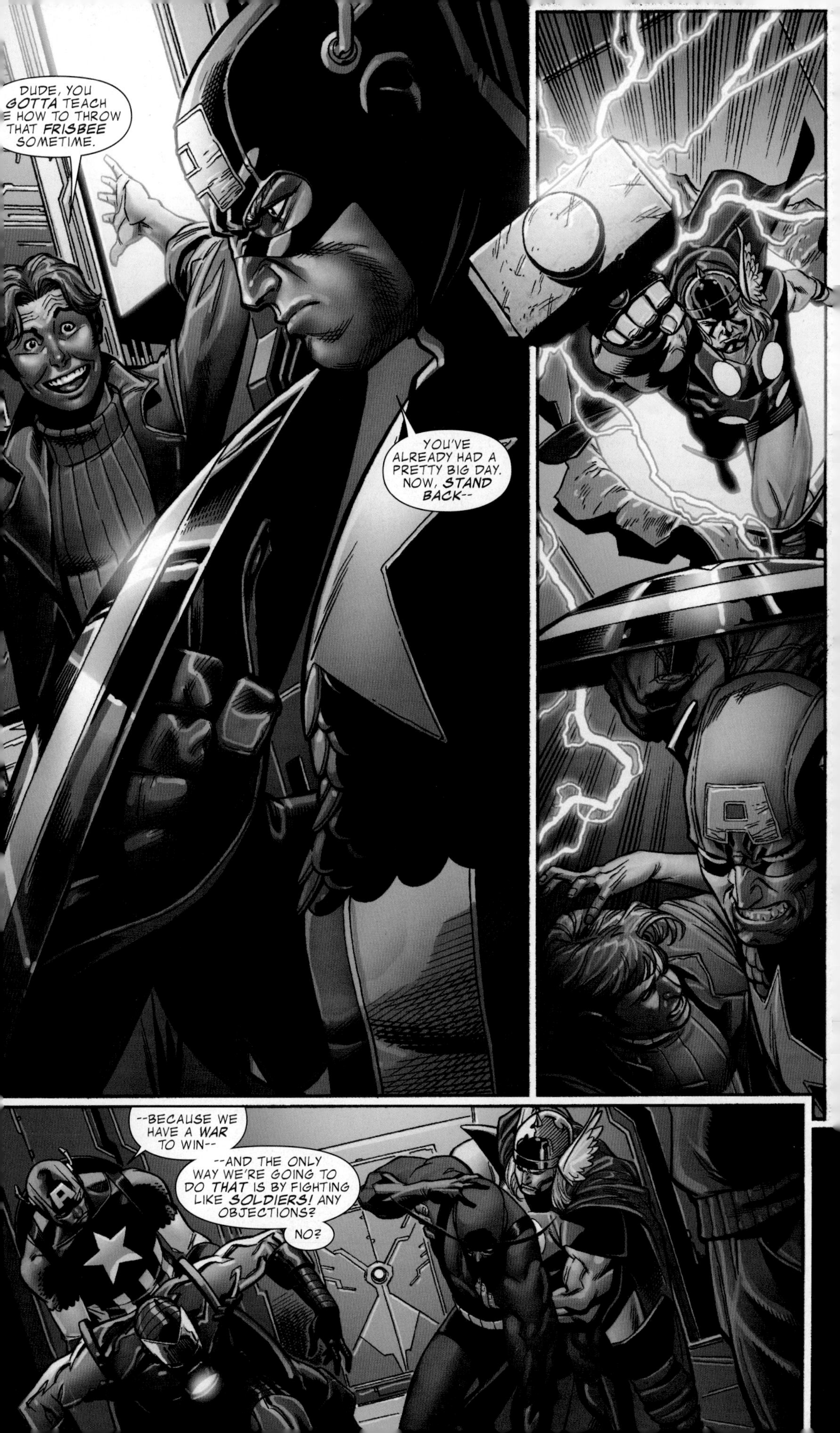
DUDE, YOU GOTTA TEACH ME HOW TO THROW THAT FRISBEE SOMETIME.
YOU'VE ALREADY HAD A PRETTY BIG DAY. NOW, STAND BACK--
--BECAUSE WE HAVE A WAR TO WIN--
--AND THE ONLY WAY WE'RE GOING TO DO THAT IS BY FIGHTING LIKE SOLDIERS! ANY OBJECTIONS?
NO?

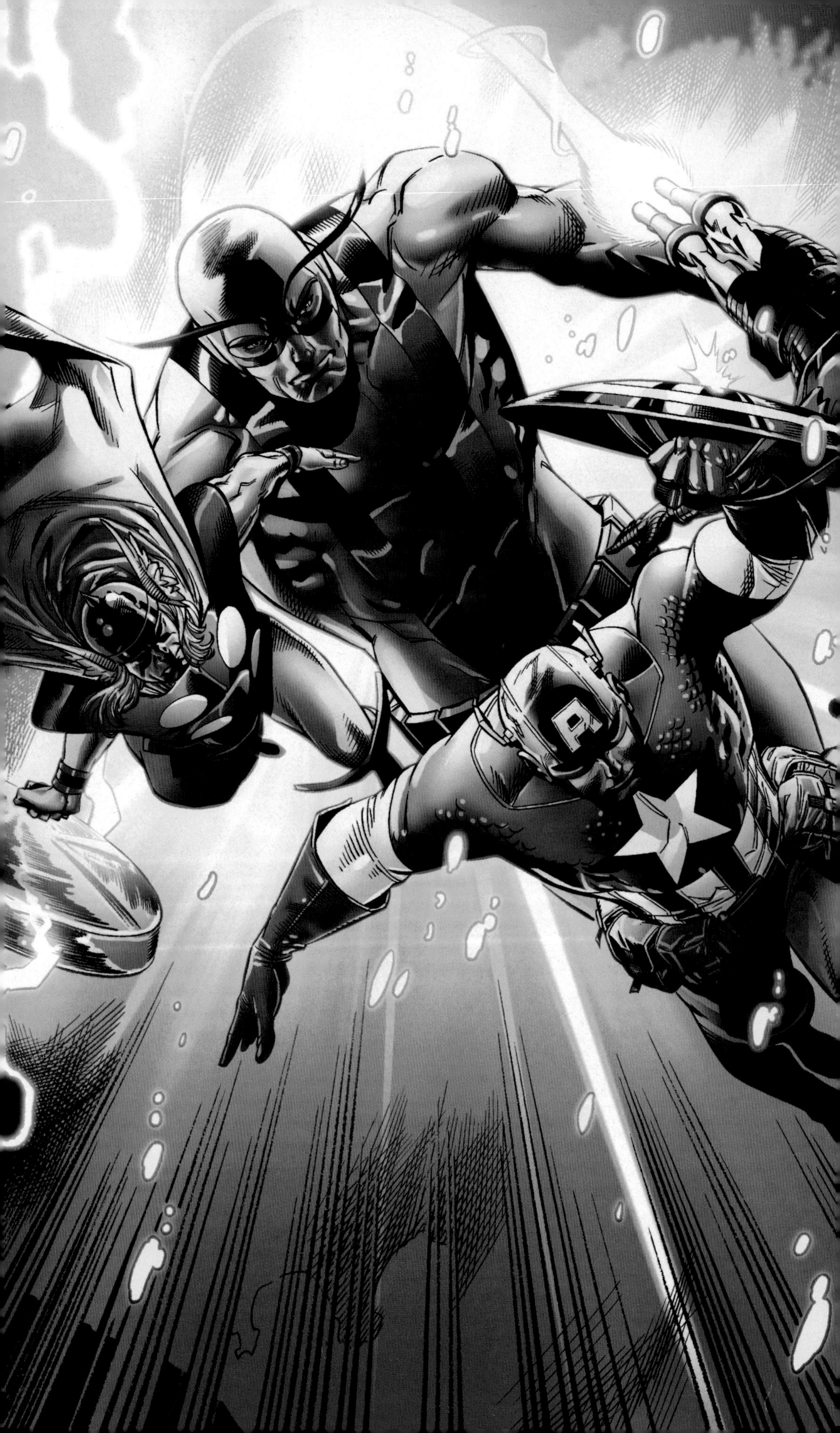

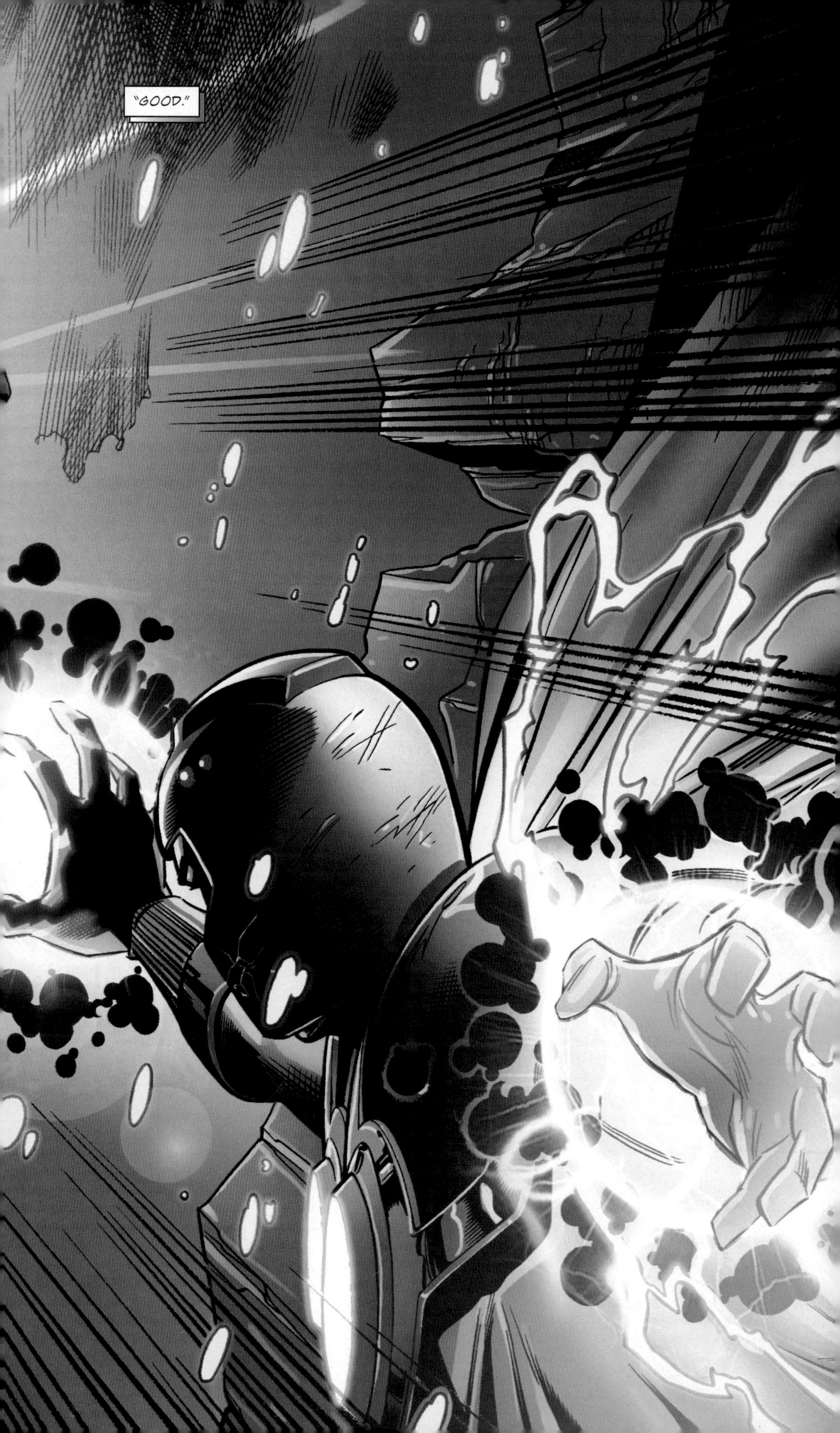
"GOOD."

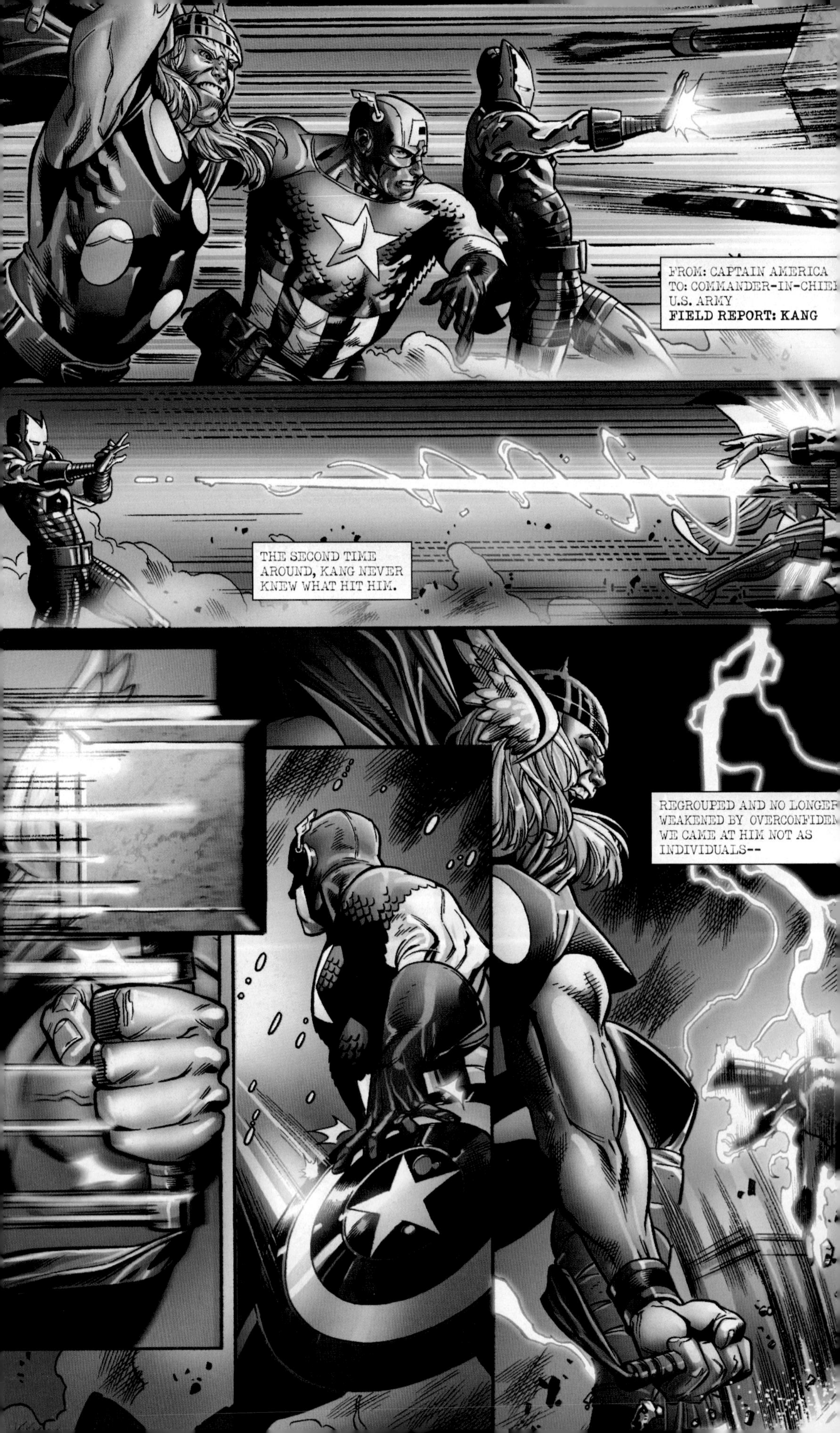
FROM: CAPTAIN AMERICA
TO: COMMANDER-IN-CHIE
U.S. ARMY
FIELD REPORT: KANG
THE SECOND TIME AROUND, KANG NEVER KNEW WHAT HIT HIM.
REGROUPED AND NO LONGER WEAKENED BY OVERCONFIDE WE CAME AT HIM NOT AS INDIVIDUALS--

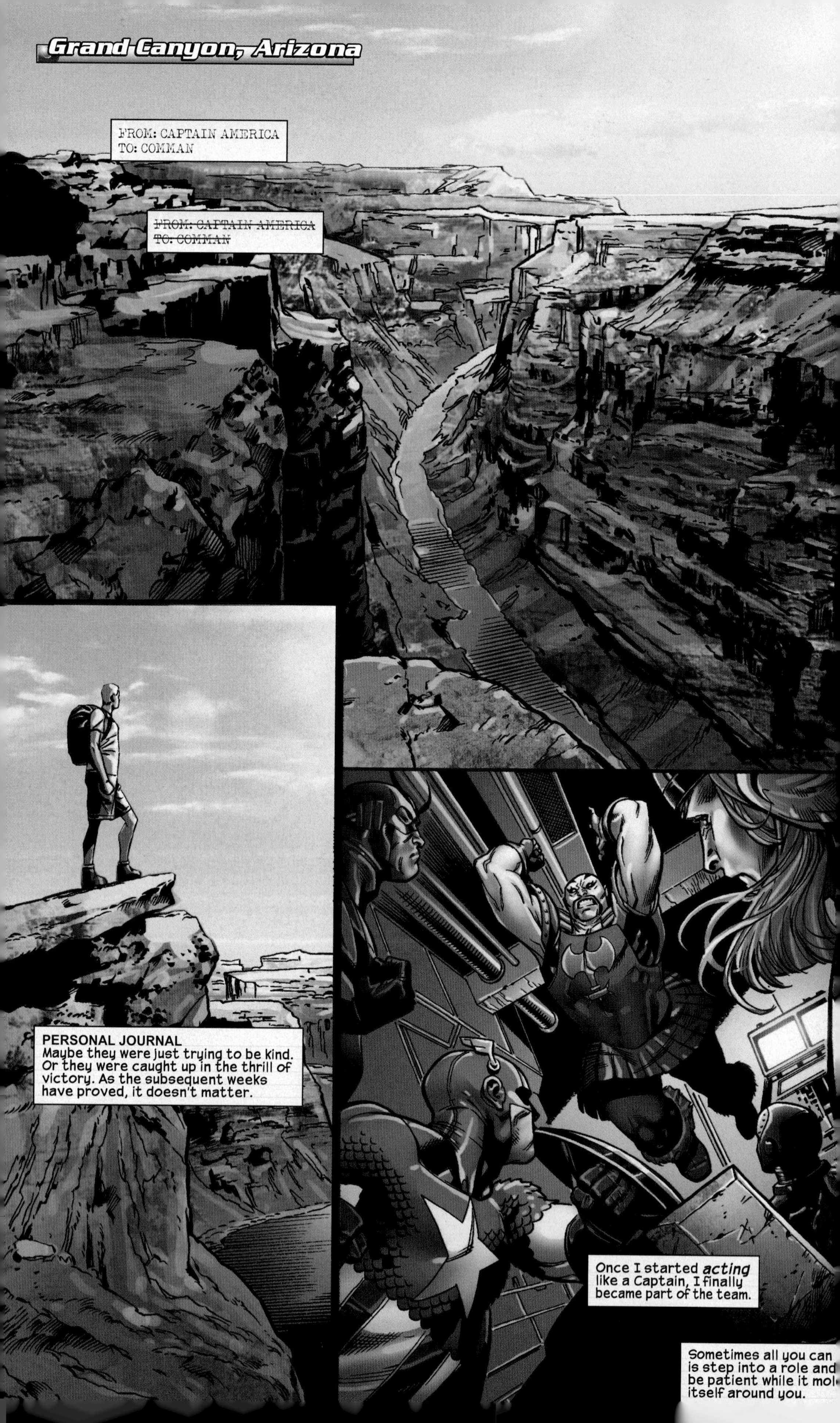
Grand Canyon, Arizona
FROM: CAPTAIN AMERICA
TO: COMMAN
FROM: CAPTAIN AMERICA
TO: COMMAN
PERSONAL JOURNAL
Maybe they were just trying to be kind. Or they were caught up in the thrill of victory. As the subsequent weeks have proved, it doesn't matter.
Once I started acting like a Captain, I finally became part of the team.
Sometimes all you can is step into a role and be patient while it mol itself around you.

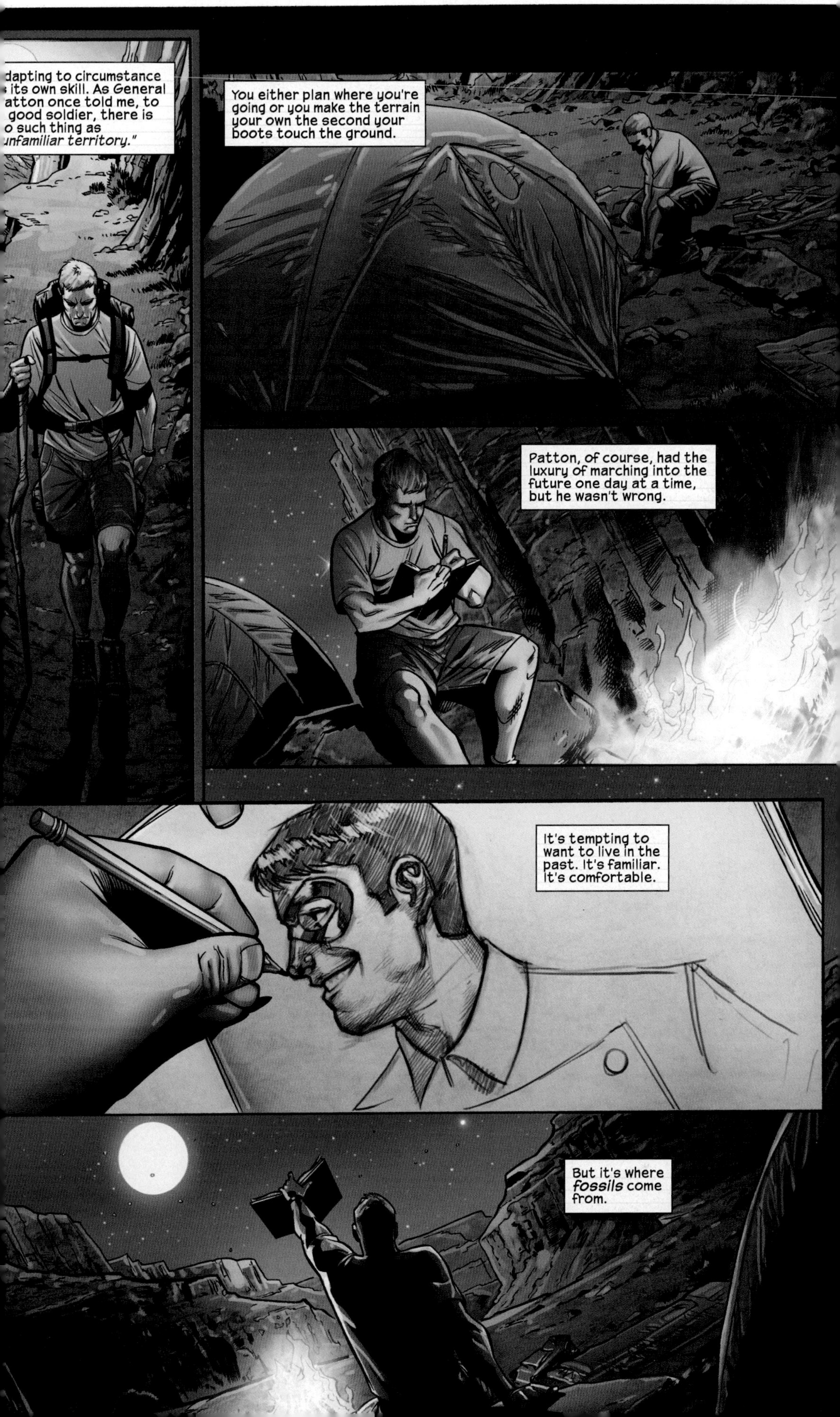
dapting to circumstance
s its own skill. As General
atton once told me, to
good soldier, there is
o such thing as
unfamiliar territory."
You either plan where you're going or you make the terrain your own the second your boots touch the ground.
Patton, of course, had the luxury of marching into the future one day at a time, but he wasn't wrong.
It's tempting to want to live in the past. It's familiar. It's comfortable.
But it's where *fossils* come from.

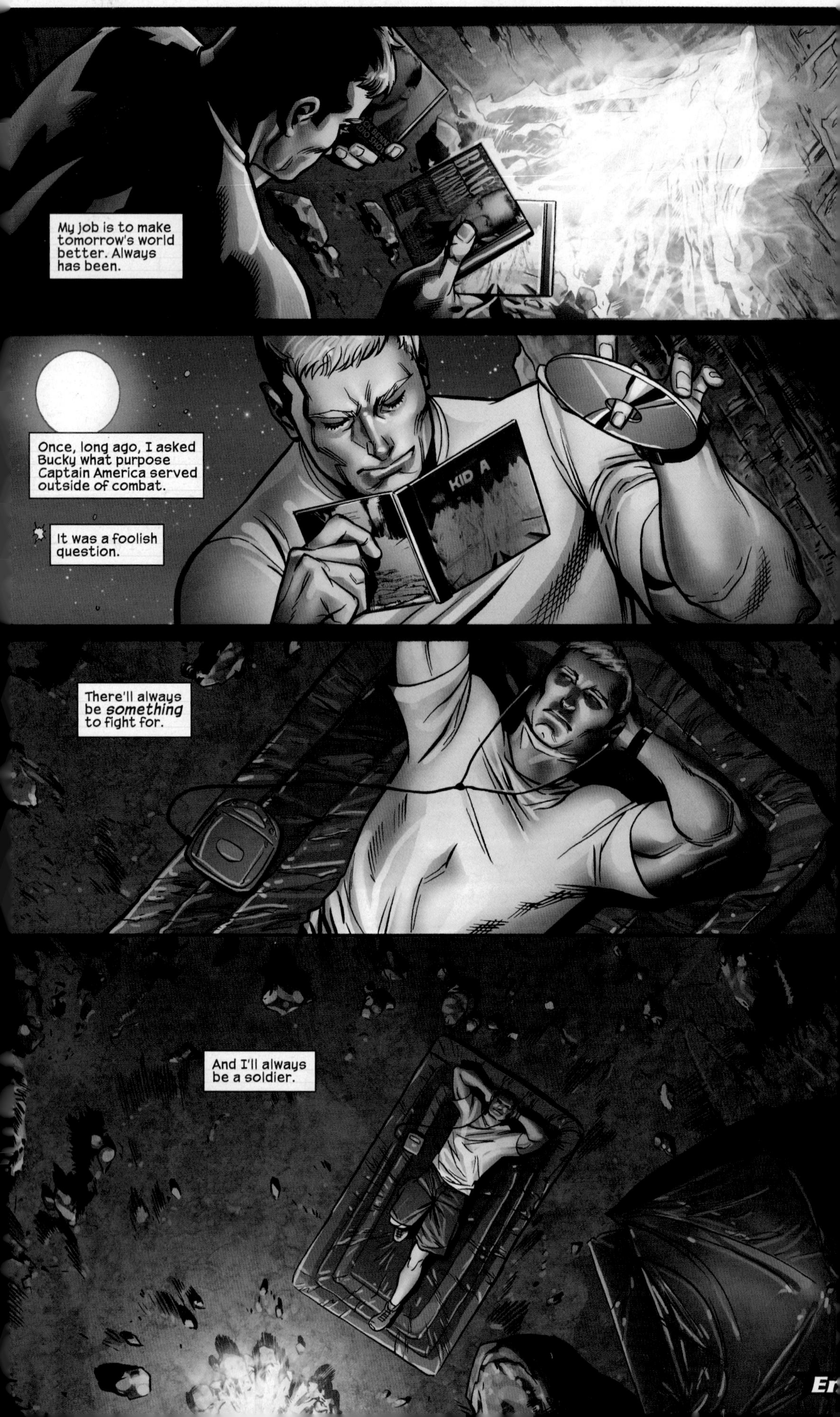
My job is to make tomorrow's world better. Always has been.
Once, long ago, I asked Bucky what purpose Captain America served outside of combat.
KID A
It was a foolish question.
There'll always be *something* to fight for.
And I'll always be a soldier.

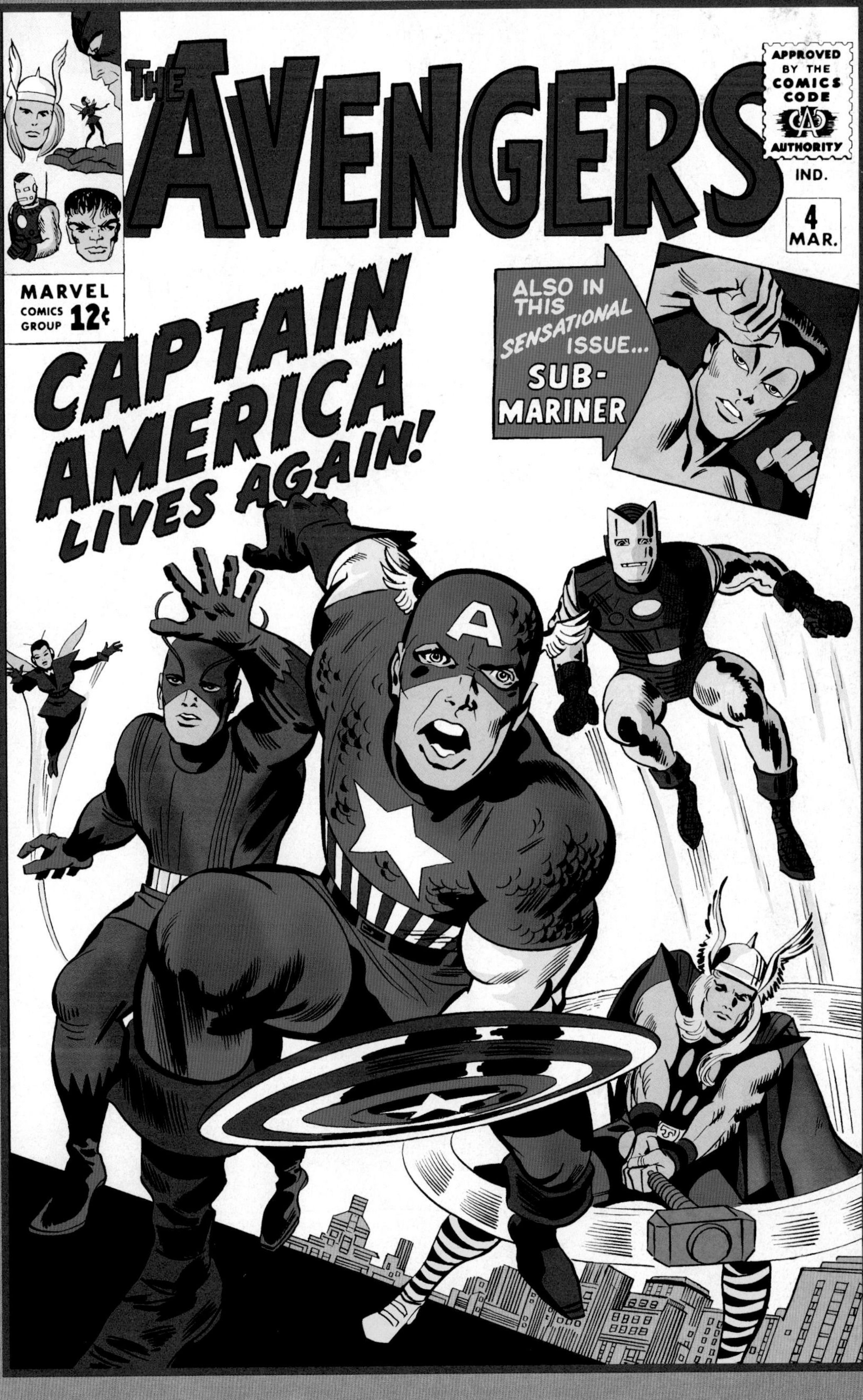
THE AVENGERS
APPROVED BY THE COMICS CODE AUTHORITY
IND.
4
MAR.
MARVEL COMICS GROUP 12¢
CAPTAIN AMERICA LIVES AGAIN!
ALSO IN THIS SENSATIONAL ISSUE... SUB-MARINER

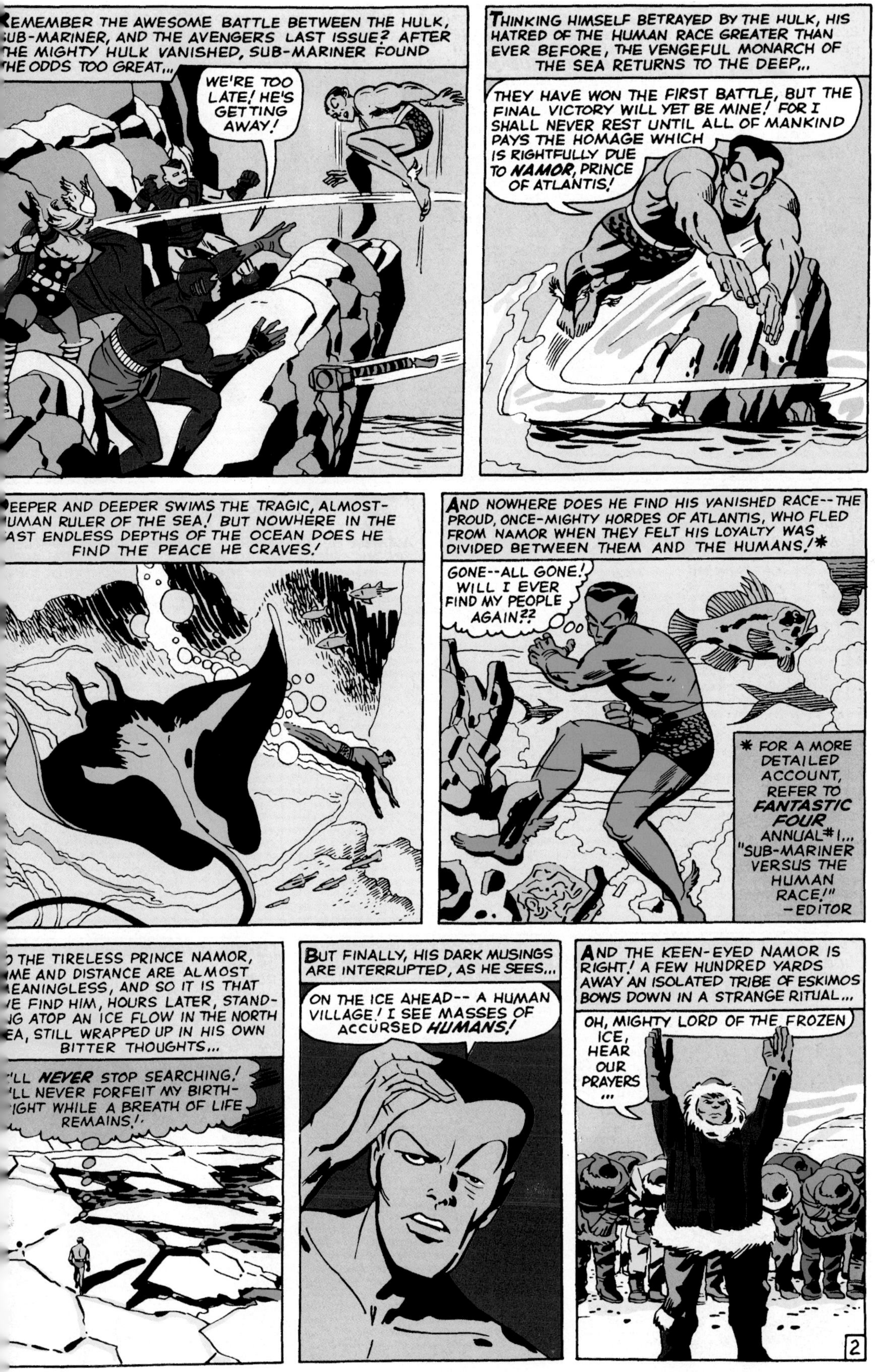

REMEMBER THE AWESOME BATTLE BETWEEN THE HULK, SUB-MARINER, AND THE AVENGERS LAST ISSUE? AFTER THE MIGHTY HULK VANISHED, SUB-MARINER FOUND THE ODDS TOO GREAT...
WE'RE TOO LATE! HE'S GETTING AWAY!
THINKING HIMSELF BETRAYED BY THE HULK, HIS HATRED OF THE HUMAN RACE GREATER THAN EVER BEFORE, THE VENGEFUL MONARCH OF THE SEA RETURNS TO THE DEEP...
THEY HAVE WON THE FIRST BATTLE, BUT THE FINAL VICTORY WILL YET BE MINE! FOR I SHALL NEVER REST UNTIL ALL OF MANKIND PAYS THE HOMAGE WHICH IS RIGHTFULLY DUE TO NAMOR, PRINCE OF ATLANTIS!
DEEPER AND DEEPER SWIMS THE TRAGIC, ALMOST-HUMAN RULER OF THE SEA! BUT NOWHERE IN THE VAST ENDLESS DEPTHS OF THE OCEAN DOES HE FIND THE PEACE HE CRAVES!
AND NOWHERE DOES HE FIND HIS VANISHED RACE--THE PROUD, ONCE-MIGHTY HORDES OF ATLANTIS, WHO FLED FROM NAMOR WHEN THEY FELT HIS LOYALTY WAS DIVIDED BETWEEN THEM AND THE HUMANS!*
GONE--ALL GONE! WILL I EVER FIND MY PEOPLE AGAIN??
* FOR A MORE DETAILED ACCOUNT, REFER TO FANTASTIC FOUR ANNUAL #1... "SUB-MARINER VERSUS THE HUMAN RACE!" -EDITOR
SO THE TIRELESS PRINCE NAMOR, TIME AND DISTANCE ARE ALMOST MEANINGLESS, AND SO IT IS THAT WE FIND HIM, HOURS LATER, STANDING ATOP AN ICE FLOW IN THE NORTH SEA, STILL WRAPPED UP IN HIS OWN BITTER THOUGHTS...
I'LL NEVER STOP SEARCHING! I'LL NEVER FORFEIT MY BIRTHRIGHT WHILE A BREATH OF LIFE REMAINS!
BUT FINALLY, HIS DARK MUSINGS ARE INTERRUPTED, AS HE SEES...
ON THE ICE AHEAD-- A HUMAN VILLAGE! I SEE MASSES OF ACCURSED HUMANS!
AND THE KEEN-EYED NAMOR IS RIGHT! A FEW HUNDRED YARDS AWAY AN ISOLATED TRIBE OF ESKIMOS BOWS DOWN IN A STRANGE RITUAL...
OH, MIGHTY LORD OF THE FROZEN ICE, HEAR OUR PRAYERS...
2

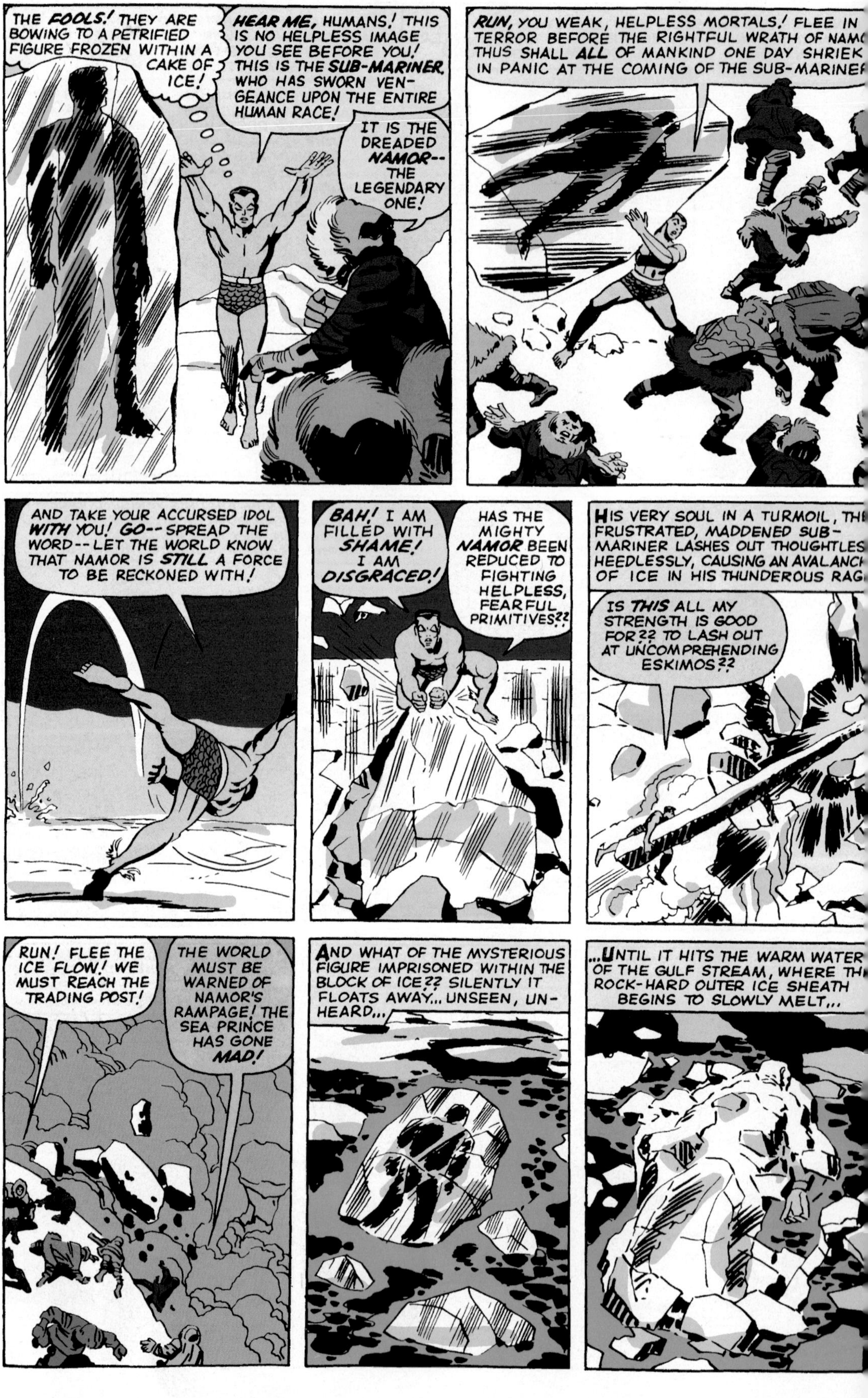
THE FOOLS! THEY ARE BOWING TO A PETRIFIED FIGURE FROZEN WITHIN A CAKE OF ICE!
HEAR ME, HUMANS! THIS IS NO HELPLESS IMAGE YOU SEE BEFORE YOU! THIS IS THE SUB-MARINER, WHO HAS SWORN VENGEANCE UPON THE ENTIRE HUMAN RACE!
IT IS THE DREADED NAMOR-- THE LEGENDARY ONE!
RUN, YOU WEAK, HELPLESS MORTALS! FLEE IN TERROR BEFORE THE RIGHTFUL WRATH OF NAMO THUS SHALL ALL OF MANKIND ONE DAY SHRIEK IN PANIC AT THE COMING OF THE SUB-MARINER
AND TAKE YOUR ACCURSED IDOL WITH YOU! GO-- SPREAD THE WORD--LET THE WORLD KNOW THAT NAMOR IS STILL A FORCE TO BE RECKONED WITH!
BAH! I AM FILLED WITH SHAME! I AM DISGRACED!
HAS THE MIGHTY NAMOR BEEN REDUCED TO FIGHTING HELPLESS, FEARFUL PRIMITIVES??
HIS VERY SOUL IN A TURMOIL, THE FRUSTRATED, MADDENED SUB-MARINER LASHES OUT THOUGHTLES HEEDLESSLY, CAUSING AN AVALANCH OF ICE IN HIS THUNDEROUS RAG
IS THIS ALL MY STRENGTH IS GOOD FOR?? TO LASH OUT AT UNCOMPREHENDING ESKIMOS??
RUN! FLEE THE ICE FLOW! WE MUST REACH THE TRADING POST!
THE WORLD MUST BE WARNED OF NAMOR'S RAMPAGE! THE SEA PRINCE HAS GONE MAD!
AND WHAT OF THE MYSTERIOUS FIGURE IMPRISONED WITHIN THE BLOCK OF ICE?? SILENTLY IT FLOATS AWAY... UNSEEN, UNHEARD...
...UNTIL IT HITS THE WARM WATER OF THE GULF STREAM, WHERE TH ROCK-HARD OUTER ICE SHEATH BEGINS TO SLOWLY MELT...

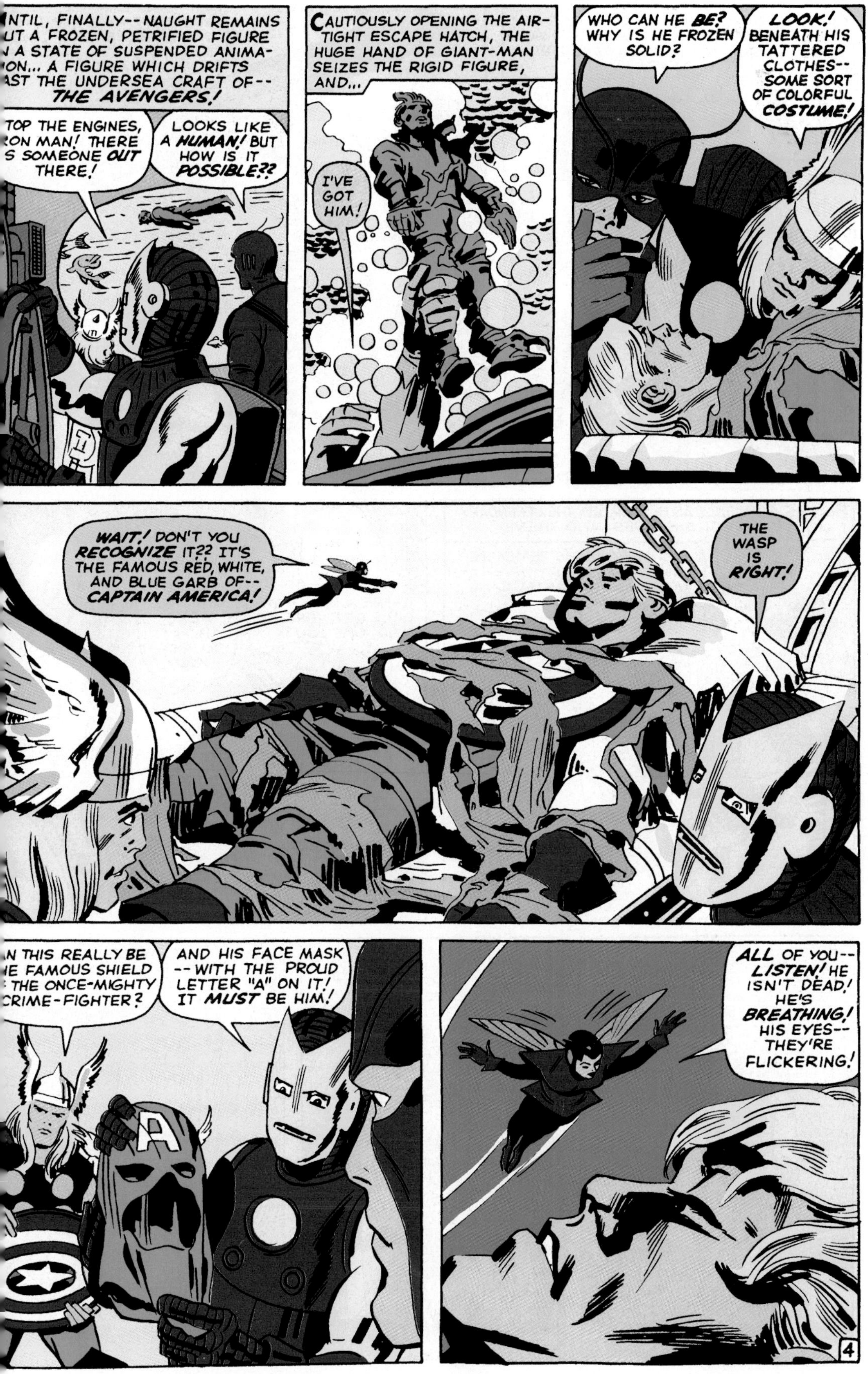
NTIL, FINALLY-- NAUGHT REMAINS UT A FROZEN, PETRIFIED FIGURE N A STATE OF SUSPENDED ANIMA-ON... A FIGURE WHICH DRIFTS AST THE UNDERSEA CRAFT OF-- THE AVENGERS!
TOP THE ENGINES, RON MAN! THERE S SOMEONE OUT THERE!
LOOKS LIKE A HUMAN! BUT HOW IS IT POSSIBLE??
CAUTIOUSLY OPENING THE AIR-TIGHT ESCAPE HATCH, THE HUGE HAND OF GIANT-MAN SEIZES THE RIGID FIGURE, AND...
I'VE GOT HIM!
WHO CAN HE BE? WHY IS HE FROZEN SOLID?
LOOK! BENEATH HIS TATTERED CLOTHES-- SOME SORT OF COLORFUL COSTUME!
WAIT! DON'T YOU RECOGNIZE IT?? IT'S THE FAMOUS RED, WHITE, AND BLUE GARB OF-- CAPTAIN AMERICA!
THE WASP IS RIGHT!
N THIS REALLY BE HE FAMOUS SHIELD THE ONCE-MIGHTY CRIME-FIGHTER?
AND HIS FACE MASK --WITH THE PROUD LETTER "A" ON IT! IT MUST BE HIM!
ALL OF YOU-- LISTEN! HE ISN'T DEAD! HE'S BREATHING! HIS EYES-- THEY'RE FLICKERING!
4

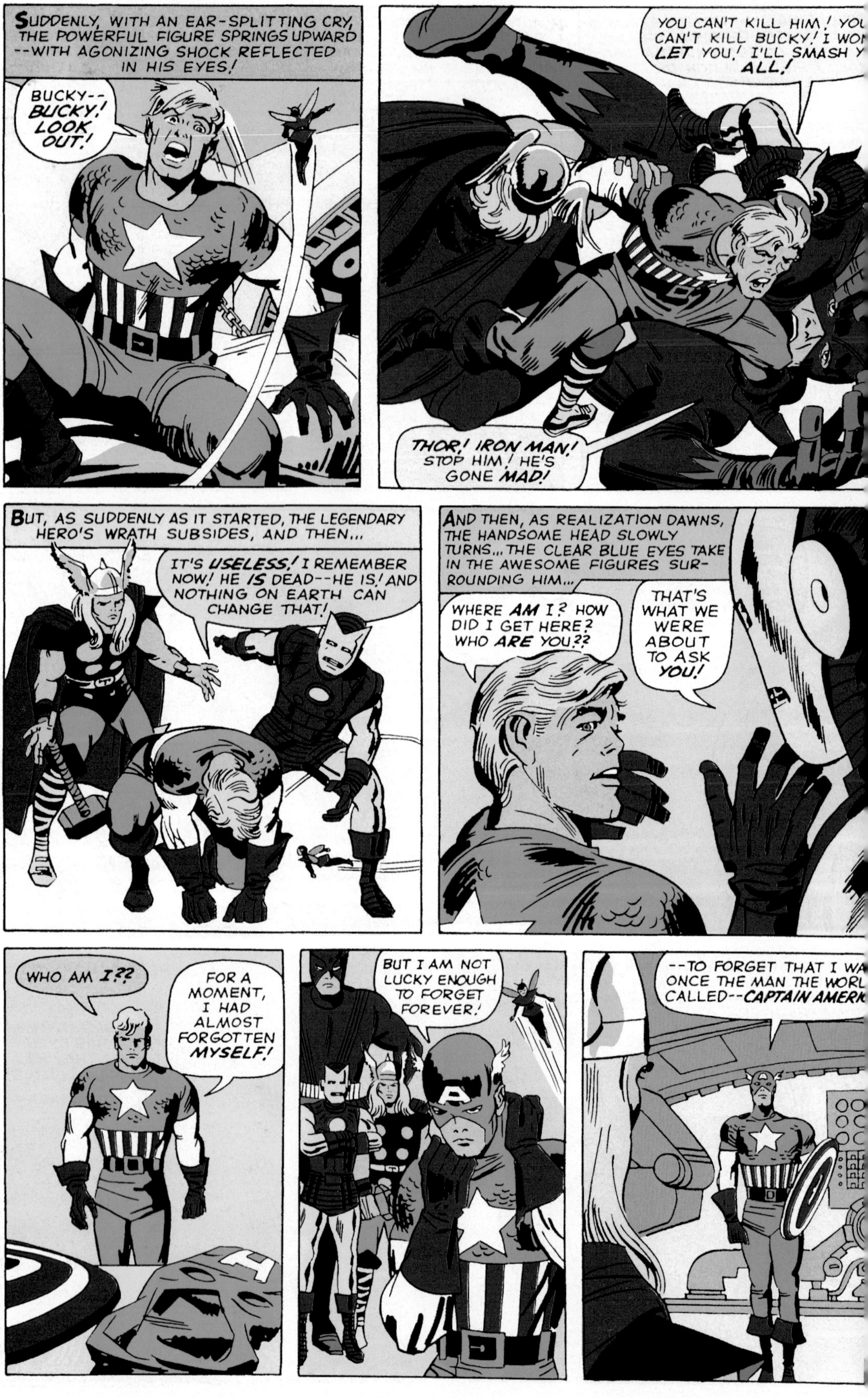
SUDDENLY, WITH AN EAR-SPLITTING CRY, THE POWERFUL FIGURE SPRINGS UPWARD --WITH AGONIZING SHOCK REFLECTED IN HIS EYES!
BUCKY-- BUCKY! LOOK OUT!
YOU CAN'T KILL HIM! YOU CAN'T KILL BUCKY! I WON'T LET YOU! I'LL SMASH YOU ALL!
THOR! IRON MAN! STOP HIM! HE'S GONE MAD!
BUT, AS SUDDENLY AS IT STARTED, THE LEGENDARY HERO'S WRATH SUBSIDES, AND THEN...
IT'S USELESS! I REMEMBER NOW! HE IS DEAD--HE IS! AND NOTHING ON EARTH CAN CHANGE THAT!
AND THEN, AS REALIZATION DAWNS, THE HANDSOME HEAD SLOWLY TURNS... THE CLEAR BLUE EYES TAKE IN THE AWESOME FIGURES SURROUNDING HIM...
WHERE AM I? HOW DID I GET HERE? WHO ARE YOU??
THAT'S WHAT WE WERE ABOUT TO ASK YOU!
WHO AM I??
FOR A MOMENT, I HAD ALMOST FORGOTTEN MYSELF!
BUT I AM NOT LUCKY ENOUGH TO FORGET FOREVER!
--TO FORGET THAT I WAS ONCE THE MAN THE WORLD CALLED--CAPTAIN AMERICA!

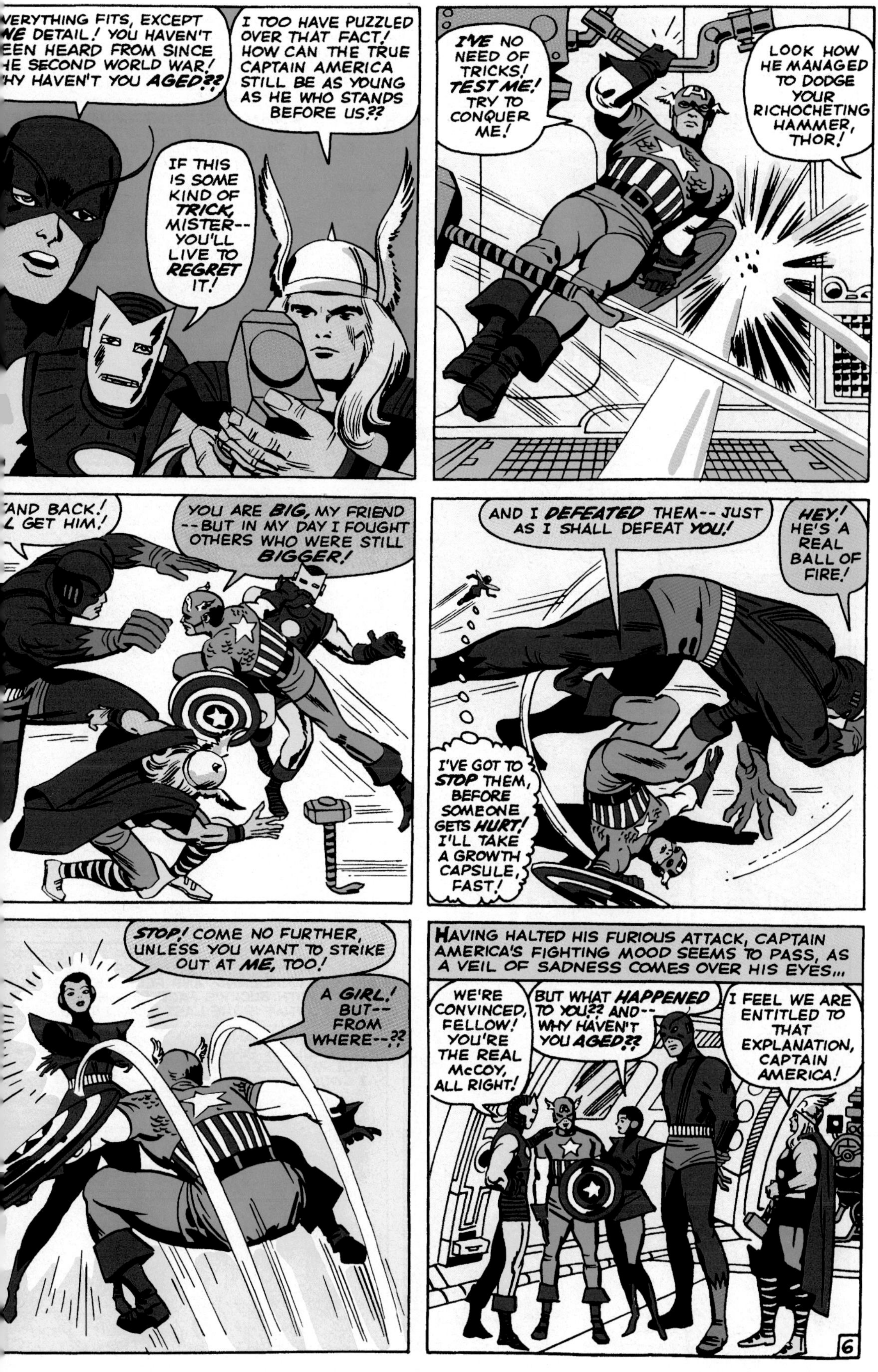
VERYTHING FITS, EXCEPT NE DETAIL! YOU HAVEN'T EEN HEARD FROM SINCE HE SECOND WORLD WAR! HY HAVEN'T YOU AGED??
I TOO HAVE PUZZLED OVER THAT FACT! HOW CAN THE TRUE CAPTAIN AMERICA STILL BE AS YOUNG AS HE WHO STANDS BEFORE US??
IF THIS IS SOME KIND OF TRICK, MISTER-- YOU'LL LIVE TO REGRET IT!
I'VE NO NEED OF TRICKS! TEST ME! TRY TO CONQUER ME!
LOOK HOW HE MANAGED TO DODGE YOUR RICHOCHETING HAMMER, THOR!
TAND BACK! L GET HIM!
YOU ARE BIG, MY FRIEND --BUT IN MY DAY I FOUGHT OTHERS WHO WERE STILL BIGGER!
AND I DEFEATED THEM-- JUST AS I SHALL DEFEAT YOU!
HEY! HE'S A REAL BALL OF FIRE!
I'VE GOT TO STOP THEM, BEFORE SOMEONE GETS HURT! I'LL TAKE A GROWTH CAPSULE, FAST!
STOP! COME NO FURTHER, UNLESS YOU WANT TO STRIKE OUT AT ME, TOO!
A GIRL! BUT-- FROM WHERE--??
HAVING HALTED HIS FURIOUS ATTACK, CAPTAIN AMERICA'S FIGHTING MOOD SEEMS TO PASS, AS A VEIL OF SADNESS COMES OVER HIS EYES...
WE'RE CONVINCED, FELLOW! YOU'RE THE REAL McCOY, ALL RIGHT!
BUT WHAT HAPPENED TO YOU?? AND-- WHY HAVEN'T YOU AGED??
I FEEL WE ARE ENTITLED TO THAT EXPLANATION, CAPTAIN AMERICA!
6

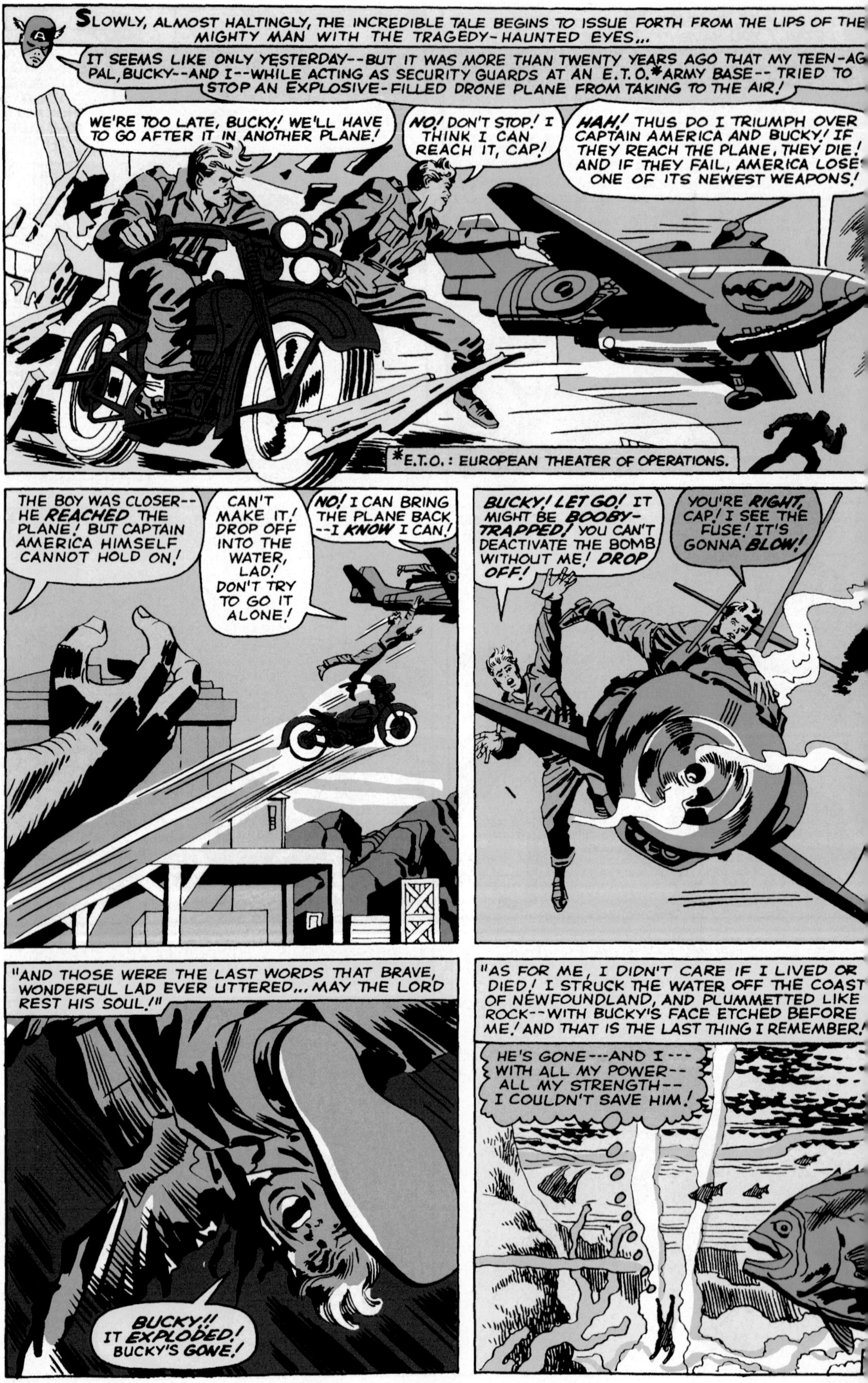
SLOWLY, ALMOST HALTINGLY, THE INCREDIBLE TALE BEGINS TO ISSUE FORTH FROM THE LIPS OF THE MIGHTY MAN WITH THE TRAGEDY-HAUNTED EYES...
IT SEEMS LIKE ONLY YESTERDAY--BUT IT WAS MORE THAN TWENTY YEARS AGO THAT MY TEEN-AG PAL, BUCKY--AND I--WHILE ACTING AS SECURITY GUARDS AT AN E.T.O.* ARMY BASE-- TRIED TO STOP AN EXPLOSIVE-FILLED DRONE PLANE FROM TAKING TO THE AIR!
WE'RE TOO LATE, BUCKY! WE'LL HAVE TO GO AFTER IT IN ANOTHER PLANE!
NO! DON'T STOP! I THINK I CAN REACH IT, CAP!
HAH! THUS DO I TRIUMPH OVER CAPTAIN AMERICA AND BUCKY! IF THEY REACH THE PLANE, THEY DIE! AND IF THEY FAIL, AMERICA LOSE ONE OF ITS NEWEST WEAPONS!
*E.T.O.: EUROPEAN THEATER OF OPERATIONS.
THE BOY WAS CLOSER--HE REACHED THE PLANE! BUT CAPTAIN AMERICA HIMSELF CANNOT HOLD ON!
CAN'T MAKE IT! DROP OFF INTO THE WATER, LAD! DON'T TRY TO GO IT ALONE!
NO! I CAN BRING THE PLANE BACK --I KNOW I CAN!
BUCKY! LET GO! IT MIGHT BE BOOBY-TRAPPED! YOU CAN'T DEACTIVATE THE BOMB WITHOUT ME! DROP OFF!
YOU'RE RIGHT, CAP! I SEE THE FUSE! IT'S GONNA BLOW!
"AND THOSE WERE THE LAST WORDS THAT BRAVE, WONDERFUL LAD EVER UTTERED... MAY THE LORD REST HIS SOUL!"
BUCKY!! IT EXPLODED! BUCKY'S GONE!
"AS FOR ME, I DIDN'T CARE IF I LIVED OR DIED! I STRUCK THE WATER OFF THE COAST OF NEWFOUNDLAND, AND PLUMMETTED LIKE ROCK--WITH BUCKY'S FACE ETCHED BEFORE ME! AND THAT IS THE LAST THING I REMEMBER!
HE'S GONE---AND I---WITH ALL MY POWER--ALL MY STRENGTH--I COULDN'T SAVE HIM!

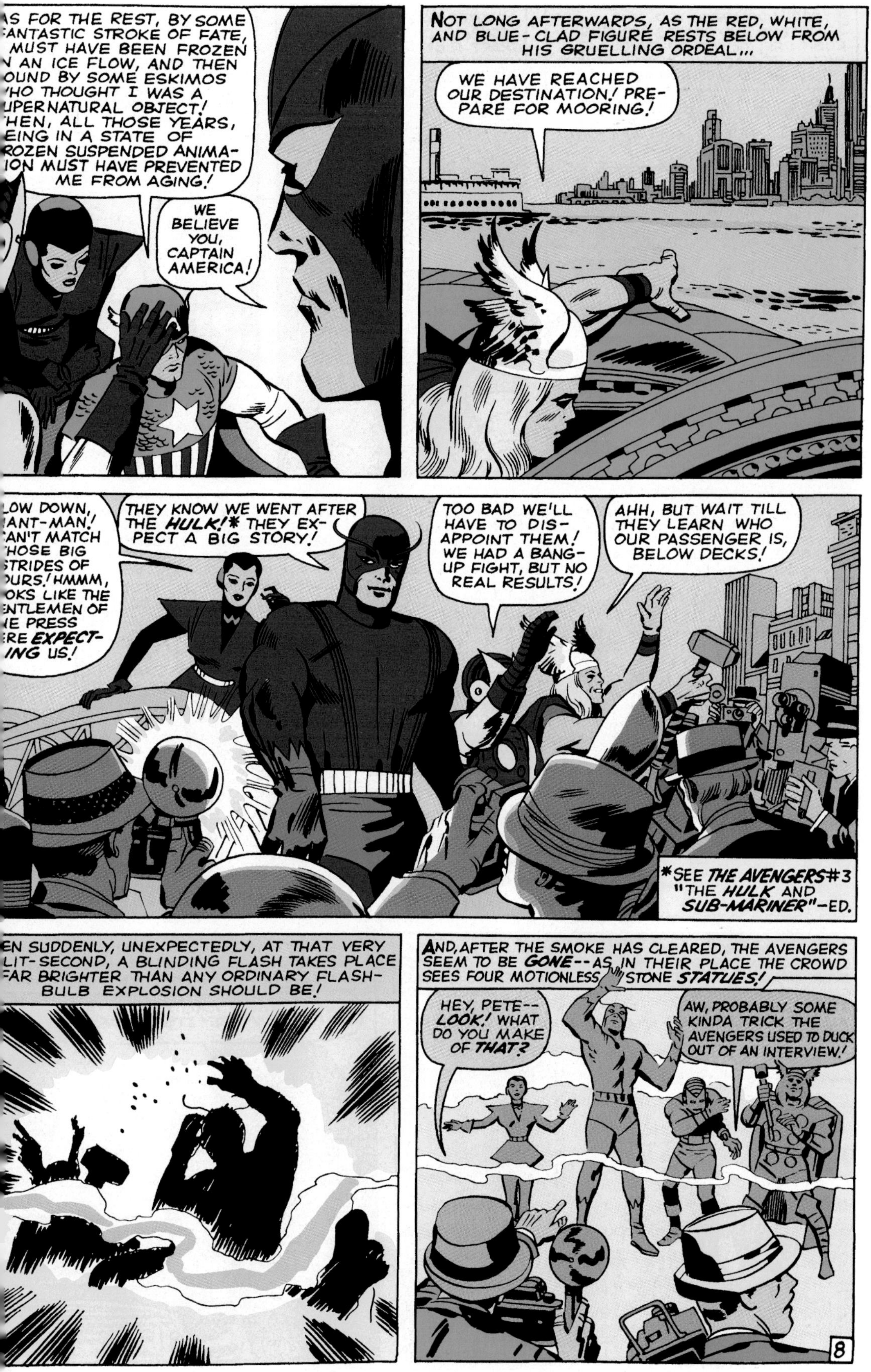

AS FOR THE REST, BY SOME FANTASTIC STROKE OF FATE, I MUST HAVE BEEN FROZEN IN AN ICE FLOW, AND THEN FOUND BY SOME ESKIMOS WHO THOUGHT I WAS A SUPERNATURAL OBJECT! THEN, ALL THOSE YEARS, BEING IN A STATE OF FROZEN SUSPENDED ANIMATION MUST HAVE PREVENTED ME FROM AGING!
WE BELIEVE YOU, CAPTAIN AMERICA!
NOT LONG AFTERWARDS, AS THE RED, WHITE, AND BLUE-CLAD FIGURE RESTS BELOW FROM HIS GRUELLING ORDEAL...
WE HAVE REACHED OUR DESTINATION! PREPARE FOR MOORING!
LOW DOWN, ANT-MAN! CAN'T MATCH THOSE BIG STRIDES OF YOURS! HMMM, LOOKS LIKE THE GENTLEMEN OF THE PRESS ARE EXPECTING US!
THEY KNOW WE WENT AFTER THE HULK!* THEY EXPECT A BIG STORY!
TOO BAD WE'LL HAVE TO DISAPPOINT THEM! WE HAD A BANG-UP FIGHT, BUT NO REAL RESULTS!
AHH, BUT WAIT TILL THEY LEARN WHO OUR PASSENGER IS, BELOW DECKS!
*SEE THE AVENGERS #3 "THE HULK AND SUB-MARINER"—ED.
THEN SUDDENLY, UNEXPECTEDLY, AT THAT VERY SPLIT-SECOND, A BLINDING FLASH TAKES PLACE FAR BRIGHTER THAN ANY ORDINARY FLASHBULB EXPLOSION SHOULD BE!
AND, AFTER THE SMOKE HAS CLEARED, THE AVENGERS SEEM TO BE GONE--AS IN THEIR PLACE THE CROWD SEES FOUR MOTIONLESS STONE STATUES!
HEY, PETE-- LOOK! WHAT DO YOU MAKE OF THAT?
AW, PROBABLY SOME KINDA TRICK THE AVENGERS USED TO DUCK OUT OF AN INTERVIEW!
8

BITTERLY DISAPPOINTED, THE REPORTERS AND PHOTOGRAPHERS RUSH OFF, TRYING TO FIND THE AVENGERS... AS THE CROWD DRIFTS AWAY TO NOTHINGNESS...

THAT'S A PRETTY CRUMMY TRICK TO PULL ON US, AFTER US WAITING ALL DAY FOR *THIS* INTERVIEW!

LET'S GO *FIND* 'EM! THEY COULDN'T HAVE GOTTEN FAR!

MINUTES LATER, THE LAST OCCUPANT OF THE UNDERSEA CRAFT SLOWLY CLIMBS UP THE HATCHWAY, HAVING BEEN AWAKENED BY THE COMMOTION ABOVE...

BUT, UPON REACHING THE SURFACE, HE FINDS...

EVERYONE'S *GONE!* THE PIER IS *DESERTED!* BUT-- WHY WOULD THEY DASH OFF *WITHOUT* ME ??

STRANGE... THOSE STATUES MUST BE IN HONOR OF THE AVENGERS! BUT THEY ARE NOT SCULPTED IN TYPICAL POSES! OH WELL, IT'S NO CONCERN OF MINE! I HAVE A WHOLE NEW WORLD TO REDISCOVER-- A WORLD WHICH HAS ADVANCED TWENTY YEARS AHEAD OF ME!

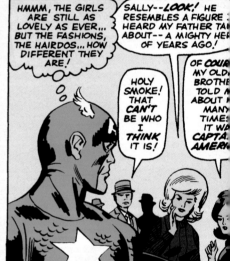

HMMM, THE GIRLS ARE STILL AS LOVELY AS EVER... BUT THE FASHIONS, THE HAIRDOS... HOW DIFFERENT THEY ARE!

SALLY--*LOOK!* HE RESEMBLES A FIGURE : HEARD MY FATHER TA ABOUT-- A MIGHTY HE OF YEARS AGO!

HOLY SMOKE! THAT *CAN'T* BE WHO I *THINK* IT IS!

OF *COUR* MY OLD BROTHE TOLD N ABOUT MANY TIMES IT WA CAPTA AMERI

AND THE NEW YORK SKY- LINE--EVER IMPRESSIVE-- EVER CHANGING! WHAT CAN *THIS* MAGNIFICENT STRUCTURE BE-- WITH ALL THE WORLD'S FLAGS ARRAYED AROUND IT ??

HEY! WATCH THE *LIGHTS* CROSSING THE STREET, MAC!

THE CARS HAVE CHANGED MOST OF ALL-- AS THEY ALWAYS DO! WE NEVER HAD SO MANY *SMALL* ONES IN THE THIRTIES AND FORTIES!

WAIT! I KNOW YOU! YOU'RE--AWW, NO! IT *CAN'T* BE! IT'S *IMPOSSIBLE!*

BUT I *CAN'T* BE WRONG! I *SAW* YOU ONCE, WHEN I WAS A KID! NEVER *FORGOT* IT!

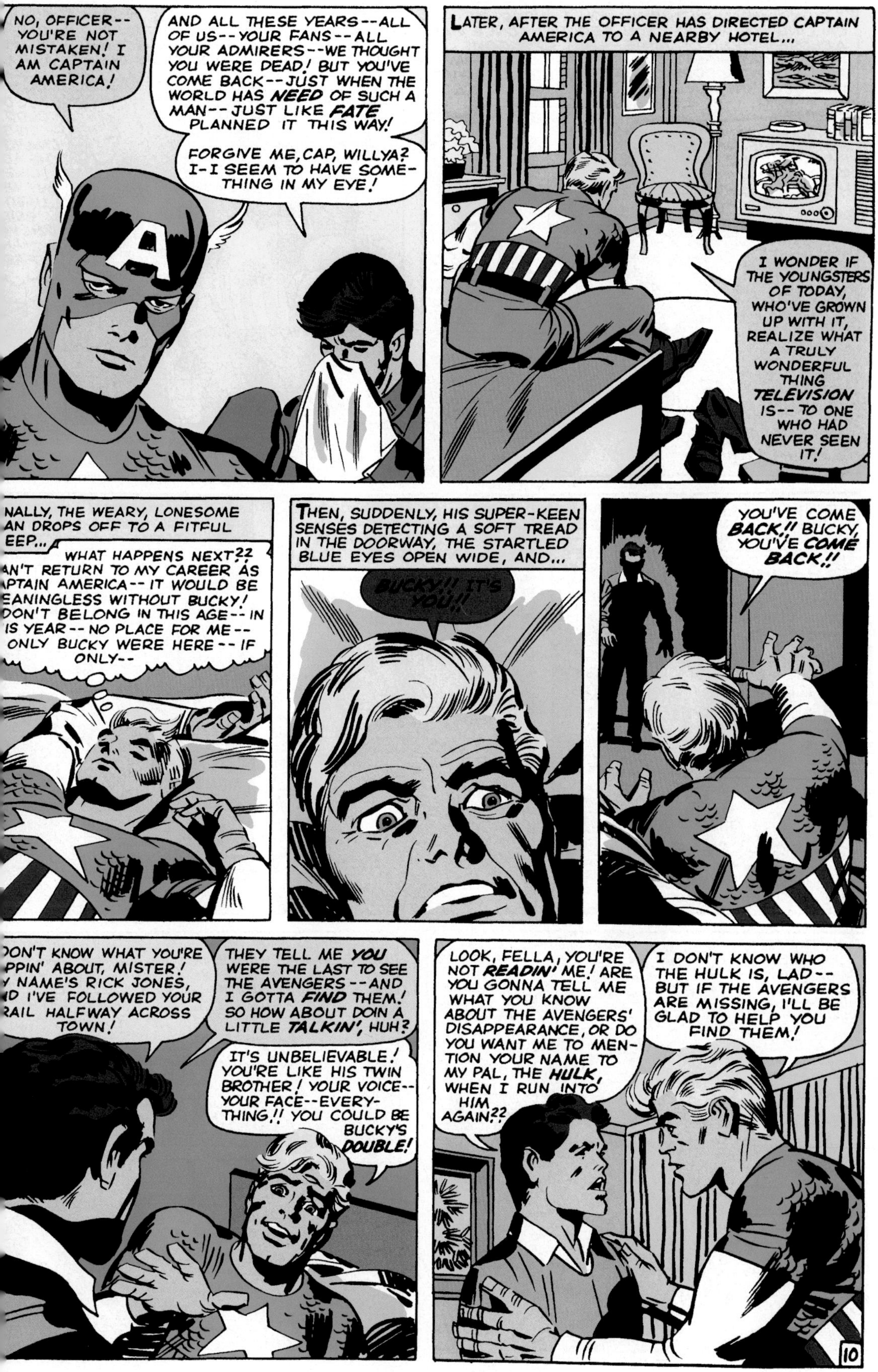

NO, OFFICER-- YOU'RE NOT MISTAKEN! I AM CAPTAIN AMERICA!
AND ALL THESE YEARS--ALL OF US--YOUR FANS--ALL YOUR ADMIRERS--WE THOUGHT YOU WERE DEAD! BUT YOU'VE COME BACK--JUST WHEN THE WORLD HAS NEED OF SUCH A MAN-- JUST LIKE FATE PLANNED IT THIS WAY!
FORGIVE ME, CAP, WILLYA? I-I SEEM TO HAVE SOMETHING IN MY EYE!
LATER, AFTER THE OFFICER HAS DIRECTED CAPTAIN AMERICA TO A NEARBY HOTEL...
I WONDER IF THE YOUNGSTERS OF TODAY, WHO'VE GROWN UP WITH IT, REALIZE WHAT A TRULY WONDERFUL THING TELEVISION IS-- TO ONE WHO HAD NEVER SEEN IT!
NALLY, THE WEARY, LONESOME AN DROPS OFF TO A FITFUL EEP...
WHAT HAPPENS NEXT?? AN'T RETURN TO MY CAREER AS APTAIN AMERICA-- IT WOULD BE EANINGLESS WITHOUT BUCKY! DON'T BELONG IN THIS AGE-- IN IS YEAR-- NO PLACE FOR ME-- ONLY BUCKY WERE HERE-- IF ONLY--
THEN, SUDDENLY, HIS SUPER-KEEN SENSES DETECTING A SOFT TREAD IN THE DOORWAY, THE STARTLED BLUE EYES OPEN WIDE, AND...
BUCKY!! IT'S YOU!!
YOU'VE COME BACK!! BUCKY, YOU'VE COME BACK!!
DON'T KNOW WHAT YOU'RE PPIN' ABOUT, MISTER! Y NAME'S RICK JONES, D I'VE FOLLOWED YOUR RAIL HALFWAY ACROSS TOWN!
THEY TELL ME YOU WERE THE LAST TO SEE THE AVENGERS--AND I GOTTA FIND THEM! SO HOW ABOUT DOIN A LITTLE TALKIN', HUH?
IT'S UNBELIEVABLE! YOU'RE LIKE HIS TWIN BROTHER! YOUR VOICE--YOUR FACE--EVERYTHING!! YOU COULD BE BUCKY'S DOUBLE!
LOOK, FELLA, YOU'RE NOT READIN' ME! ARE YOU GONNA TELL ME WHAT YOU KNOW ABOUT THE AVENGERS' DISAPPEARANCE, OR DO YOU WANT ME TO MENTION YOUR NAME TO MY PAL, THE HULK, WHEN I RUN INTO HIM AGAIN??
I DON'T KNOW WHO THE HULK IS, LAD-- BUT IF THE AVENGERS ARE MISSING, I'LL BE GLAD TO HELP YOU FIND THEM!
10

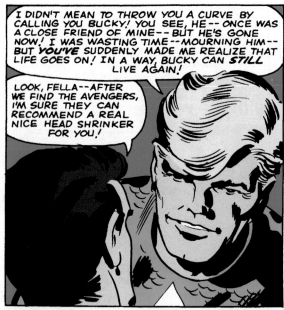

WITHIN AN HOUR, THE SEARCH IS ON, AS SHARP EYED TEEN-AGERS COVER THE CITY, SEEKING A PASTY-FACED MAN, WEARING OVAL SUN-GLASSES, WITH JET BLACK HAIR! NOT MUCH TO GO ON, PERHAPS, BUT STILL A STARTING POINT FOR THE EAGER BRIGADERS...

THAT'S NOT HIM! HAIR'S NOT BLACK ENOUGH!

THOUGHT I HAD HIM-- BUT HE'S MUCH TOO OLD!

WORKING AROUND THE CLOCK, THE ALERT TEEN-BRIGADE TAKES CANDID CAMERA SNAP-SHOTS OF ALL POSSIBLE SUS-PECTS, SENDING THEM IMMEDIATELY TO RICK JONES...

THAT GUY'S ANOTHER FALSE ALARM, BUT I'VE GOT A HALF-DOZEN SNAPS TO SEND RICK ANYWAY!

THEN, RACING THRU THE VAST CITY LIKE AN AVENGING STREAK, THE NIMBLE, SEEMINGLY TIRELESS CAPTAIN AMERICA FOLLOWS UP EACH LEAD, NO MATTER WHERE IT MAY TAKE HIM...

IT'S LIKE OLD TIMES AGAIN, BEING IN COSTUME-- ON THE TRAIL OF SOME STRANGE, UNKNOWN MENACE!

THIS IS WHAT I WAS MEANT TO DO! THIS IS THE DESTINY I CAN NEVER ESCAPE!

AND THEN, FINALLY...

IT'S HIM! THE ONE WE'RE AFTER!

WITHOUT A MOMENT'S HESITATION, TWO HUNDRED POUNDS OF FIGHTING FURY CRASH THRU THE SHATTERING WINDOW...

BUT, IN HIS EAGERNESS, THE ATTACKING CRIME-FIGHTER HAS FAILED TO NOTICE THE GUNMEN IN THE ADJOINING ROOM--GUNMEN WHO HEAR THE CRASH AND RACE TO THE SCENE, THEIR WEAPONS THUNDERING!!

GET THAT COSTUMED CLOWN, WHO-EVER HE IS!

IT'LL BE A CINCH!

12

THERE'S ALWAYS THE CHANCE YOU *MAY* GET ME! BUT "A CINCH"? *NEVER!*

H-HE SLICED OUR GUNS IN TWO WITH THAT *SHIELD* OF HIS!

WHO *IS* HE, ANY-WAY??

I'VE BEEN CALLED *MANY* THINGS-- BUT I'VE COME TO PREFER THE NAME *CAPTAIN AMERICA!*

I SHOULDA *KNOWN!* I *READ* ABOUT HIM WHEN I WAS A KID!

HE MUST BE A *PHONY!* HE'S T YOUNG TO BE TH *REAL* CAPTAIN AMERICA!

OWWW! THERE'S NO *STOPPIN'* HIM! HE'S LIKE A *WHIRLWIND!*

OOOF! IF *HE'S* A PHONY, I'M LITTLE RED RIDING HOOD!

NO ONE CAN PAY U ENOUGH TO FIGHT *HIM!* KNOCK IT OFF MASKED MAN-- WE GIVE UP!

AND THAT LEAVES *YOU*, FELLA! *YOU'VE* GOT THE KEY TO THE DISAPPEAR-ANCE OF THE AVENGERS!

BUT *YOU'LL* NEVER LEARN THE SECRET!

IT'S *UNCANNY!* HE MOVES SO FAST, MY RAY CAN'T STRIKE HIM!

THAT "GUN" YOU USED CAME FROM SOME PLACE *OTHER* THAN EARTH! AND SO, I SUSPECT, DID *YOU!* NOW *TALK--* WHILE YOU STILL *CAN!*

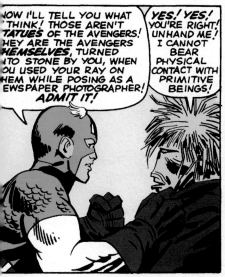

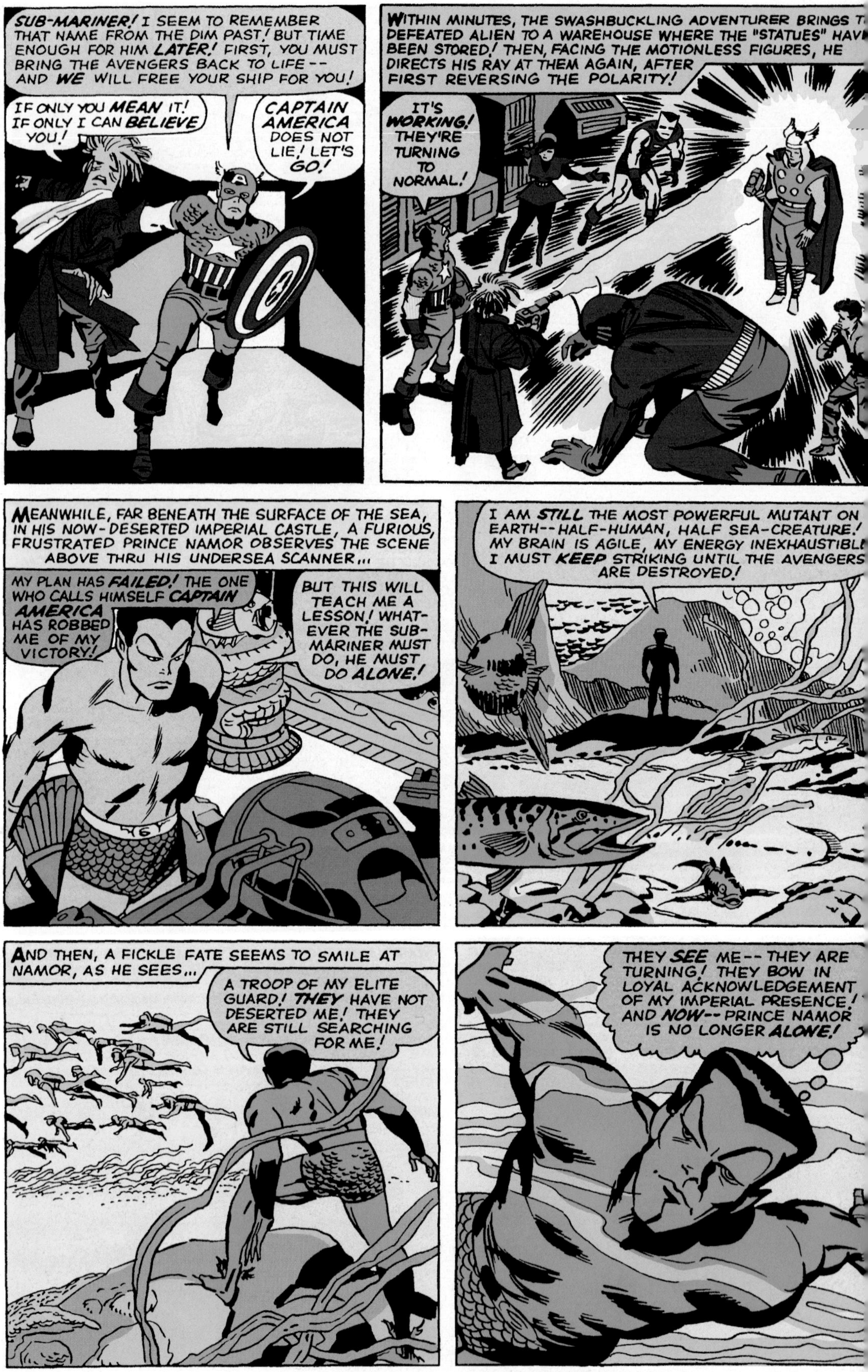
SUB-MARINER! I SEEM TO REMEMBER THAT NAME FROM THE DIM PAST! BUT TIME ENOUGH FOR HIM LATER! FIRST, YOU MUST BRING THE AVENGERS BACK TO LIFE -- AND WE WILL FREE YOUR SHIP FOR YOU!
IF ONLY YOU MEAN IT! IF ONLY I CAN BELIEVE YOU!
CAPTAIN AMERICA DOES NOT LIE! LET'S GO!
WITHIN MINUTES, THE SWASHBUCKLING ADVENTURER BRINGS THE DEFEATED ALIEN TO A WAREHOUSE WHERE THE "STATUES" HAVE BEEN STORED! THEN, FACING THE MOTIONLESS FIGURES, HE DIRECTS HIS RAY AT THEM AGAIN, AFTER FIRST REVERSING THE POLARITY!
IT'S WORKING! THEY'RE TURNING TO NORMAL!
MEANWHILE, FAR BENEATH THE SURFACE OF THE SEA, IN HIS NOW-DESERTED IMPERIAL CASTLE, A FURIOUS, FRUSTRATED PRINCE NAMOR OBSERVES THE SCENE ABOVE THRU HIS UNDERSEA SCANNER...
MY PLAN HAS FAILED! THE ONE WHO CALLS HIMSELF CAPTAIN AMERICA HAS ROBBED ME OF MY VICTORY!
BUT THIS WILL TEACH ME A LESSON! WHATEVER THE SUB-MARINER MUST DO, HE MUST DO ALONE!
I AM STILL THE MOST POWERFUL MUTANT ON EARTH--HALF-HUMAN, HALF SEA-CREATURE! MY BRAIN IS AGILE, MY ENERGY INEXHAUSTIBLE! I MUST KEEP STRIKING UNTIL THE AVENGERS ARE DESTROYED!
AND THEN, A FICKLE FATE SEEMS TO SMILE AT NAMOR, AS HE SEES...
A TROOP OF MY ELITE GUARD! THEY HAVE NOT DESERTED ME! THEY ARE STILL SEARCHING FOR ME!
THEY SEE ME-- THEY ARE TURNING! THEY BOW IN LOYAL ACKNOWLEDGEMENT OF MY IMPERIAL PRESENCE! AND NOW-- PRINCE NAMOR IS NO LONGER ALONE!

IT **WORKED!** YOU FREED THE SHIP, THOR!

WHY DO YOU SOUND SURPRISED? WAS THAT NOT MY **INTENTION??**

YOU KEPT YOUR WORD! NOW I CAN REPAIR MY SHIP IN MINUTES, AND DEPART FROM THIS WRETCHED PLANET!

NOW THAT IT'S FLOATING FREE, THE WATER MAKES IT ALMOST WEIGHTLESS!

LEAVE IT HERE! I'LL MAKE MY REPAIRS UNDER WATER, SAFE FROM ANY PRYING EYES!

SUIT YOURSELF, M TER! AS LONG AS HIT THE ROAD, W DON'T CARE HO YOU DO

AND THAT'S THAT! I WONDER WHAT THE A.A.A. WOULD HAVE SAID IF THE ALIEN HAD CALLED **THEM** FOR EMERGENCY REPAIRS.!??

Y'KNOW, GIANT-MAN, I LIKE YOUR STYLE! YOU **AVENGERS** MAKE A GREAT TEAM! IN FACT, I WAS WON- DERING...

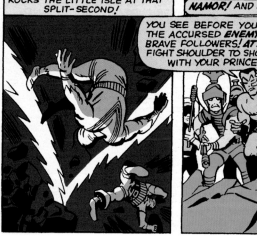

BUT CAPTAIN AMERICA'S SEN- TENCE IS CUT SHORT BY A THUNDEROUS EXPLOSION WHICH ROCKS THE LITTLE ISLE AT THAT SPLIT-SECOND!

AND, WHEN THE STARTLED AVENGE RECOVER THEIR EQUILIBRIUM, THE ARE AMAZED TO SEE...

NAMOR! AND A SQUAD OF UNDE SEA WARRIOR

YOU SEE BEFORE YOU THE ACCURSED **ENEMY,** MY BRAVE FOLLOWERS! **ATTACK!** FIGHT SHOULDER TO SHOULDER WITH YOUR PRINCE!

THOUGH THE FIRST ONSLAUGHT IS UNEX- PECTED AND DEVESTATING, THE AVENGERS' BATTLE- TRAINED REFLEXES ARE EQUAL TO THE CHALLENGE!

YOU'LL HAVE TO DO BETTER THAN **THAT,** LAUGH- ING BOY!

YOU'LL **GET** YOUR WISH, IRON MAN! **NAMOR** WILL DO BETTER! YOUR IRON ARMOR CANNOT SAVE YOU FROM THE SEA MONARCH'S ATTACK!!

I'LL HAVE TO ACT **FAST!** HIS FISTS ARE LIKE LIVIN SLEDGE-HAMMERS! MY ARMOR CAN'T TAKE IT MUC LONGER!

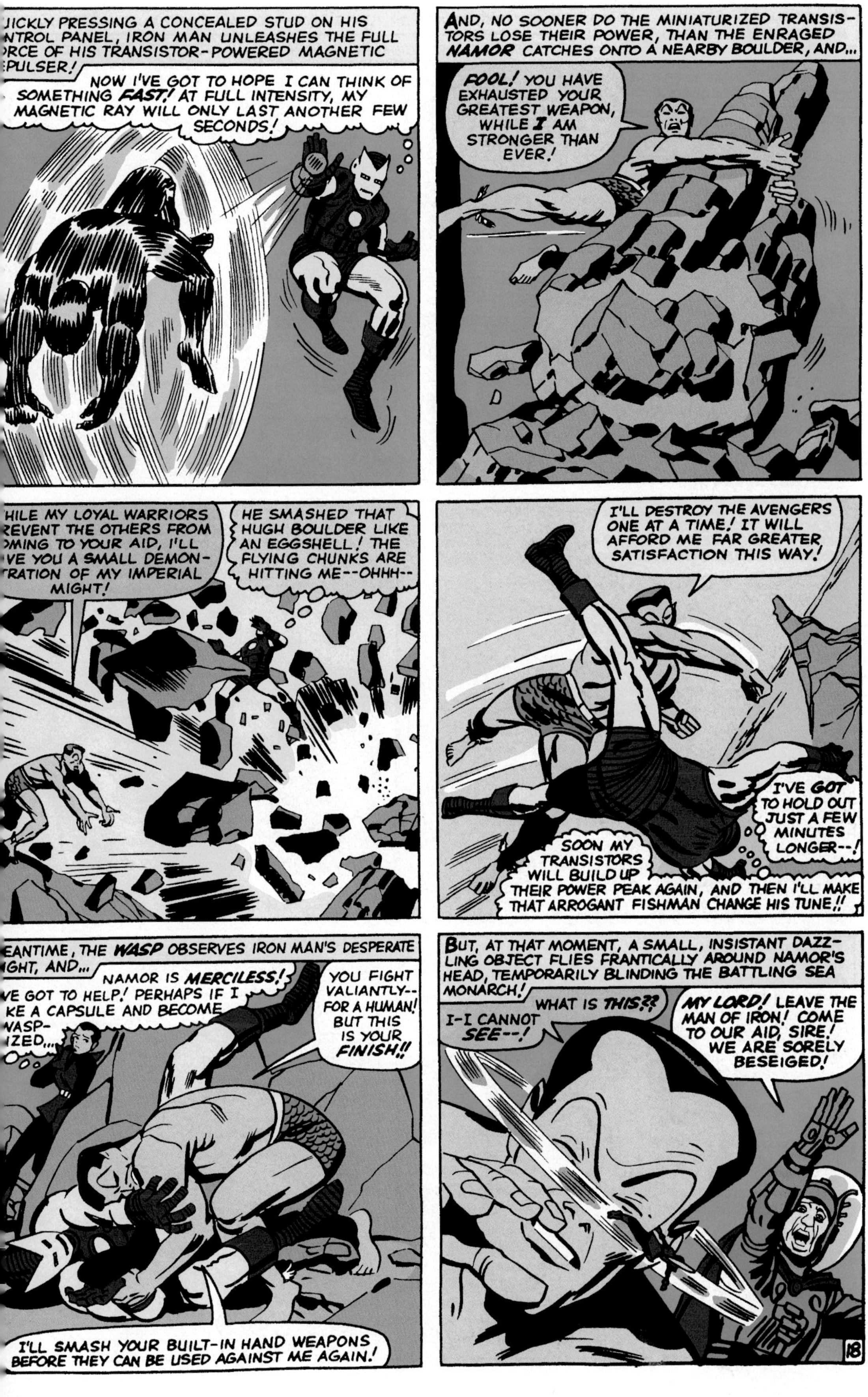

UICKLY PRESSING A CONCEALED STUD ON HIS
NTROL PANEL, IRON MAN UNLEASHES THE FULL
RCE OF HIS TRANSISTOR-POWERED MAGNETIC
PULSER!
NOW I'VE GOT TO HOPE I CAN THINK OF SOMETHING FAST! AT FULL INTENSITY, MY MAGNETIC RAY WILL ONLY LAST ANOTHER FEW SECONDS!
AND, NO SOONER DO THE MINIATURIZED TRANSISTORS LOSE THEIR POWER, THAN THE ENRAGED NAMOR CATCHES ONTO A NEARBY BOULDER, AND...
FOOL! YOU HAVE EXHAUSTED YOUR GREATEST WEAPON, WHILE I AM STRONGER THAN EVER!
HILE MY LOYAL WARRIORS
REVENT THE OTHERS FROM
OMING TO YOUR AID, I'LL
VE YOU A SMALL DEMON-
TRATION OF MY IMPERIAL
MIGHT!
HE SMASHED THAT HUGH BOULDER LIKE AN EGGSHELL! THE FLYING CHUNKS ARE HITTING ME--OHHH--
I'LL DESTROY THE AVENGERS ONE AT A TIME! IT WILL AFFORD ME FAR GREATER SATISFACTION THIS WAY!
I'VE GOT TO HOLD OUT JUST A FEW MINUTES LONGER--!
SOON MY TRANSISTORS WILL BUILD UP THEIR POWER PEAK AGAIN, AND THEN I'LL MAKE THAT ARROGANT FISHMAN CHANGE HIS TUNE!!
EANTIME, THE WASP OBSERVES IRON MAN'S DESPERATE
IGHT, AND...
NAMOR IS MERCILESS!
VE GOT TO HELP! PERHAPS IF I
KE A CAPSULE AND BECOME
WASP-
IZED...
YOU FIGHT VALIANTLY-- FOR A HUMAN! BUT THIS IS YOUR FINISH!!
I'LL SMASH YOUR BUILT-IN HAND WEAPONS BEFORE THEY CAN BE USED AGAINST ME AGAIN!
BUT, AT THAT MOMENT, A SMALL, INSISTANT DAZZLING OBJECT FLIES FRANTICALLY AROUND NAMOR'S HEAD, TEMPORARILY BLINDING THE BATTLING SEA MONARCH!
WHAT IS THIS??
I-I CANNOT SEE--!
MY LORD! LEAVE THE MAN OF IRON! COME TO OUR AID, SIRE! WE ARE SORELY BESEIGED!
18

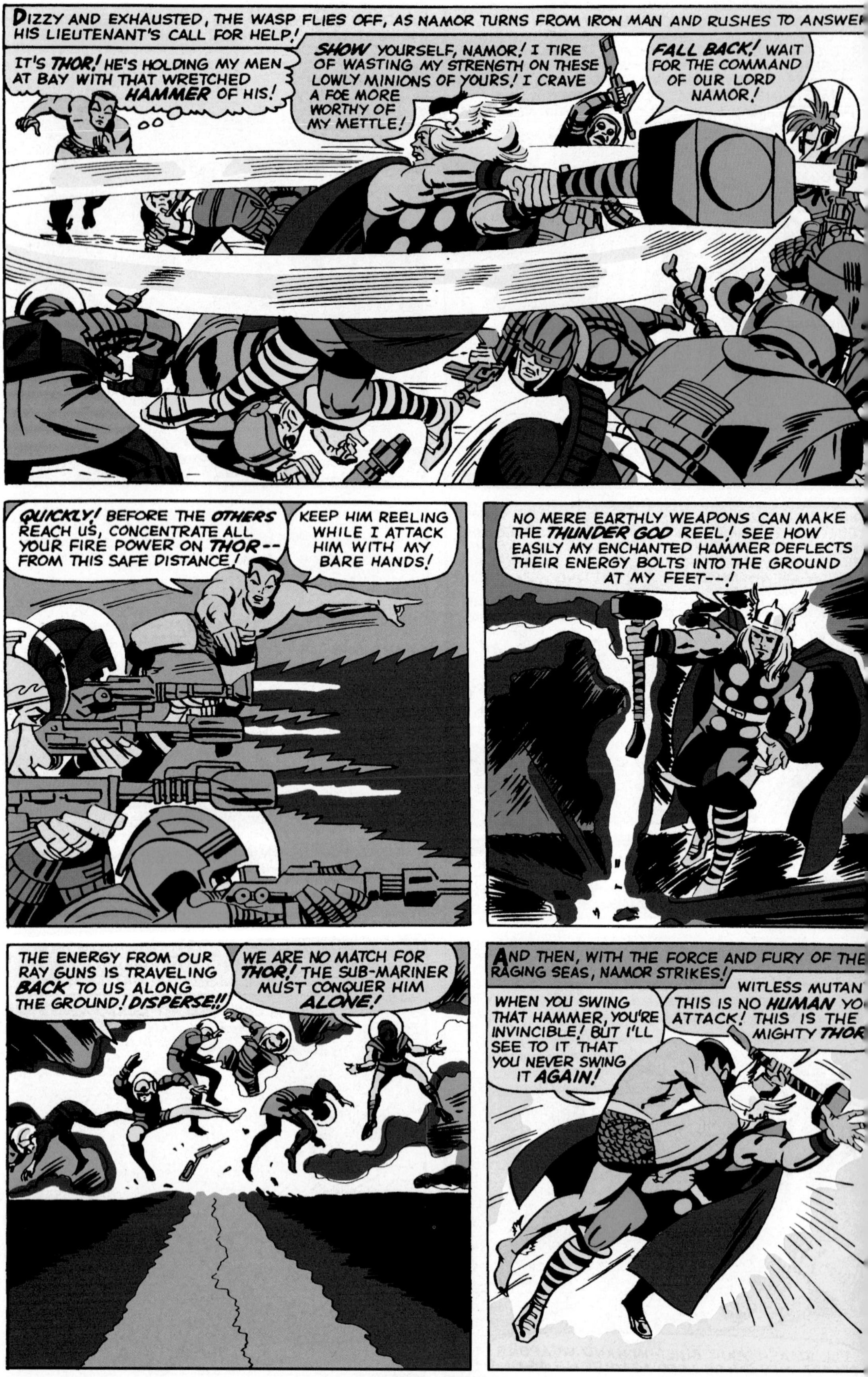
DIZZY AND EXHAUSTED, THE WASP FLIES OFF, AS NAMOR TURNS FROM IRON MAN AND RUSHES TO ANSWER HIS LIEUTENANT'S CALL FOR HELP!
IT'S THOR! HE'S HOLDING MY MEN AT BAY WITH THAT WRETCHED HAMMER OF HIS!
SHOW YOURSELF, NAMOR! I TIRE OF WASTING MY STRENGTH ON THESE LOWLY MINIONS OF YOURS! I CRAVE A FOE MORE WORTHY OF MY METTLE!
FALL BACK! WAIT FOR THE COMMAND OF OUR LORD NAMOR!
QUICKLY! BEFORE THE OTHERS REACH US, CONCENTRATE ALL YOUR FIRE POWER ON THOR-- FROM THIS SAFE DISTANCE!
KEEP HIM REELING WHILE I ATTACK HIM WITH MY BARE HANDS!
NO MERE EARTHLY WEAPONS CAN MAKE THE THUNDER GOD REEL! SEE HOW EASILY MY ENCHANTED HAMMER DEFLECTS THEIR ENERGY BOLTS INTO THE GROUND AT MY FEET--!
THE ENERGY FROM OUR RAY GUNS IS TRAVELING BACK TO US ALONG THE GROUND! DISPERSE!!
WE ARE NO MATCH FOR THOR! THE SUB-MARINER MUST CONQUER HIM ALONE!
AND THEN, WITH THE FORCE AND FURY OF THE RAGING SEAS, NAMOR STRIKES!
WHEN YOU SWING THAT HAMMER, YOU'RE INVINCIBLE! BUT I'LL SEE TO IT THAT YOU NEVER SWING IT AGAIN!
WITLESS MUTAN THIS IS NO HUMAN YO ATTACK! THIS IS THE MIGHTY THOR

MEANWHILE, WHAT OF THE THIRD AVENGER--AND CAPTAIN AMERICA?? THEY HAD BOTH BEEN HURLED BACK INTO THE SEA BY THE EARTH-SHATTERING BLAST WHICH HERALDED NAMOR'S ATTACK! AND NOW, WE FIND GIANT-MAN, AT THE BRINK OF DISASTER...

CAN'T HOLD MY BREATH MUCH LONGER! ONLY ONE CHANCE --MY REDUCING CAPSULE... THERE! I SWALLOWED IT!

IN THE WINK OF AN EYE, THE DOUBLE-SIZED ADVENTURER BECOMES ANT MAN, AND EASILY SWIMS TO FREEDOM THRU THE NOW-LIMP ROPES!

MADE IT! WONDER WHAT HAPPENED TO CAPTAIN AMERICA?? WELL, NO TIME TO SEARCH FOR HIM NOW!

OH! MY ANT-SIZE IS FINE FOR ESCAPING FROM ROPES, BUT IF I DON'T WANNA END MY DAYS AS FISH FOOD, I'D BETTER BECOME GIANT-MAN AGAIN-- AND PRONTO!

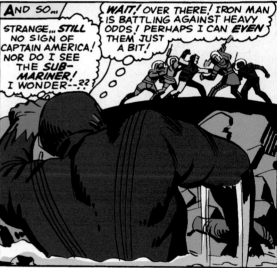

AND SO...

STRANGE,... STILL NO SIGN OF CAPTAIN AMERICA! NOR DO I SEE THE SUB-MARINER! I WONDER--??

WAIT! OVER THERE! IRON MAN IS BATTLING AGAINST HEAVY ODDS! PERHAPS I CAN EVEN THEM JUST A BIT!

ALL YOU BULLY-BOYS ENJOY GANGING UP ON ONE MAN, TRY ME FOR SIZE! HEY, I NOTICE YOU'RE NOT WHOOPING IT UP SO MUCH NOW!

GO ON BACK TO THE DEPTHS YOU CAME FROM! WE'VE NO QUARREL WITH YOU! IT'S THAT POWER-MAD PRINCE OF YOURS WE'RE AFTER!

20

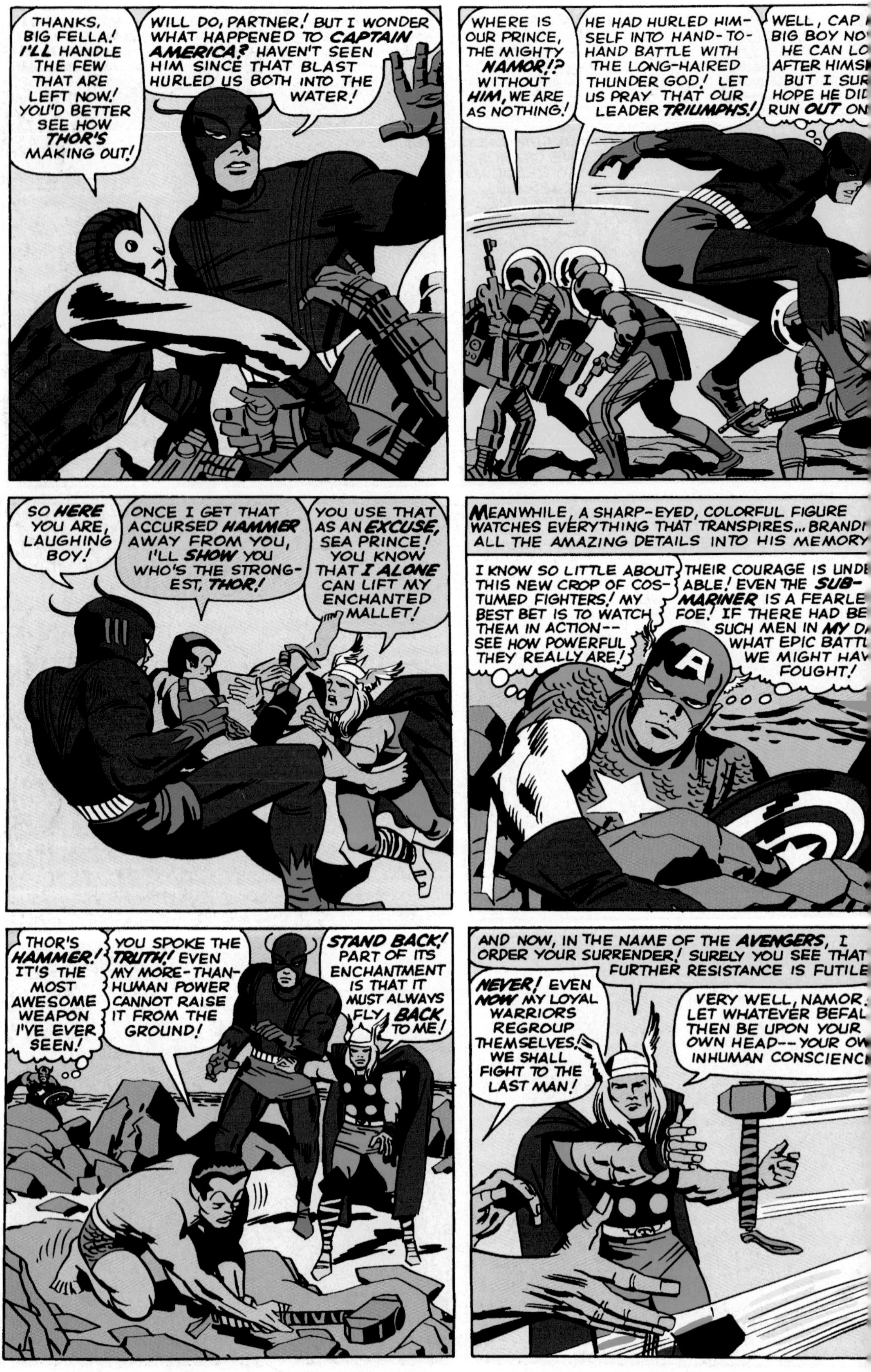
THANKS, BIG FELLA! I'LL HANDLE THE FEW THAT ARE LEFT NOW! YOU'D BETTER SEE HOW THOR'S MAKING OUT!
WILL DO, PARTNER! BUT I WONDER WHAT HAPPENED TO CAPTAIN AMERICA? HAVEN'T SEEN HIM SINCE THAT BLAST HURLED US BOTH INTO THE WATER!
WHERE IS OUR PRINCE, THE MIGHTY NAMOR!? WITHOUT HIM, WE ARE AS NOTHING!
HE HAD HURLED HIMSELF INTO HAND-TO-HAND BATTLE WITH THE LONG-HAIRED THUNDER GOD! LET US PRAY THAT OUR LEADER TRIUMPHS!
WELL, CAP BIG BOY NO HE CAN LO AFTER HIMS BUT I SUR HOPE HE DI RUN OUT ON
SO HERE YOU ARE, LAUGHING BOY!
ONCE I GET THAT ACCURSED HAMMER AWAY FROM YOU, I'LL SHOW YOU WHO'S THE STRONGEST, THOR!
YOU USE THAT AS AN EXCUSE, SEA PRINCE! YOU KNOW THAT I ALONE CAN LIFT MY ENCHANTED MALLET!
MEANWHILE, A SHARP-EYED, COLORFUL FIGURE WATCHES EVERYTHING THAT TRANSPIRES... BRANDI ALL THE AMAZING DETAILS INTO HIS MEMORY
I KNOW SO LITTLE ABOUT THIS NEW CROP OF COSTUMED FIGHTERS! MY BEST BET IS TO WATCH THEM IN ACTION-- SEE HOW POWERFUL THEY REALLY ARE!
THEIR COURAGE IS UNDE ABLE! EVEN THE SUB-MARINER IS A FEARLE FOE! IF THERE HAD BE SUCH MEN IN MY D WHAT EPIC BATTL WE MIGHT HAV FOUGHT!
THOR'S HAMMER! IT'S THE MOST AWESOME WEAPON I'VE EVER SEEN!
YOU SPOKE THE TRUTH! EVEN MY MORE-THAN-HUMAN POWER CANNOT RAISE IT FROM THE GROUND!
STAND BACK! PART OF ITS ENCHANTMENT IS THAT IT MUST ALWAYS FLY BACK TO ME!
AND NOW, IN THE NAME OF THE AVENGERS, I ORDER YOUR SURRENDER! SURELY YOU SEE THAT FURTHER RESISTANCE IS FUTILE
NEVER! EVEN NOW MY LOYAL WARRIORS REGROUP THEMSELVES! WE SHALL FIGHT TO THE LAST MAN!
VERY WELL, NAMOR LET WHATEVER BEFAL THEN BE UPON YOUR OWN HEAD--YOUR OW INHUMAN CONSCIENC

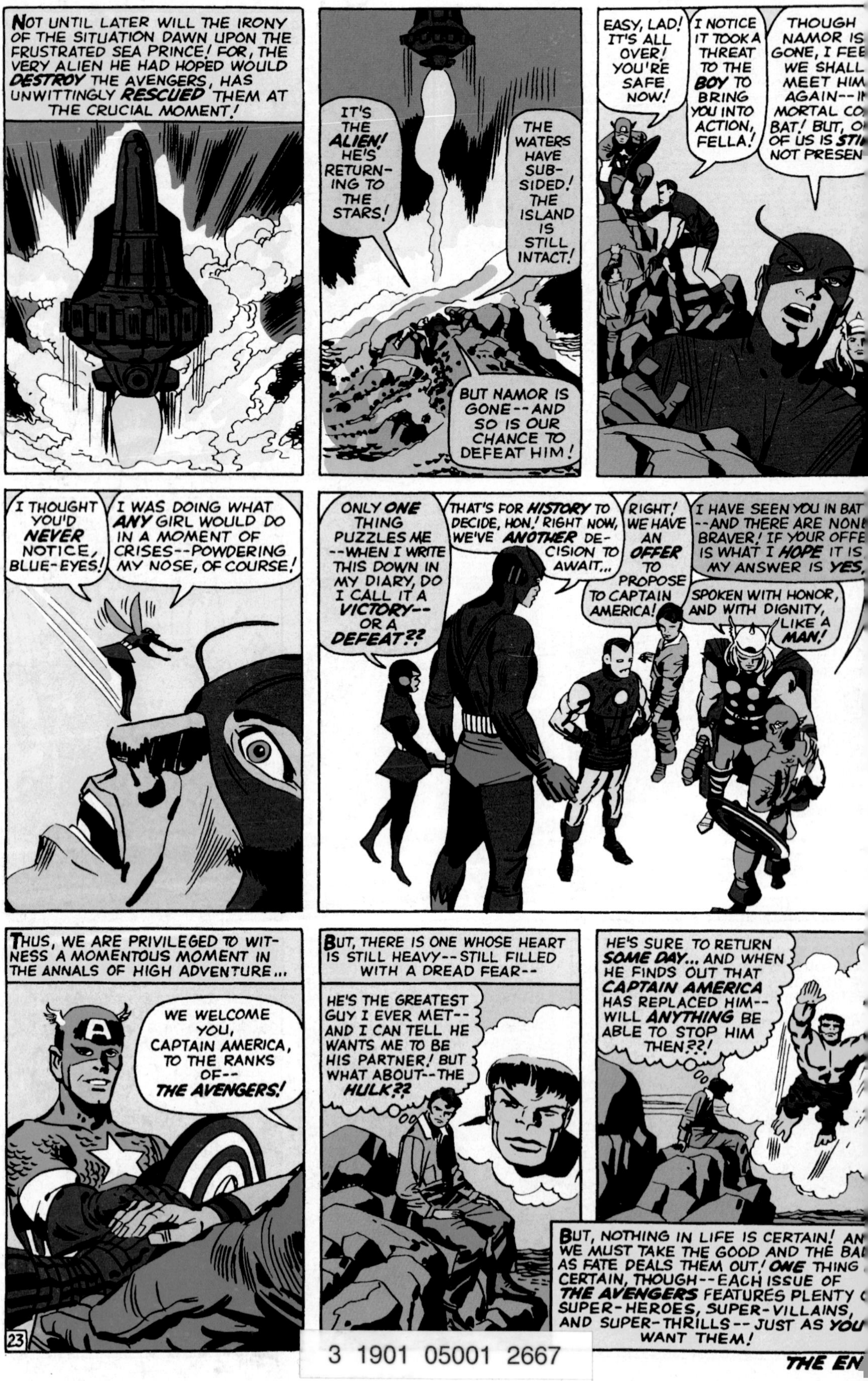
NOT UNTIL LATER WILL THE IRONY OF THE SITUATION DAWN UPON THE FRUSTRATED SEA PRINCE! FOR, THE VERY ALIEN HE HAD HOPED WOULD DESTROY THE AVENGERS, HAS UNWITTINGLY RESCUED THEM AT THE CRUCIAL MOMENT!
IT'S THE ALIEN! HE'S RETURNING TO THE STARS!
THE WATERS HAVE SUBSIDED! THE ISLAND IS STILL INTACT!
BUT NAMOR IS GONE--AND SO IS OUR CHANCE TO DEFEAT HIM!
EASY, LAD! IT'S ALL OVER! YOU'RE SAFE NOW!
I NOTICE IT TOOK A THREAT TO THE BOY TO BRING YOU INTO ACTION, FELLA!
THOUGH NAMOR IS GONE, I FEE WE SHALL MEET HIM AGAIN--I MORTAL CO BAT! BUT, O OF US IS STI NOT PRESEN
I THOUGHT YOU'D NEVER NOTICE, BLUE-EYES!
I WAS DOING WHAT ANY GIRL WOULD DO IN A MOMENT OF CRISES--POWDERING MY NOSE, OF COURSE!
ONLY ONE THING PUZZLES ME--WHEN I WRITE THIS DOWN IN MY DIARY, DO I CALL IT A VICTORY--OR A DEFEAT??
THAT'S FOR HISTORY TO DECIDE, HON! RIGHT NOW, WE'VE ANOTHER DECISION TO AWAIT...
RIGHT! WE HAVE AN OFFER TO PROPOSE TO CAPTAIN AMERICA!
I HAVE SEEN YOU IN BAT --AND THERE ARE NON BRAVER! IF YOUR OFFE IS WHAT I HOPE IT IS MY ANSWER IS YES
SPOKEN WITH HONOR, AND WITH DIGNITY, LIKE A MAN!
THUS, WE ARE PRIVILEGED TO WITNESS A MOMENTOUS MOMENT IN THE ANNALS OF HIGH ADVENTURE...
WE WELCOME YOU, CAPTAIN AMERICA, TO THE RANKS OF--THE AVENGERS!
23
BUT, THERE IS ONE WHOSE HEART IS STILL HEAVY--STILL FILLED WITH A DREAD FEAR--
HE'S THE GREATEST GUY I EVER MET--AND I CAN TELL HE WANTS ME TO BE HIS PARTNER! BUT WHAT ABOUT--THE HULK??
HE'S SURE TO RETURN SOME DAY... AND WHEN HE FINDS OUT THAT CAPTAIN AMERICA HAS REPLACED HIM--WILL ANYTHING BE ABLE TO STOP HIM THEN??!
BUT, NOTHING IN LIFE IS CERTAIN! AN WE MUST TAKE THE GOOD AND THE BA AS FATE DEALS THEM OUT! ONE THING CERTAIN, THOUGH--EACH ISSUE OF THE AVENGERS FEATURES PLENTY O SUPER-HEROES, SUPER-VILLAINS, AND SUPER-THRILLS--JUST AS YOU WANT THEM!
THE EN